CIM
PRACTICE & REVISION KIT

Diploma

Strategic Marketing Management: Planning and Control

BPP Publishing
September 2000

First edition 1999
Second edition September 2000

ISBN 0 7817 4915 X (previous edition 0 7517 4130 3)

British Library Cataloguing-in-Publication Data
A catalogue record for this book
is available from the British Library

Published by

BPP Publishing Limited
Aldine House, Aldine Place
London W12 8AW

www.bpp.com

in association with
Nottingham Business School
Nottingham Trent University

Printed in England by W M Print
Frederick Street
Walsall
West Midlands WS2 9NE

All our rights reserved. No part of this publication may be reproduced, stored in a retrieval system or transmitted, in any form or by any means, electronic, mechanical, photocopying, recording or otherwise, without the prior written permission of BPP Publishing Limited.

We are grateful to the Chartered Institute of Marketing for permission to reproduce past examination questions. The suggested solutions to past examination questions have been prepared by BPP Publishing Limited.

Authors
Valerie Youngson and Brian Searle

Series editor
Paul Brittain, Senior Lecturer in Marketing and Retailing at Nottingham Business School, Nottingham Trent University

©
BPP Publishing Limited
2000

Contents

	Page
CONTENTS	
Question and answer checklist/index	(iv)
About this kit	(vii)
Revision	(viii)
Question practice	(ix)
Exam technique	(x)
Approaching mini-cases	(xii)
The exam paper	(xv)
Syllabus	(xix)
QUESTION BANK	3
ANSWER BANK	29
TEST YOUR KNOWLEDGE	
Questions	185
Answers	187
TEST PAPER	
June 2000 paper questions	192
June 2000 paper suggested answers	199
TOPIC INDEX	
ORDER FORMS	
REVIEW FORM & FREE PRIZE DRAW	

Question and answer checklist/index

The headings indicate the main topics of questions, but questions often cover several different topics.

Tutorial questions, listed in italics, are followed by **guidance notes** on how to approach the question, thus easing the transition from study to examination practice.

A date alone (12/96, say) after the question title refers to a past examination question.

Questions marked by * are **key questions** which we think you must attempt in order to pass the exam. Tick them off on this list as you complete them.

		Marks	Time allocation mins	Page number Question	Answer

PART A: MARKET-LED APPROACH TO PLANNING

		Marks	Time allocation mins	Question	Answer
*1	*Tutorial question: Marketing and corporate planning*	-	-	4	29
*2	Marketing and corporate strategy	20	32	4	30
3	Marketing task (12/97)	20	32	4	32
4	Developing marketing orientation	20	32	4	34
5	Information for franchising decision (12/98)	20	32	4	36
6	Effective marketing planning (12/99)	20	32	4	38

PART B: ANALYSIS

		Marks	Time allocation mins	Question	Answer
*7	*Tutorial question: Marketing audit*	-	-	6	40
*8	Marketing analysis: Buyer behaviour	20	32	6	42
9	Social change (12/96)	20	32	6	44
10	Overseas buyer behaviour (6/96)	20	32	6	47
11	Competitor response profiles (6/96)	20	32	6	48
*12	Information about competitors (6/97)	20	32	6	50
13	Internal cultural barriers (6/99)	20	32	6	51
14	Potential market segments (6/99)	20	32	6	52

PART C: TECHNIQUES FOR ANALYSIS AND STRATEGY DEVELOPMENT

Where do we want to be

		Marks	Time allocation mins	Question	Answer
15	*Tutorial question: SWOT analysis*	-	-	8	54
16	*Tutorial question: Sales forecasting*	-	-	8	56
*17	SWOT: need for rigour (6/97)	20	32	8	57
*18	Portfolio analysis: BCG and others (12/98)	20	32	8	59
19	Product life cycle (12/98)	20	32	8	62
20	New product potential (12/97)	20	32	8	64
21	Laser drill life cycle (6/98)	20	32	8	66

Developing strategies

		Marks	Time allocation mins	Question	Answer
22	Life cycles and high-tech products (6/97)	20	32	9	68
*23	Decline stage (6/96)	20	32	9	70
24	Portfolio review (12/97)	20	32	9	72
25	Analysis techniques (12/99)	20	32	9	74

PART D: STRATEGY FORMULATION AND SELECTION

		Marks	Time allocation Mins	Page number Question	Answer
*26	Tutorial question: Marketing plan	-	-	11	77
27	Tutorial question: Competitive strategy	-	-	11	79
28	Tutorial question: New product development	-	-	11	81
29	Strategic objectives trade off (12/99)	20	32	11	83
*30	Strategic wear-out (12/99)	20	32	11	85
31	Mission and objectives	20	32	11	87
*32	Importance of market share (12/96)	20	32	11	89
33	Industrial segmentation	20	32	12	92
34	Information for segmentation and positioning (6/98)	20	32	12	94
35	Lifestyle segmentation (12/98)	20	32	12	95
*36	Geodemographical segmentation (12/99)	20	32	12	98
37	Customer profiles and software (6/97)	20	32	12	99
38	Marketing strategy development (12/97)	20	32	12	101
*39	Developing a strategy (6/96)	20	32	12	101
40	Competitive advantages (6/95)(12/98)	20	32	12	103
*41	Defending position (12/98)	20	32	13	105
42	Critical factors for success	20	32	13	107
43	Price-based strategies (12/97)	20	32	13	109
44	Evaluation criteria	20	32	13	111
45	Effect of technology on customers (6/98)	20	32	13	113
46	Brand stretching (6/98)	20	32	13	114
*47	Brand strategy (6/96)	20	32	13	115
48	Innovation: implementation issues (12/98)	20	32	13	117
*49	Loyalty marketing (12/97)	20	32	14	119
*50	Product development (12/99)	20	32	14	121
*51	Feasibility studies and risk evaluation	20	32	14	124
*52	Criteria for a new proposal (6/98)	20	32	14	126
53	Pan-European branding (6/99)	20	32	14	127
54	PIMS (6/99)	20	32	14	129
55	Relationship marketing strategy (6/99)	20	32	14	132

PART E: IMPLEMENTATION AND CONTROL

56	Tutorial question: Budgets	-	-	16	133
*57	Implementation problems	20	32	16	134
*58	Internal marketing (6/96)	20	32	16	136
59	Internal marketing in a hotel (6/98)	20	32	16	138
60	Effective controls (12/96)	20	32	16	140
*61	Control systems (6/97)	20	32	16	142
62	Market-led strategic changes (6/99)	20	32	16	143

Question and answer checklist/index

MINI-CASES

Examination standard mini-cases

		Marks	Time allocation mins	Page number Question	Answer
*63	The Legal Business (12/96)	50	80	17	146
*64	MJS Catering Supplies (6/97)	50	80	18	153
*65	Wild Outdoors (12/97)	50	80	19	158
*66	TMM (6/98)	40	64	21	164
*67	The wet shave market (6/99)	40	64	22	168
*68	The Lens Shop Ltd (12/98)	40	64	23	173
*69	Easyjet (12/99)	40	64	24	178

ABOUT THIS KIT

You're taking your professional CIM exams in December 2000 and June 2001. You're under time pressure to get your exam revision done and you want to pass first time. Could you make better use of your time? Are you sure that your revision is really relevant to the exam you will be facing?

If you use this BPP Practice & Revision Kit you can be sure that the time you spend revising and practising questions is time well spent.

The BPP Practice & Revision Kit: Strategic Marketing Management: Planning and Control

The BPP Practice & Revision Kit, produced in association with Nottingham Trent University Business School, has been specifically written for the syllabus by experts in marketing education, Valerie Youngson and Brian Searle.

- We give you a **comprehensive question and answer checklist** so you can see at a glance which are the key questions that we think you should attempt in order to pass the exam, what the mark and time allocations are and when they were set (where this is relevant)
- We offer **vital guidance** on revision, question practice and exam technique
- We show you the **syllabus** examinable in December 2000 and June 2001. We **analyse the papers** set so far, with summaries of the examiner's comments
- We give you a **comprehensive question bank** containing:
    - *Do You Know* checklists to jog your memory
    - *Tutorial questions* to warm you up
    - *Exam-standard questions*, including questions set up until December 1999 and the new syllabus specimen paper
    - *Full suggested answers* - with summaries of the examiner's comments
- A **Test Your Knowledge quiz** covering selected areas from the entire syllabus
- A **Test Paper** consisting of the June 2000 exam, again with full suggested answers, for you to attempt just before the real thing
- A **Topic Index** for ready reference

The Study Text: further help from BPP

The other vital part of BPP's study package is the Study Text. The Study Text features:

- Structured, methodical syllabus coverage
- Lots of case examples from real businesses throughout, to show you how the theory applies in real life
- Action programmes and quizzes so that you can test that you've mastered the theory
- A question and answer bank
- Key concepts and full index

There's an order form at the back of this Kit.

Help us to help you

Your feedback will help us improve our study package. Please complete and return the Review Form at the end of this Kit; you will be entered automatically in a Free Prize Draw.

BPP Publishing
September 2000

To learn more about what BPP has to offer, visit our website: www.bpp.co.uk

REVISION

This is a very important time as you approach the exam. You must remember three things.

> Use time sensibly
> Set realistic goals
> Believe in yourself

Use time sensibly

1   **How much study time do you have?** Remember that you must EAT, SLEEP, and of course, RELAX.

2   **How will you split that available time between each subject?** What are your weaker subjects? They need more time.

3   **What is your learning style?** AM/PM? Little and often/long sessions? Evenings/weekends?

4   **Are you taking regular breaks?** Most people absorb more if they do not attempt to study for long uninterrupted periods of time. A five minute break every hour (to make coffee, watch the news headlines) can make all the difference.

5   **Do you have quality study time?** Unplug the phone. Let everybody know that you're studying and shouldn't be disturbed.

Set realistic goals

1   Have you set a **clearly defined objective** for each study period?

2   Is the objective **achievable**?

3   Will you **stick to your plan**? Will you make up for any **lost time**?

4   Are you **rewarding yourself** for your hard work?

5   Are you leading a **healthy lifestyle**?

Believe in yourself

Are you cultivating the right attitude of mind? There is absolutely no reason why you should not pass this exam if you adopt the correct approach.

- **Be confident** - you've passed exams before, you can pass them again
- **Be calm** - plenty of adrenaline but no panicking
- **Be focused** - commit yourself to passing the exam

QUESTION PRACTICE

Do not simply open this Kit and, beginning with question 1, start attempting all of the questions. You first need to ask yourself three questions.

> **Am I ready to answer questions?**
> **Do I know which questions to do first?**
> **How should I use this Kit?**

Am I ready to answer questions?

1   Check that you are familiar with the material on the **Do you know?** page for a particular syllabus area.

2   If you are happy, you can go ahead and start answering questions. If not, go back to your BPP Study Text and revise first.

Do I know which questions to do first?

1   **Start with tutorial questions**. They warm you up for key and difficult areas of the syllabus. Try to produce at least a plan for these questions, using the guidance notes following the question to ensure your answer is structured so as to gain a good pass mark.

2   Don't worry about the time it takes to answer these questions. Concentrate on producing good answers. There are 8 tutorial questions in this Kit.

How should I use this Kit?

1   Once you are confident with the Do you know? checklists and the tutorial questions, you should try as many as possible of the exam-standard questions; at the very least you should attempt the **key questions**, which are highlighted in the **question and answer checklist/index** at the front of the Kit.

2   Try to **produce full answers under timed conditions**; you are practising exam technique as much as knowledge recall here. Don't look at the answer, your BPP Study Text or your notes for any help at all.

3   **Mark your answers to the non-tutorial questions as if you were the examiner**. Only give yourself marks for what you have written, not for what you meant to put down, or would have put down if you had had more time. If you did badly, try another question.

4   Read the **Tutorial notes** in the answers very carefully and take note of the advice given and any **comments by the examiner**.

5   When you have practised the whole syllabus, go back to the areas you had problems with and **practise further questions**.

6   When you feel you have completed your revision of the entire syllabus to your satisfaction, answer the **test your knowledge** quiz on pages 88 to 91. This covers selected areas from the entire syllabus and answering it unseen is a good test of how well you can recall your knowledge of diverse subjects quickly.

7   Finally, when you think you really understand the entire subject, **attempt the test paper** at the end of the Kit. Sit the paper under strict exam conditions, so that you gain experience of selecting and sequencing your questions, and managing your time, as well as of writing answers.

Exam technique

EXAM TECHNIQUE

Passing professional examinations is half about having the knowledge, and half about doing yourself full justice in the examination. You must have the right approach to two things.

The day of the exam
Your time in the exam hall

The day of the exam

1 Set at least one alarm (or get an alarm call) for a morning exam.

2 Have something to eat but beware of eating too much; you may feel sleepy if your system is digesting a large meal.

3 Allow plenty of time to get to the exam hall; have your route worked out in advance and listen to news bulletins to check for potential travel problems.

4 Don't forget pens, pencils, rulers, erasers.

5 Put new batteries into your calculator and take a spare set (or a spare calculator).

6 Avoid discussion about the exam with other candidates outside the exam hall.

Your time in the exam hall

1 **Read the instructions (the 'rubric') on the front of the exam paper carefully**

   Check that the exam format hasn't changed. It is surprising how often examiners' reports remark on the number of students who attempt too few - or too many - questions, or who attempt the wrong number of questions from different parts of the paper. Make sure that you are planning to answer the right number of questions.

2 **Select questions carefully**

   Read through the paper once, then quickly jot down key points against each question in a second read through. Select those questions where you could latch on to 'what the question is about' - but remember to check carefully that you have got the right end of the stick before putting pen to paper.

3 **Plan your attack carefully**

   Consider the order in which you are going to tackle questions. It is a good idea to start with your best question to boost your morale and get some easy marks 'in the bag'.

4 **Check the time allocation for each question**

   Each mark carries with it a time allocation of 1.6 minutes (including time for selecting and reading questions). A 20 mark question therefore should be completed in 32 minutes. When time is up, you must go on to the next question or part. Going even one minute over the time allowed brings you a lot closer to failure.

5 **Read the question carefully and plan your answer**

   Read through the question again very carefully when you come to answer it. Plan your answer to ensure that you keep to the point. Two minutes of planning plus eight minutes of writing is virtually certain to earn you more marks than ten minutes of writing.

6 Produce relevant answers

Particularly with written answers, make sure you answer the question set, and not the question you would have preferred to have been set.

7 Gain the easy marks

Include the obvious if it answers the question and don't try to produce the perfect answer.

Don't get bogged down in small parts of questions. If you find a part of a question difficult, get on with the rest of the question. If you are having problems with something, the chances are that everyone else is too.

8 Produce an answer in the correct format

The examiner will state in the requirements the format in which the question should be answered, for example in a report or memorandum.

9 Follow the examiner's instructions

You will annoy the examiner if you ignore him or her. The examiner will state whether he or she wishes you to 'discuss', 'comment', 'evaluate' or 'recommend'.

10 Present a tidy paper

Students are penalised for poor presentation and so you should make sure that you write legibly, label diagrams clearly and lay out your work neatly. Markers of scripts each have hundreds of papers to mark; a badly written scrawl is unlikely to receive the same attention as a neat and well laid out paper.

11 Stay until the end of the exam

Use any spare time checking and rechecking your script.

12 Don't worry if you feel you have performed badly in the exam

It is more than likely that the other candidates will have found the exam difficult too. Don't forget that there is a competitive element in these exams. As soon as you get up to leave the exam hall, forget that exam and think about the next - or, if it is the last one, celebrate!

13 Don't discuss an exam with other candidates

This is particularly the case if you still have other exams to sit. Even if you have finished, you should put it out of your mind until the day of the results. Forget about exams and relax!

Approaching mini-cases

APPROACHING MINI-CASES

What is a mini-case?

The mini-case in the examination is a description of an organisation at a moment in time. You first see it in the examination room and so you have 64 minutes to read, understand, analyse and answer the mini-case.

The mini-case (Part A of the paper) carries 40% of the available marks in the examination.

As mini-cases are fundamental to your exam success, you should be absolutely clear about what mini-cases are, the CIM's purpose in using them, and what the examiner seeks; then, in context, you must consider how best they should be tackled.

The purpose of the mini-case

The examiner requires students to demonstrate not only their knowledge of the fundamentals of marketing, but also their ability to use that knowledge in a commercially credible way in the context of a 'real' business scenario.

The examiner's requirements

The examiner is the 'consumer' of your examination script. You should remember first and foremost that a paper is needed which makes his or her life easy. That means that the script should be well laid out, with plenty of white space and neat readable writing. All the basic rules of examination technique discussed earlier must be applied, but because communication skills are fundamental to the marketer, the ability to communicate clearly is particularly important.

An approach to mini-cases

Mini-cases are easy once you have mastered the basic techniques. The key to success lies in adopting a logical sequence of steps which, with practice, you will master. You must enter the exam room with the process as second nature, so you can concentrate your attention on the marketing issues which face you.

Students who are at first apprehensive when faced with a mini-case often come to find them much more stimulating and rewarding than traditional examination questions. There is the added security of knowing that there is no single correct answer to a case study.

Suggested mini-case method

You have about 64 minutes in total.

Stage		Minutes
1	Read the mini-case and questions set on it very quickly.	2
2	Read the questions and case again, but carefully. Make brief notes of significant material. Determine key issues in relation to the questions etc.	5
3	Put the case on one side and turn to your notes. What do they contain? A clear picture of the situation? Go back if necessary and concentrate on getting a grip on the scenario outlined.	4
4	Prepare an answer structure plan for question (a) following exactly the structure suggested in the question, highlighting your decisions supported by case data and theory if appropriate. Follow the process outlined for question (b), etc.	3
5	Prepare a timeplan for each part of the question, according to the marks allocated.	1
6	Write your answer	44
7	Read through and correct errors, improve presentation	5
		64

A good answer will be a document on which a competent manager can take action.

Notes

(a) It is not seriously suggested that you can allocate your time quite so rigorously! The purpose of showing detailed timings is to demonstrate the need to move with purpose and control through each stage of the process.

(b) Take time to get the facts into your short term memory. Making decisions is easier once the facts are in your head.

(c) Establish a clear plan and you will find that writing the answers is straightforward.

(d) Some candidates will be writing answers within five minutes. The better candidates will ignore them and concentrate on planning. This is not easy to do, but management of your examination technique is the key to your personal success.

(e) Presentation is crucial. Your answer should be written as a final draft that would go to typing. If the typist could understand every word and replicate the layout, then the examiner will be delighted and it will be marked highly.

Handling an unseen mini-case or caselet in the examination

The following extract is taken from the Chartered Institute of Marketing's Tutor's/Student Guide to the treatment of mini-cases.

Tutor's/Student Guide to the treatment of mini-cases

'It needs to be stated unequivocally that the type of extremely short case (popularly called the mini-case) set in the examinations for Certificate and Diploma subjects cannot be treated in exactly the same way as a long case study issued in advance. If it could there would be little point of going to all the trouble of writing an in-depth case study.

'Far too many students adopt a maxi-case approach using a detailed marketing audit outline which is largely inappropriate to a case consisting only of two or three paragraphs. Others use the SWOT analysis and simply re-write the case under the four headings of strengths, weaknesses, opportunities and threats.

'Some students even go so far as to totally ignore the specific questions set and present a standard maxi-case analysis outline including environmental reviews through to contingency plans.

'The "mini-case" is not really a case at all, it is merely an outline of a given situation, a scenario. Its purpose is to test whether examinees can apply their knowledge of marketing theory and techniques to the company or organisation and the operating environment described in the scenario. For example answers advocating retail audits as part of the marketing information system for a small industrial goods manufacturer demonstrate a lack of practical awareness. Such answers confirm that the examinee has learned a given MIS outline by rote and simply regurgitated this in complete disregard of the scenario. Such an approach would be disastrous in the real world and examinees adopting this approach cannot be passed, ie gain the confidence of the Institute as professional marketing practitioners. The correct approach to the scenario is a mental review of the area covered by the question and the *selection* by the examinee of those particular parts of knowledge or techniques which apply to the case. This implies a rejection of those parts of the student's knowledge which clearly do not apply to the scenario.

'All scenarios are based upon real world companies and situations and are written with a fuller knowledge of how that organisation actually operates in its planning environments. Often the organisation described in the scenario will not be a giant fast moving consumer goods manufacturing and marketing company since this would facilitate mindless regurgitation of textbook outlines and be counter to the intention of this section of the examination.

'More often the scenarios will involve innovative small or medium sized firms which comprise the vast majority of UK companies which lack the resources often assumed by the textbook approach. These firms do have to market within these constraints however and are just as much concerned with marketing communications, marketing planning and control and indeed (proportionately) in international marketing, particularly the Common Market, as are larger enterprises.

Approaching mini-cases

'However, as marketing applications develop and expand and as changes take root, the Institute (through its examiners) will wish to test students' knowledge and awareness of these changes and their implication with regard to marketing practice. For example in the public sector increasing attention is being paid to the marketing of leisure services and the concept of "asset marketing" where the "product" is to a greater extent fixed and therefore the option of product as a variable in the marketing mix is somewhat more constrained.

'Tutors and students are referred to Examiners' Reports which repeatedly complain of inappropriateness of answer detail which demonstrates a real lack of *practical* marketing grasp and confirms that a leaned by rote textbook regurgitation is being used. Examples would include:

- The recommendation of national TV advertising for a small industrial company with a local market
- The overnight installation of a marketing department comprising Marketing Director, Marketing Manager, Advertising Manager, Distribution Manager, Sales Manager, etc into what has been described as a very small company
- The inclusion of packaging, branded packs, on-pack offers, etc, in the marketing mix recommendations for a service

'It has to be borne in mind that the award of the Diploma is in a very real sense the granting of a licence to practice marketing and certainly an endorsement of the candidate's practical as well as theoretical grasps of marketing. In these circumstances such treatments of the mini-case as described above cannot be passed and give rise to some concern that perhaps the teaching/learning approach to mini-cases has not been sufficiently differentiated from that recommended for maxi-cases.

'Tutors/distance-learning students are recommended to work on previously set mini-cases and questions and review results against published specimen answers. They are also advised to use course-members' companies/organisations as examples in the constraints/limitations of marketing techniques and how they might need to be modified.

'Students are also advised to answer the specified questions set and if for example a question was on objectives, then undue reference to market analysis and strategies would be treated as extraneous.'

THE EXAM PAPER

Format of the exam

	Number of marks
Part A: one compulsory minicase	40
Part B: three questions from six (equal marks)	60
	100

Time allowed: 3 hours

Analysis of past papers

June 2000

Part A

1   Profile of a cereal manufacturer
    (a) Strategic options in a price war
    (c) Auditing process necessary to review innovation activities

Part B

2   Value chain
3   Evaluation of target markets
4   Balanced score card approach
5   Branding issues
6   Motivation for strategic partnership and critical success issues
7   Scenario planning

> This paper forms the Test Paper at the end of this Kit, so only an outline of its contents is given here.

December 1999

Question number in this Kit

Part A

1   Profile of a low cost UK based airline — 69
    (a) Identification of core capabilities, using the value chain
    (c) Branding strategy for future developments

Part B

2	Problems in effective marketing planning	6
3	Geodemographic segmentation and direct marketing	36
4	Formulation of, and influences on, strategic objectives	29
5	Forming a view of the future: market sensing and market research	25
6	New product development	50
7	Danger and causes of strategic wear out	30

> **Examiner's comments.**
> - Candidates had to ensure that they answered all elements of the question asked.
> - Candidates needed to concentrate on the strategic aspects of marketing and not make the mistake of drifting into tactical answers.

The exam paper

June 1999

Part A

The wet shave market   67
1 (a) Briefing paper on new product development and promotion
  (b) Evaluate the strategic options

Part B

2	Pan-European branding	53
3	PIMS	54
4	Internal cultural barriers	13
5	Market-led strategic change	62
6	Potential market segments	14
7	Relationship marketing strategy	55

> **Examiner's comments summarised by BPP**
>
> - Candidates needed to ensure that they concentrated on the specifics of the question set, rather than answering in a generalised way.
>
> - For example in question 7, the question related to a company in the 'business to business' sector. To gain high marks, the candidates needed to relate their answer specifically to issues in the business to business sector.

December 1998

Part A

A UK retailer specialises in selling photographic equipment.   68
1 (a) Competitive position and competitive advantage
  (b) Internal marketing

Part B

2	Weakness of BCG	18
3	Defending position	41
4	Franchising	5
5	Lifestyle segmentation and international markets	35
6	Innovation in a domestic appliance business	48
7	Product life cycle	19

> **Examiner's comments**
>
> The overall standard achieved was similar to June 1998. Where poor results were achieved, this was generally due to the following factors.
>
> - failure to answer the required number of questions
> - failure to answer the question set
> - superficiality
> - lack of strategic insight or international dimension
> - poor writing style and grammar
> - little application of relevant concepts, theories or examples
> - use of bullet point checklists
>
> Of all these points, the lack of an international dimension to many answers was particularly worrying and indicates a need to read more widely.

The exam paper

The analysis below shows the topics that have been examined in the sittings of the old syllabus **Strategic Marketing Management: Planning and Control** since 1997

		Question number in this Kit
June 1998		
Part A		
A German packaging company, organised into three SBUs, markets all over Europe. Despite technological and product excellence, market share is falling.		66
1(a)	How to respond to price competition	
1(b)	Developing an effective environmental monitoring system	
Part B		
2	Internal marketing	59
3	Segmentation and positioning in business-to-business markets	34
4	IT and managing customers	45
5	Brand strategy in financial services	46
6	Evaluating a new service proposal	52
7	Forecasting the life cycle	21

Examiner's comments

Candidates should have related the answer to the specific context of the question, and answered all parts in the required format.

December 1997

Part A

1	A middle ranking manufacturer of mountain bikes is facing competitive pressures	65
	(a) Challenging leaders	
	(b) Brand strategy	

Part B

2	Market potential and information	20
3	Divisional product portfolio	24
4	Price-based strategy	43
5	Marketing strategy for marketing manager	38
6	Loyalty marketing	49
7	Changes in marketing	3

Examiner's comments, summarised by BPP

The examiner was disappointed that, despite this straightforward paper, there were still some very poor papers, and a greater polarisation between good and bad answers than before. Answers to the mini-case were sometimes problematic.

The exam paper

June 1997 | Question number
| In this kit

Part A

1. A supplier of ready-made re-heatable meals has grown rapidly, relying on its product and reputation. New competitive pressures have led to a more offensive approach — 64

   (a) Offensive marketing towards challenges and focus
   (b) Relationship marketing

Part B

2. Bring rigour to SWOT — 17
3. Life cycle analysis and high-tech products — 22
4. Customer profiles in business-to-business marketing — 37
5. Direct marketing — -
6. Marketing control for a brand manager and multiple distribution systems — 61
7. Competitor information system — 12

Examiner's comments

The scripts tended to be very variable. In general, there was a greater understanding of strategic issues. Some candidates still fell into the trap of ignoring the specific issues raised by the questions and producing very general answers.

SYLLABUS

Aims and objectives

- To enable students to develop a sound theoretical and practical understanding of marketing planning and control
- To enable students to understand the theoretical concepts, techniques and models that underpin the marketing planning process
- To build practical skills associated with the management of planning process
- To develop an understanding of the barriers that exist to effective implementation of strategy
- To appreciate the need to tailor marketing plans and process to allow for the specific sector and situational factors that apply to any given organisation
- To develop an awareness of the techniques that underpin innovation and creativity in organisations

Learning outcomes

Students will be able to:

- Understand and critically appraise a wide variety of marketing techniques, concepts and models
- Conduct and evaluate a detailed marketing audit, both internally and externally
- Compare and contrast strategic options
- Specify a clear rationale when choosing between strategic alternatives
- Prepare effective and realistic marketing plans
- Initiate control systems for marketing planning
- Understand and evaluate the processes that can be used to overcome barriers to effective implementation of marketing strategies and plans
- Evaluate a range of techniques that facilitate innovation in organisations

Indicative content and weighting

1 Market-led approach to planning (10%)

1.1 Adopting a market-led orientation
   - Marketing orientation
   - Role of marketing in market-led strategic management
   - Drivers of change in the business environment

1.2 The strategic marketing process
   - Corporate strategy/marketing interface
   - The basis of planning and control: the structure of planning and the cycle of control
   - The nature of strategic, tactical and contingency planning

2 Analysis (20%)

2.1 External analysis
   - Environmental analysis, industry analysis
   - Market analysis
   - Competitor analysis, customer analysis

Syllabus

2.2 Internal analysis

- Resource-based approach:
  Organisational assets, capabilities and competencies
  Technical resources
  Financial standing
  Managerial skills
  Organisation
  Information systems
- Asset-based approach:
  Customer-based assets
  Distribution-based assets
  Alliance-based asset
  Internal assets
- Marketing activities audit
  Marketing strategy audit
  Marketing structures audit
  Marketing systems audit
  Productivity audit
  Marketing functions audit
- Innovation audit:
  The organisational climate
  Rate of new product development
  Customer satisfaction ratings
  The innovation/value matrix
  The balance of cognitive styles of the senior management team

3 Techniques for analysis and strategy development (20%)

3.1 Techniques for developing a future orientation

- Trend extrapolation
- Modelling
- Intuitive forecasting
  Individual of genius forecasting
  Consensus forecasting
  Jury forecasting
  Delphi forecasts
  Scenario planning
- Market sensing - examines the way in which managers develop new ways of looking at the outside world, in order to improve the way they develop market strategies and delivery marketing programmes

3.2 Auditing tools

- Portfolio analysis
- Value chain
- PIMS
- Experience curves
- Financial
  Ratio analysis
  Productivity analysis
  Segmental analysis
  Balance sheet evaluation
  Profit and loss accounts
- SWOT analysis
- GAP analysis

4 Strategy formulation and selection (30%)

4.1 The strategic intent

- Mission
- Objectives
- Stakeholders
- Customer/competitor orientation

4.2 Approaches to creating strategic advantage

- Generic strategies
- Developing sustainable advantage
  - Superior product or service
  - Perceived advantage
  - Global skills
  - Low-cost operator
  - Superior competences
  - Superior assets
  - Scale advantages
  - Attitude advantages
  - Legal advantages
  - Superior relationships
- Alliances and networks
- Offensive/defensive strategies
- Competitive positions and strategy
  - Strategies for market leaders
  - Strategies for market challengers
  - Strategies for followers
  - Strategies for market nichers
- Product/market strategy
  - Product/market matrix
  - PLC
  - PIMS
  - Portfolio analysis
- Strategies for declining and hostile markets
- Strategic wear-out and renewal

4.3 Developing a specific competitive position

- Strategic alignment process
  Assets/competencies
- Segmentation and targeting
  Evaluation of balanced score card
- Positioning
- Branding strategy
- Innovation and product development
- Building customer relationships

4.4 Strategic marketing plans

- Process and structure of marketing planning
- Strategic and tactical marketing decisions

Syllabus

5 Implementation and control (15%)

5.1 Key elements of implementation
- Leadership
- Internal marketing
- Project management
  Systems
  Skills
  Management of change-

5.2 Key elements of control
- The dimensions of effective marketing feedback and control systems
- Basic control concepts and their application throughout the planning and implementation process
- Financial control
  Budgets
  Ratios
- Benchmarking

Question bank

DO YOU KNOW? - THE MARKET LED APPROACH TO PLANNING

- *Check that you know the following basic points before you attempt any question. If in doubt, you should go back to your BPP Study Text and revise first.*

- Marketing is the management process responsible for identifying, anticipating and satisfying customer requirements profitably.

- A strategic perspective to marketing centres around planning for the future. It expands the marketer's role from an emphasis on tactical marketing mix detail to include decisions about the organisation's future direction.

- Marketing orientation is the way by which an enterprise's target customers' needs are effectively and efficiently satisfied within the resource limitations and long term survival requirements of that enterprise.

- The process of planning can be split into five stages.
    - Where are we now? Strategic and market analysis.
    - Where are we going? Strategic direction and strategy formulation.
    - How can we get there? Strategic choice.
    - Which is the best route? Strategic evaluation.
    - How can we ensure arrival? Strategic implementation and control.

- Corporate planning involves consideration of the future direction of all the functional areas of a business: production; finance; personnel; marketing. Marketing planning provides the focus on products and markets.

- Tactical planning is more detailed and short term. Tactics are the way in which the operations required to implement the strategy are broken down into individual responsibilities, time schedules and budgets.

- Contingency plans are developed to ensure that the organisation is prepared for an event that is liable, but not certain, to occur which may adversely affect the marketing plan.

- A marketing research plan should contain background information, research objectives, research proposal, method of reporting and a budget.

- MkIS stands for a Marketing Information System. Four subsystems make up the MkIS: the internal reports system; the marketing intelligence system; the analytical marketing system; and the marketing research system.

- The sales force can be used to collect continuous and specific information about the marketplace.

- Advertising campaigns can be pre-tested using tests of consumer opinion, individual interviews, focus groups, physiological measurement, readability tests and test marketing.

- The main types of primary research methods are observation, surveys (personal, telephone, mail) and experimentation.

Question bank

1   TUTORIAL QUESTION: MARKETING AND CORPORATE PLANNING

How does corporate planning differ from marketing planning?

Guidance note

Outline the stages of the corporate planning process and indicate how marketing contributes at each stage.

2   MARKETING AND CORPORATE STRATEGY   *32 mins*

What are the characteristics of strategic decisions at the corporate and marketing level, and how can a strategic perspective at the marketing level be developed?
(20 marks)

3   MARKETING TASK (12/97)   *32 mins*

As markets fragment and life cycles get shorter and less predictable, the nature of the marketing task is changing. Identify the causes of these changes and how a marketing manager might possibly respond. **(20 marks)**

4   DEVELOPING MARKETING ORIENTATION   *32 mins*

How important is the development of a marketing orientation for the effective development and implementation of a marketing plan? **(20 marks)**

5   INFORMATION FOR FRANCHISING DECISION (12/98)   *32 mins*

Your Taiwan based organisation has been approached by a major UK clothing retailer with a view to franchising their operation in your home market. Write a report outlining the information that is needed in order to make a management decision on this proposal. Show how you would acquire this data. **(20 marks)**

6   EFFECTIVE MARKETING PLANNING (12/99)   *32 mins*

What are the potential problems faced by an organisation attempting to make marketing planning effective? How can the impact of these problems be minimised? **(20 marks)**

DO YOU KNOW? - ANALYSIS

- Check that you know the following basic points before you attempt any question. If in doubt, you should go back to your BPP Study Text and revise first.

- SWOT analysis assesses the organisation's Strengths and Weaknesses in relation to external Opportunities and Threats.

- A marketing audit covers six areas: the external environment audit; the strategy audit; the systems audit; the functions audit; the structure audit; and the productivity audit.

- The macro environment consists of four sets of factors: politico-legal; economic; socio-cultural and technological.

- Consumer buyer behaviour is affected by cultural, social, personal and psychological factors.

- Industrial buying behaviour is affected by environmental, organisational, interpersonal and individual factors.

- The general model of the consumer decision-making process has five stages: identification of needs; gathering of information; comparison of alternatives; selection; and post-purchase evaluation.

- Four types of buying behaviour have been identified (by Assael): habitual, dissonance reducing, variety seeking and complex.

- The DMU (decision making unit) is responsible for buying decisions and comprises users, influencers, deciders, approvers, buyers and gatekeepers.

- The family life cycle model can be used to track buyer behaviour over time. One such model (Wells and Gubar's) suggests nine stages beginning with the bachelor stage and ending with the solitary survivor, retired.

- Competitor response profiles as suggested by Porter should be developed. These consist of each competitor's current strategy, capabilities, assumptions and future goals.

- The balance sheet is a snap-shot of a business's financial position at a particular time. The profit and loss account shows the excess of income over expenditure. Profit and cash are *not* the same: a company can be profitable, but, for various reasons, can run out of cash. The cash flow statement acts as a link between the balance sheet and the profit and loss account. It shows all sources of funding whether capital or revenue in nature.

- Ratio analysis is used to indicate the financial health of an organisation either internally over time or against budget, or externally in comparison with other companies.

- Kotler suggests that five issues are important when reviewing marketing effectiveness.
  - A customer-orientated philosophy
  - An integrated marketing organisation
  - Adequate marketing information
  - A strategic orientation
  - Operational efficiency

- Strategic wear-out refers to the problems organisations face when they do not continually review and update their marketing strategies.

Question bank

7 TUTORIAL QUESTION: MARKETING AUDIT

To what areas should managers pay attention when conducting a marketing audit?

Guidance note

Remember to include the three levels of analysis: macro-environmental; micro-environmental and internal analysis.

8 MARKETING ANALYSIS: BUYER BEHAVIOUR *32 mins*

In what ways does **organisational** buyer behaviour differ from **consumer** buyer behaviour? How can an understanding of these differences be used in the planning of the sales strategy?

(20 marks)

9 SOCIAL CHANGE (12/96) *32 mins*

Societies are changing in a wide variety of ways. Identify the nature and significance of two such changes that are taking place within your own society and discuss their implications for the marketing planning and control process. **(20 marks)**

10 OVERSEAS BUYER BEHAVIOUR (6/96) *32 mins*

Your company is thinking of entering a number of foreign markets with a range of fashion products that it has previously only sold in its home markets. What factors would you take into account in analysing patterns of customer buying behaviour in the new markets?

(20 marks)

11 COMPETITOR RESPONSE PROFILES (6/96) *32 mins*

Your company is coming under increasing attack from a number of competitors. Identify the information that you would need in order to develop competitive response profiles and how this information might subsequently be used in the development of a marketing strategy. **(20 marks)**

12 INFORMATION ABOUT COMPETITORS (6/97) *32 mins*

Your company's markets are becoming increasingly competitive. Explain how you would develop an effective competitive information system in these circumstances, the nature of the inputs that the system would require and how the outputs from the system might be used to improve the strategic marketing process. **(20 marks)**

13 INTERNAL CULTURAL BARRIERS (6/99) *32 mins*

Many organisations wish to build or maintain a high degree of market orientation or customer focus. How can they overcome the internal cultural barriers that may oppose this approach? **(20 marks)**

14 POTENTIAL MARKET SEGMENTS (6/99) *32 mins*

A small chain of independent hotels has undertaken thorough market research that has identified a range of market segments they could pursue. Write a report outlining how this organisation can evaluate the attractiveness of the potential segments in order to decide which ones it should serve. **(20 marks)**

DO YOU KNOW? - TECHNIQUES FOR ANALYSIS AND STRATEGIC DEVELOPMENT

- *Check that you know the following basic points before you attempt any question. If in doubt, you should go back to your BPP Study Text and revise first.*

- Mission statements should at least describe the firm's basic business in terms of products and/or services to provide and markets to serve. The identification of future directions to be pursued by the firm and the establishment of business values, attitudes and beliefs.

- The basis for deciding on a mission statement is the firm's response to two fundamental questions: 'Where is our business now?' 'Where should our business go in the future?'

- Objectives are clear statements of what the business or function intends to achieve. Objectives should be hierarchical, measurable, realistic and consistent.

- Marketing objectives are usually expressed in sales terms: market share, sales revenue and sales volume. These are then translated down into tactical objectives for product, pricing, promotion and distribution plans.

- Five stages of environmental analysis (as suggested by Wilson, Gilligan and Pearson) are as follows.
    - Audit of environmental influences
    - Assessment of the nature of the environment
    - Identification of key environmental forces
    - Identification of the competitive position
    - Identification of the principal opportunities and threats

- Four bases for segmenting consumer markets are: demographic; geographic; behavioural and psychographic.

- Market targeting involves two steps. Step 1 is the evaluation of the potential and attractiveness of each segment. Step 2 is the selection of the target segment(s).

- The four stages of the product life cycle are: introduction, growth, maturity and decline.

- A number of criticisms have been levelled at the Boston Consulting Group portfolio model which relates market growth and market share. One of the key criticisms is that more than two factors affect cash flow.

- Porter suggests there are three broad generic competitive strategies; overall cost leadership, overall differentiation and focus (segmentation based on cost or differentiation).

- Kotler and Singh propose five offensive competitive marketing strategies which are effective in challenging market leaders. The most direct form of attack is a frontal strategy.

- In marketing, generally applicable critical success factors (CSFs) include sales volume, market share and gross margin.

- Time series analysis, leading indicators, simulation and diffusion models are quantitative sales forecasting methods which marketers can employ.

15 TUTORIAL QUESTION: SWOT ANALYSIS

What practical contribution is SWOT analysis capable of making to the marketing planning and control process? What role does the marketing audit play in SWOT analysis?

Guidance note

In addition to outlining each element of a SWOT analysis, also point out the contribution it can make to effective planning and control, together with any limitations you think it might have.

16 TUTORIAL QUESTION: SALES FORECASTING

What are the organisational implications of both underestimating and overestimating the expected level of sales in the annual sales forecast?

Guidance note

Outline what sales forecasting is, and the implications of having too few goods on the one hand and too many on the other. Conclude by discussing how sales forecasting can be made more accurate.

17 SWOT: NEED FOR RIGOUR (6/97) *32 mins*

It has been suggested that the majority of SWOT analyses are far too bland and of little real planning value. Explain how you would go about conducting a **rigorous** SWOT analysis and how the results might then be used strategically. **(20 marks)**

18 PORTFOLIO ANALYSIS: BCG AND OTHERS (12/98) *32 mins*

Several models have been developed to provide a more flexible approach to portfolio analysis than that developed by the Boston consultancy Group Matrix (BCG). What are the weaknesses of the BCG approach? Using an alternative model of your choice show how it tries to overcome the limitations of the BCG. **(20 marks)**

19 PRODUCT LIFE CYCLE (12/98) *32 mins*

'Far from providing any useful insights the concept of the product life cycle is likely to mislead marketing Managers.' Discuss this statement and illustrate with examples from your own experience. **(20 marks)**

20 NEW PRODUCT POTENTIAL (12/97) *32 mins*

Your company has been offered the production and marketing rights for an innovatory new product aimed at the manufacturing sector. Explain, in detail, how you would assess the product's market potential and how the information might be used in developing the company's marketing strategy for the product. **(20 marks)**

21 LASER DRILL LIFE CYCLE (6/98) *32 mins*

Your company is in the process of developing a laser drill. How would you go about evaluating the market potential of the product and forecasting the probably shape of the product life cycle? **(20 marks)**

Question bank

22 LIFE CYCLES AND HIGH-TECH PRODUCTS (6/97) *32 mins*

To what extent is traditional thinking on product and market life cycles a useful tool for forecasting the length and shape of the life cycles of high technology products in fast moving markets? How, if at all, might thinking on life cycles need to develop in order to reflect more accurately the particular challenges of these types of market? **(20 marks)**

23 DECLINE STAGE (6/96) *32 mins*

You have recently taken responsibility for a product which your company has marketed for several years, but which now appears to be entering the decline stage of the product life cycle. Identify the strategic alternatives that are open to you and the criteria that should be used in deciding between these alternatives. **(20 mins)**

24 PORTFOLIO REVIEW (12/97)

As a newly appointed Marketing Manager, you have decided to review your division's product portfolio. Explain how you would go about this task and how the results might possibly be used. **(20 marks)**

25 ANALYSIS TECHNIQUES (12/99) *32 mins*

Your Marketing Director has asked you to write a briefing paper, outlining and evaluating the techniques available to help the organisation form a view of the future. In particular, she has asked you to explain the difference between the concept of market sensing and market research. **(20 marks)**

DO YOU KNOW? - STRATEGY FORMULATION AND SELECTION

- *Check that you know the following basic points before you attempt any question. If in doubt, you should go back to your BPP Study Text and revise first.*

- The 4Ps are product, price, promotion and place. Each element has a sub-mix. Promotion, for example, consists of advertising, sales promotion, PR and selling.

- The service marketing mix (developed by Booms and Bitner) has 7 'Ps'; the four above, plus physical evidence, process and people.

- To develop a new product a number of stages of development are necessary. In Booz, Allen and Hamilton's model, these are idea generation, screening, concept development and testing, marketing strategy, business analysis, product development, market testing and commercialisation.

- Sales promotions can be aimed at consumers, industrial customers, resellers and the sales force.

- When setting the price of a product, five broad factors should be considered: costs; demand; competitor pricing; company objectives and the product itself.

- The first stage in the development of an advertising campaign is to conduct research. This should cover background information on the consumers, on the product and competitors.

- The AIDA model (developed by Strong) describes the consumer's response to the promotion in terms of communication theory. AIDA stands for Awareness, Interest, Desire and Action.

- Intensive, selective and exclusive strategies are the three possible distribution channel strategies.

- There are three strategy-determined methods to set the advertising budget: objective-task; mathematical models; and the experimental approach.

- Profitability, liquidity and value-added are examples of financial evaluation criteria. Sales volume, customer satisfaction and growth rate are examples of non-financial criteria.

- SWOT analysis, portfolio models, CVP analysis, decision trees and networks are all examples of models which can be used to aid decision-making in the planning and control process.

- Pearson suggests a feasibility study should include:
    - Corporate audit
    - The scenario or project
    - Assumptions
    - Feasibility research: technical; marketing; and financial

26 TUTORIAL QUESTION: MARKETING PLAN

Identify the key elements of the marketing plan and its relationship with the total planning process.

Guidance note

The marketing plan is generated from the corporate plan, but the relationship between them means that marketing considerations are at the heart of the corporate plan.

27 TUTORIAL QUESTION: COMPETITIVE STRATEGY

Making reference to examples, discuss how Michael Porter's ideas of generic competitive strategies can be used by the marketing planner.

Guidance note

This is fundamental to the strategic approach, as it has implications for all business functions, not just marketing.

28 TUTORIAL QUESTION: NEW PRODUCT DEVELOPMENT

What guidelines has research in recent years provided on how the new product development process might most effectively be organised?

Guidance note

This question is not asking you simply to outline the NPD process but to consider the various ways the process can *be organised*.

29 STRATEGIC OBJECTIVES TRADE OFF (12/99) *32 mins*

The strategic direction of an organisation is subject to a number of influences. Discuss the trade-offs that managers should consider when formulating an organisation's strategic objectives. **(20 marks)**

30 STRATEGIC WEAR-OUT (12/99) *32 mins*

Your Managing Director has asked you to write a report on the dangers and causes of strategic wear-out in an organisation. In particular the report should identify ways in which this danger can be avoided. **(20 marks)**

31 MISSION AND OBJECTIVES *32 mins*

Illustrate the essential differences between an organisation's mission, policies, aims and objectives. **(20 marks)**

32 IMPORTANCE OF MARKET SHARE (12/96) *32 mins*

Why is the pursuit of market share typically seen to be such an important marketing objective? In what circumstances would you recommend to an organisation that market share or market share increases would be an inappropriate objective? **(20 marks)**

Question bank

33 INDUSTRIAL SEGMENTATION *32 mins*

Evaluate the proposition that our knowledge of how to segment industrial markets effectively now lags a considerable way behind how this might be done in consumer markets. **(20 marks)**

34 INFORMATION FOR SEGMENTATION AND POSITIONING (6/98) *32 mins*

Your company has developed a computer software package targeted at specialist distribution companies. Identify the information you would use in order to develop a clear understanding of the market and how this information might then be used to develop an effective segmentation and positioning policy. **(20 marks)**

35 LIFESTYLE SEGMENTATION (12/98) *32 mins*

What advantages do lifestyle segmentation techniques offer over other methods of segmenting a market? For an organisation operating internationally what difficulties may they encounter using this approach? **(20 marks)**

36 GEODEMOGRAPHICAL SEGMENTATION (12/99) *32 mins*

What advantages would a geodemographic segmentation approach offer a financial services organisation, expanding into the insurance market, using direct marketing techniques?
(20 marks)

37 CUSTOMER PROFILES AND SOFTWARE (6/97) *32 mins*

Your company is about to launch a new computer software package into the airline and hotel reservations market. Prepare a report for your marketing director identifying the information needed to develop customer profiles and how these profiles might then be used to develop the segmentation, targeting and positioning strategy. **(20 marks)**

38 MARKETING STRATEGY DEVELOPMENT (12/97) *32 mins*

What factors should a marketing manager take into account in developing a marketing strategy? **(20 marks)**

39 DEVELOPING A STRATEGY (6/96) *32 mins*

What factors should be taken into account in the development of a marketing strategy?
(20 marks)

40 COMPETITIVE ADVANTAGES (6/95) (12/96) *32 mins*

> **Tutorial note.** This question has two dates as it has been set twice.

It has long been recognised that effective marketing is based upon the identification and exploitation of meaningful competitive advantage(s). Making reference to the possible bases of competitive advantage, explain why so many marketing campaigns fail to do this and reflect instead a 'me-too' approach. **(20 marks)**

Question bank

41 DEFENDING POSITION (12/98) *32 mins*

A major bank has declared that it is going to enter an already very competitive motor insurance market and offer highly competitive prices to customers. You have been asked to provide a briefing paper advising a financial services company, which is a well established direct insurer, on the options open to them when faced by this new discount orientated competitor. **(20 marks)**

42 CRITICAL FACTORS FOR SUCCESS *32 mins*

How can an understanding of critical success factors be used to aid an organisation's planning and control? **(20 marks)**

43 PRICE-BASED STRATEGIES (12/97) *32 mins*

Faced with an increasingly competitive market, your Marketing Director is thinking of pursuing an aggressive price-based strategy. Identify the criteria which should be used in deciding whether to cut prices and how you would go about forecasting the probable effects of any price cuts upon demand. **(20 marks)**

44 EVALUATION CRITERIA *32 mins*

As a marketing manager working within a multinational, you have been asked to evaluate the organisation's performance in a variety of product and market sectors. What financial and non-financial criteria would you recommend be used to develop a clear picture of past and probable future performance? **(20 marks)**

45 EFFECT OF TECHNOLOGY ON CUSTOMERS (6/98) *32 mins*

Making reference to examples, discuss how either the Internet or developments in database management are changing managers' thinking on the marketing strategy and how customers might be managed. **(20 marks)**

46 BRAND STRETCHING (6/98) *32 mins*

As a Marketing Planner for a financial services company, identify the key elements of a brand strategy and the criteria which should be used in brand stretching decisions. **(20 marks)**

47 BRAND STRATEGY (6/96) *32 mins*

You are a marketing analyst of a company that manufactures and markets soft drinks. Your newly appointed marketing director feels that the company has no real brand strategy. You are required therefore to prepare a report which identifies the key elements of a brand strategy. **(20 marks)**

48 INNOVATION: IMPLEMENTATION ISSUES (12/98) *32 mins*

A domestic appliance manufacturer is concerned that its main competitor is delivering new products to the market more quickly than they are. You have been asked to provide a report to this company on how it can increase its pace on innovation. Any implementation issues that might cause particular difficulties should be highlighted. **(20 marks)**

Question bank

49 LOYALTY MARKETING (12/97) *32 mins*

Your Marketing Director has returned from a seminar at which reference was made to 'loyalty marketing'. Prepare a briefing paper explaining what is meant by loyalty marketing and how a loyalty marketing campaign might be introduced by an organisation. **(20 marks)**

50 PRODUCT DEVELOPMENT (12/99) *32 mins*

Evaluate the alternative means by which the new product development process could be organised by an organisation which manufactures electrical cooking equipment for both domestic and commercial customers. **(20 marks)**

51 FEASIBILITY STUDIES AND RISK EVALUATION *32 mins*

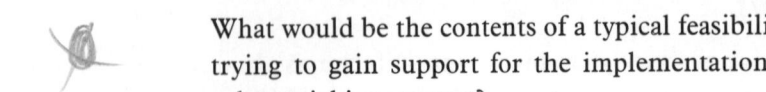

What would be the contents of a typical feasibility study developed by a marketing manager trying to gain support for the implementation of a new leisure centre venture requiring substantial investment? **(20 marks)**

52 NEW CRITERIA FOR A NEW PROPOSAL (6/98) *32 mins*

Identify the financial and marketing criteria which should be used to evaluate a new service proposal and how these criteria might be applied. **(20 marks)**

53 PAN-EUROPEAN BRANDING (6/99) *32 mins*

Your organisation is a large confectionery manufacturer operating in Europe. You have been asked to write a report outlining and evaluating the various strategic options available for pan-European branding. **(20 marks)**

54 PIMS (6/99) *32 mins*

Write a report critically evaluating the usefulness of Profit Impact On Marketing Strategy (PIMS) in the analysis of marketing performance, and in the formulation of marketing strategies. **(20 marks)**

55 RELATIONSHIP MARKETING STRATEGY (6/99) *32 mins*

How can an information technology company in the 'business-to-business' sector build a relationship marketing programme? **(20 marks)**

DO YOU KNOW? - IMPLEMENTATION AND CONTROL

- *Check that you know the following basic points before you attempt any question. If in doubt, you should go back to your BPP Study Text and revise first.*

- Kotler suggests there are four steps in the control process: goal setting, performance measurement, performance diagnosis and corrective action.

- Bonoma and Clark's implementation model suggests four skills are required for the effective implementation of marketing plans: allocating; monitoring; organising; and interacting skills.

- Frequently encountered implementation problems include: weak support from senior management; the degeneration of the planning process into an annual ritual; failure to integrate planning into the total corporate planning system; and too much detail projected too far ahead.

- Internal marketing involves selling the external marketing plan to internal customers (ie employees).

- For internal marketing to be effective, an analysis of the internal 'political' situation can be helpful, as well as an analysis of the case to be sold, on its rational merits.

- Ratios are often grouped into four areas.

    - Profitability ratios, for example return on capital employed
    - Debt and gearing ratio; for example cash flow ratio
    - Liquidity ratios (eg stock turnover period, creditors ageing, debtors ageing)
    - Shareholders' investment ratios (eg earnings per share)

- Profitability, sales analysis, market share analysis and sales/expense ratios are useful in the implementation of marketing plans.

- To monitor a sales representative's performance, certain quantitative data would be useful:

    - The number of locations of the accounts to be visited/contacted
    - The 'call frequency' relating to the various types/groups of customer
    - Achievement of average or budgeted call rates
    - Time spent in selling
    - Call rates for existing/new customers
    - Time expended on repeat/new business
    - The number of working days available to each representative
    - Time allowed for travelling, contact, and report writing

- An internal marketing audit should be comprehensive, systematic, independent and it should be performed regularly.

- The information derived from using the audit in the control process feeds into the next planning cycle at the situation analysis.

Question bank

56 TUTORIAL QUESTION: BUDGETS

Discuss the behavioural arguments for and against involving those members of management who are responsible for the implementation of the budget in the annual budget setting process. Explain how the methods by which annual budgets are formulated might help to overcome behavioural factors likely to limit the efficiency and effectiveness of the budget.

57 IMPLEMENTATION PROBLEMS *32 mins*

'Marketing planning is a generally straightforward exercise; the marketer's real problems are those of effective implementation.' (Anonymous). Identify the barriers to effective implementation that marketers typically encounter. **(20 marks)**

58 INTERNAL MARKETING (6/96) *32 mins*

Explain what is meant be 'internal marketing' and how you would go about introducing an effective internal marketing programme to an organisation. **(20 marks)**

59 INTERNAL MARKETING IN A HOTEL (6/98) *32 mins*

As the Marketing Manager for a chain of hotels, you have decided to develop an internal marketing programme. Prepare a briefing paper for your Marketing Director outlining the key elements of an internal marketing programme, how such a programme might be developed and implemented, and the nature of any problems which are likely to be encountered. **(20 marks)**

60 EFFECTIVE CONTROLS (12/96) *32 mins*

It is increasingly being recognised that marketing managers often pay more attention to planning that to control processes. Explain why this should be the case, the probable consequences, and how an effective marketing control system might be established.
(20 marks)

61 CONTROL SYSTEMS (6/97) *32 mins*

As the brand manager with profit responsibility for a range of personal computers sold through a variety of different types of distribution channel, identify the types of marketing and financial information you would require for an effective marketing control system and how this information might be used. **(20 marks)**

62 MARKET-LED STRATEGIC CHANGE (6/99) *32 mins*

Your Managing Director has returned from a conference at which reference was made to market-led strategic change. Prepare a briefing paper explaining what market-led strategic change entails. **(20 marks)**

DO YOU KNOW? - MINI-CASES

- If you are in any doubt as to how you should tackle a mini-case go back to page (xi).
- The mini-case is compulsory and comprises 40% of the marks. Ignore it at your peril.
- Consequently, **all** the mini-cases given below should be attempted. However, if really pressed, do questions 66 to 69 inclusive.

63 THE LEGAL BUSINESS (12/96) *80 mins*

The Legal Business is an ambitious and growth-orientated medium-sized firm of lawyers with offices in three major cities. The firm operates with 35 partners supported by 97 other fee earners and 100 support staff. The annual turnover is currently around £10 million. The legal services offered include matrimonial, commercial litigation, insolvency, debt recovery, licensing, intellectual property, and private client work. The fee earning potential and the firm's capabilities in each of these areas varies significantly. Each area is the responsibility of one of the senior partners. Until recently, the managing partner has taken responsibility for the marketing effort, but has found the task to be increasingly demanding and difficult.

Because of this, the managing partner hired a marketing consultant to conduct a brief and general review of the firm's current marketing activities. The results of the review have been summarised for the firm's partners and are as follows.

1. Levels of client satisfaction and client care are far lower than had been expected, with a high proportion of clients suggesting that they were not kept fully or sufficiently informed of the progress of their case.

2. Existing and potential clients appear to have little awareness of the full range of the services that the firm is able to offer. This problem is compounded by the ways in which the individual partners fiercely guard client relationships. The result of this is that although there are often opportunities for the cross-selling of services, this seldom happens.

3. There is no real sense of a long term direction for the firm or of a true competitive stance.

4. There is little planning and no obvious attempt to capitalise upon the firm's strengths.

5. Although there is some advertising, there is no advertising or promotional strategy.

6. Levels of client retention and new client attraction have dropped significantly over the past two years.

7. Market research suggests that the firm is perceived generally to be rather staid.

8. A number of the younger and more promising staff have been attracted away by competitors over the past two years.

9. A number of the companies both regionally and nationally have recently become far more aggressive in their search for new business, with the result that the firm's overall share of market is dropping.

In discussion with the partners and staff, the marketing consultant discovered that many are unclear about what is meant by marketing or indeed how it might contribute to the development of the firm. Instead, there is a culture based on a 'professional approach' characterised by a lack of commerciality and an attitude which prefers to wait for business to come in rather than going out to get it. This was reflected in comments such as:

Question bank

'Isn't marketing just a different name for selling?'

'Marketing is a cost and so whatever we spend will reduce our profits for the year.'

'If I had wanted to be a salesman, I would have chosen a different career path. I become a lawyer because I want to practise law. It isn't my job to do all this selling and marketing, is it? Don't expect me to change how I operate.'

Given this, the consultant recommended that a marketing manager be appointed to develop and co-ordinate an external and an internal marketing programme. You are the person who has been appointed to do this.

(a) As the first step, you have decided to carry out a detailed marketing audit of the firm. You should therefore prepare a briefing paper for the managing partner in which you explain the purpose, focus and components of the audit, how it might be conducted, and how the results might be used. (20 marks)

(b) Against the background of your comments in 1a, you are required to prepare a report for the managing partner recommending how a strategic marketing orientation might be introduced to the firm. In going this, you must make SPECIFIC reference to the particular problems that are likely to be encountered within a professional services organisation and how these problems might possibly be overcome. (30 marks)

(50 marks)

64 MJS CATERING SUPPLIES (6/97) *80 mins*

The MJS Catering Supplies Company

The MJS Catering Supplies Company is a specialist supplier of ready prepared meals which are then reheated before serving. The company operates with four principal strategic business units serving the airlines, restaurants, hotels and educational markets; selected sales and market data appear in Figure 1.

Figure 1	Selected sales and market data	
	Sales (1996/97)	Annual forecast market growth rate: 1997 - 2000
	£ million	%
Airlines	190	12
Hotels	163	10
Restaurants	120	8.5
Educational institutions	105	6.2
	578	

The company has grown rapidly over the past few years and has seen little need for detailed environmental analysis. Equally, little thought has been given by the management team to the development of an explicit marketing strategy. Instead, they have operated with a strong sales orientation and what they believe is an instinctive and unerring feel for the market which has led to the company identifying and exploiting a series of market opportunities.

The company's selling propositions have traditionally centred around the quality of its products, its innovative recipes, strong service backup and a high value for money offer. Although MJS is not a market leader in any of the sectors in which it operates, the company is seen by industry analysts to be a major player in all four of its markets.

Over the past two years, a number of changes have occurred in the catering supplies market, the three most significant of which have been the entry to the market of several new competitors; the take-over of two medium-sized firms by cash-rich and growth-oriented firms; and the merger of three of the smaller players. The net effect of this has been that the structure of the market has begun to change fairly dramatically, as have the nature and bases of competition.

Although MJS has not previously viewed its competitors as a real threat and has relied instead upon its strong market position and established reputation, there is now a recognition that patters of competition in the future will be very different. The company has recently lost two of its most profitable airline and hotel customers to medium-sized and increasingly aggressive organisations, and has been unsuccessful in five of the last six contracts for which it has submitted tenders. The majority of these tenders appear to have been lost to relatively small companies which have been market niching within the airlines and hotels markets.

Because of this, an element of panic has hit the company and there is now a recognition of the need for a far more offensive approach to its markets. In commenting on this, the managing director said, 'As a company, we're fat, lazy and complacent. If we carry on like this, we simply won't survive'.

As the firm's marketing manager, you have the responsibility for advising on the development and implementation of a new and more offensive marketing approach.

Required

(a) Prepare a briefing paper for the main board outlining the dimensions of an offensive marketing strategy and, in particular, how the company might fight off the emerging market challengers and nichers. You should also include within the paper comments on the organisational and cultural implications for MJS of adopting a more offensive competitive stance. **(30 marks)**

(b) In response to the finding of a market research exercise (see Figure 2 below), prepare a report for the managing director outlining the principal dimensions of a relationship marketing programme and how such a programme might most effectively be implemented. **(20 marks)**

Figure 2

A summary of market research findings

MJS's customers' perceptions of MJS

	1994	1995	1996
Product quality	4.3	3.9	3.1
Product innovation	4.6	4.1	3.3
Customer support	4.0	2.9	2.9
Value for money	4.2	3.8	3.7
Breadth of the product range	4.1	3.6	3.6

(**Note**. Scores are based on a five-point scale: 1 = very poor, 5 = very good)

(50 marks)

65 WILD OUTDOORS (12/97) *80 mins*

Background

The first mountain or off-road bikes were made in California in the late 1970s. Throughout the 1980s and 1990s, the market grew rapidly. Although initially slow to recognise the growing market opportunities, Wombat, a manufacturer of road bikes aimed at adults and children and racing bikes aimed at the enthusiastic amateur, entered the market in 1987 with a small range of medium quality, medium priced mountain bikes which it sold throughout Europe. In common with most other bicycle companies, the majority of their manufacturing was carried out in China and Taiwan.

At the beginning of the 1990s, the company restructured and concentrated its mountain bike operations in a new division which it called The Wild Outdoors Bicycle Company (referred to hereafter as WOBC); the division now accounts for 75% of the company's overall sales.

By the middle of 1997, the company was firmly established as a middle ranking player in the mountain bike market with annual sales of £126 million.

The 1998 Planning meeting

In October 1997, the marketing planning team met to update the company's annual plan and develop the 3 - 5 year strategic marketing plan for Europe. The meeting began with the Marketing Director giving an overview of the market and WOBC's performance. Amongst the points made were:

(a) The market is becoming increasingly competitive and showing all the signs of polarisation, with customers and retailers at the bottom end becoming more and more price sensitive, while at the top end they are looking for more sophisticated and innovative products.

(b) One of the most important critical success factors is access to a broad distribution network. Increasingly, the big three manufacturers are trying to tie up distribution with a series of special offers and incentives.

(c) The bigger retailers are looking for more promotional and merchandising support and over the next year or so will probably begin rationalising the ranges they offer. Because of this, some of the smaller and less specialised players will find it increasingly difficult to get wide distribution.

(d) Margins throughout the industry have been dropping over the past two years.

Turning to WOBC's performance, he highlighted the company's **slightly** higher than average sales and profit growth from 1993-96.

Leaning forward and looking intensely at his colleagues, he paused for dramatic effect before saying, 'It's obvious that the market out there is changing. Everything points to a shake-out over the next 2 - 3 years. To make sure that we survive, we need to be much more aggressive than we have been in the past. One of the problems that we face though is that we haven't done enough brand building and don't have a sufficiently strong brand strategy. It's obvious that there's a lot of potential out there. We can see that some of the competition is vulnerable. They're vulnerable because they've made a lot of money in the past and now they're fat, lazy and complacent. With margins dropping, they simply don't know how to respond. So let's get out there and start winning some market share. Let's stop talking about being a challenger, let's go and do it.'

As the others around the table needed, the Marketing Director turned to the newly appointed Marketing Analyst. 'As a first step, let's get some ideas on how to go about this. I suggest that we meet in a week or so and look at the situation again. So, I'd like you to prepare the papers on how we might go about challenging some of the others in the market and how we can go about developing a stronger branding strategy.'

As the analyst, you have the task of preparing the briefing papers for the meeting.

(a) In the first of these, you should outline the possible dimensions of a market challenger strategy for WOBC. In doing this, you should make reference to the probable resource, cultural and implementation implications of such a strategy.

(30 marks)

(b) You should then prepare a paper detailing the key elements of a brand strategy and how such a strategy might be developed and implemented over a 3 - 5 year period.

(20 marks)

(50 marks)

66 TMM INDUSTRIES (6/98) *64 mins*

The company

TMM Industries is a German packaging company with markets its products across Northern Europe through independent distributors. These distributors have typically been given the exclusive rights to a geographic area for a given period are able to call upon TMM for specialist sales and technical support. Promotional material is supplied by TMM, which also provides firm guidelines on prices and discount structures. Sales targets are agreed annually between TMM and the distributor.

The company's operations are divided between three strategic business units (SBUs): packaging machinery, packaging materials and specialist consultancy services which are offered to organisations with complex packaging problems. Selected sales and financial data appear in Figure 1.

Figure 1. Selected Sales and Financial Data

	TMM Sales (1997) £M £m	Number of perceived direct competitors	TMM's perception of its position in the market 1995	1997	Forecast Annual Market Growth Rate (1998- 2001)
Packaging machinery	140	9	3	5	6
Packaging materials	86	34	9	12	11
Consultancy services	35	5	2	1	8

The problem

For the past forty years, the company's marketing strategy has been based upon the technological superiority and technical excellence of its products, premium prices and high levels of after-sales service. However, since 1995, the market shares of each of its two biggest SBUs have dropped significantly. In the case of packaging machinery, the principal causes of this appear to have been an increased emphasis on innovation on the part of the traditional competitors, the entry to the market of an aggressively-priced and technically sophisticated company from South-east Asia which is targeting TMM's customers, and a general shortening of delivery times which TMM has not yet been able to match. The effects of this have been seen not just in an erosion of market share, but also in four of the company's largest distributors having taken the decision at the beginning of 1998 to drop their TMM franchise.

Question bank

The solution?

Following a crisis meeting of the firm's main board at the end of the first quarter of 1998, the decision was taken to appoint the company's first Marketing Director; prior to this, the responsibility for marketing within what is undoubtedly a product-led organisation was unclear. The new Marketing Director has begun by reviewing the entire sales strategy. His initial conclusions are that:

1. The company has too little formal market information and no clear idea of how its markets are likely to develop over the next few years.

2. The competitive stance is generally unfocused and appears to be based on assumptions that are no longer necessarily valid.

3. The product range and approach to selling/distribution are both in need of review.

TMM's Marketing Director has two priorities; deciding whether to respond to the competitive attacks the company is currently facing, and developing a far clearer and more strategic view of the market.

As the Market Analyst, working with the Marketing Director, you have been given two tasks.

(a) Prepare a briefing paper identifying the criteria which should be used in deciding whether and how to respond to the price-based attack from the South East Asian competitors. **(20 marks)**

(b) Prepare a report recommending how an effective environmental monitoring system for the company should be developed. Included within the report should be your suggestions on the structure of the system, the expected inputs and outputs, the likely organisational and resource implications, and the way in which the outputs might be used in developing TMM's future marketing strategy. **(20 marks)**

(40 marks)

67 THE WET SHAVE MARKET (6/99) — 64 mins

Gillette is launching a new wet shave razor system, called Mach 3, onto the global market. This product cost £460 million and took seven years to develop. The company aims to spend around £215 million launching this product globally of which approximately 10% will be spent in the UK. The main feature of this shaving system is that it has three blades. The key benefit is that it cuts 40% more hair than Gillette's previous shaving system Sensor Excel, and gives an extra-smooth shave. It also exerts less friction making shaving more comfortable. The Mach 3 is forecast to generate 17% category growth over two years, equivalent to selling 1.2 billion blades globally.

Wet shave customers can buy a shaving system or a disposable razor. With shaving systems the customer buys a razor handle which is refillable with blades that they can buy separately. The three main competitors in the wet shave market in the UK have the following market shares:

	Number of users of wet shave razors (Millions)
Gillette	9.0
Wilkinson Sword	2.8
Biro Bic	2.6

Note: Biro Bic concentrate on disposable razors.

The UK market is split between 54% on systems and 46% on disposables. 74% of blade and razor purchases (shaving systems and disposables) are made by men for themselves. The male grooming market has grown over the last two years by £50 million. The shaving systems market alone is worth £113 million. This is broken down as follows:

Gillette	£105m	65%
Wilkinson Sword	£32m	20%
Biro Bic	£11m	7%
Other brands, retailers own label	£13m	8%

When Gillette launched Sensor (a new razor system) in 1989 it went on to generate £3.65 billion in worldwide brand sales and sold nearly 400 million razor handles and eight billion blades. At the same time because Sensor was an innovative product Gillette was able to charge a high price for the product. The fact that there was little interchangability of the blades with other systems meant that the customer was restricted to purchasing Gillette blades. Previous launches of new systems have typically been priced 15% higher than the most expensive product available. The Mach 3 will be around 35% more expensive. Replacement blades will cost £1.12 each.

The aim with the Mach 3 is to capture new users into the Gillette franchise, to encourage millions of current Gillette users to trade up to the new system, and to move current users of disposables into the refillable shaving systems sector.

Advertising for the Mach 3 will be identical globally. Television advertisements will use the same film from Asia to Europe, with only minor modifications to the script. The aim of the campaign will be to steal customers from its competitors, (Wilkinson Sword in particular, as it is the only major competitor in the systems market) and to aggressively grow the sector. Prior to the launch of the Mach 3 Gillette ran a television advertising campaign with the aim of persuading customers to move from disposable razors to the Gillette system.

This mini-case study has been prepared from secondary sources.

(a) As a marketing manager for Wilkinson Sword write a briefing paper to your marketing director explaining why Gillette continue to spend large amounts of money on new product development and promotion. **(20 marks)**

(b) Outline and evaluate the strategic options that are available to Wilkinson Sword in this market. **(20 marks)**

(40 marks)

68 THE LENS SHOP LTD (12/98) *64 mins*

The Lens Shop Ltd (TLS) is a camera retailer based in the UK. It currently has 15 outlets based in the major centres of population.

There are two types of retailers selling cameras in the UK. On the one hand stores that sell a limited range of cameras amongst a range of other electrical and domestic appliances. These are mainly large department stores and electrical retailers that sell computers, hi-fi's, televisions and cameras. then there are specialist camera stores that only sell photographic products. TLS is one of major retailers in this more specialist camera sector.

TLS sells the majority of the leading brands. it also is the largest and most well established outlet for discontinued products, used by all the distributors to clear their shelves of 'old' product lines. These products are discounted heavily by TLS. TLS are able to buy in bulk and as a result can negotiate extra discounts.

All TLS stores are small and are located on less expensive secondary sites in the city centre but away from the main, high rent, shopping centre locations. The outlets are small they

Question bank

need less stock for display purposes and have very limited stock room space. Management feel that small stores have a better atmosphere, are less formal, hectic, yet friendly.

TLS's main promotional vehicle is a colour catalogue, which is described as '16 great pages of bargains'. This is very much seen as a 'fun' brochure promoting products in a positive light-hearted way by mixing illustrations, technical details and humour. The catalogue is distributed in a number of ways; to people coming into the stores, from racks outside the store, by 'freephone' telephone hotline and via a database of past customers. Media advertising is also used. Typically camera magazines will carry a five-page advertisement which highlights current bargains and often contains a promotional voucher for discounts or free accessories.

Prices are highly competitive, often discounted below recommended retail levels. The customer is provided with a price guarantee that TLS will beat any current local price by £10 for a similar brand of camera. TLS also offer a three year extended warranty at an extremely low price. Additionally, their warranty offers a unique guaranteed buy-back service for customers wishing to upgrade their photographic equipment. Management sees this as a genuine customer service which will hopefully encourage customer loyalty. All goods are subject to a 14-day exchange.

The company also aims to give high levels of customer service. Members of staff have a high degree of product knowledge. Sales assistants are particularly helpful, advising on the best purchases for any given budget. Staff are also happy to demonstrate the equipment. Selections of recent reviews from camera magazines are also available in the store to provide further information to customers.

To maintain required levels of customer service all customers are given a short questionnaire and asked to return them to the Managing Directors of TLS by freepost. The managing Director reviews all comments relating to customer service, and responds where appropriate.

As the new Marketing Manager for 'TLS' you have been asked to:

(a) Identify and explain the sources of the organisation's competitive advantage and whether their current position is sustainable. **(20 marks)**

(b) The Managing Directors of 'TLS' has heard that internal marketing might be a useful approach to adopt in her business. You have been asked to write a report illustrating how an internal marketing programme could be implemented. This report should also highlight the benefits of such a programme and the potential problems. **(20 marks)**

(40 marks)

69 EASYJET (12/99) *64 mins*

EasyJet is a low fare airline that operates a number of routes within the European market. Haji-Ioannou, the owner of Easyjet, founded the airline based on the belief that reduced prices would lead to more people flying. EasyJet's prices are low, for instance a return flight from Luton to Amsterdam costs between £70 to £130. Flights, with an airline offering full customer service package, could cost around £315 upwards.

The organisation's main base is at Luton airport from where flights to European destinations such as Amsterdam, Geneva, Nice, Barcelona, Palma and Athens are available. The airline also flies UK domestic routes from Luton to Edinburgh, Glasgow, Belfast and Liverpool. Liverpool allows the company to gain access into the lucrative North of England market and is becoming a growing centre of activity for EasyJet. Flights can now be taken from Liverpool to Nice, Amsterdam and Belfast.

Luton airport is around 30 minutes by road from north London and only 15 minutes from London's main orbital motorway, the M25. The airport is ten minutes away from Luton railway from where a 27-minute rail connection to London is available. A shuttle bus to the station is available every 10 minutes. A return rail journey for EasyJet passengers is available at around £8 (sterling). Liverpool airport also has good motorway connections.

Connecting flights are not part of EasyJet's product offering. The airline merely carries passengers to and from single destinations. This allows the airline to eliminate costly ticketing processes as well as intermediaries, such as travel agents. The company operates a paperless office policy and non-ticket flights. Simply by ringing the company's telephone number or using the company's Internet site customers can book a seat immediately by credit card. In autumn 1998, 40% of bookings for a major promotion in the Times newspaper were via the Internet. Although a confirmation of the booking will be sent if requested, customers only have to produce identification at the airport and quote the booking reference number to be given a boarding pass for their flight.

EasyJet flights are 'free seating'. Passengers are not allocated a specific seat when they check-in, instead they are given a boarding card that carries a priority number. The first person to check-in gets boarding card No.1, the next passenger, boarding card No. 2 and so on. Customers are then asked to board according to the order in which they checked-in occupying whichever seat they wish. The result is that passengers board the plane faster and tend to sit down faster than is the case when they have to search for an allocated seat, as is the situation in the more traditional airline operations. The faster passengers board an aircraft the quicker the plane can take off and the less time it spends on the tarmac. This results in reduced airport fees.

The fact that EasyJet is not hindered by connections to other flights allows it to operate out of cheaper secondary airports such as Luton and Liverpool, rather than larger airports like Heathrow or Manchester. EasyJet also exploits the lack of competition for time slots at Luton and Liverpool to keep the length of time its aircraft are on the tarmac to a minimum. EasyJet's aircraft are therefore airborne longer, creating more hours of revenue earning per aircraft, than companies operating out of larger and busier airports.

Premium priced airlines offer business class seats, which take up more room on an aircraft, and will normally operate with 109 seats on a Boeing 737-300. These airlines also require additional cabin crew in order to provide the level of service business class passengers demand. EasyJet operates without offering business class seats, which allows it to create 148 passenger places on a Boeing 737-300. Catering consists of a trolley from which cabin staff will sell drinks and a limited range of snacks to passengers. The only 'freebie' on the flight is a copy of the airlines in-flight magazine called 'Easy Rider', which is printed on recycled paper. Cabin staff look more casual in orange polo shirts and black jeans than traditional airlines and have a more relaxed attitude. They appear equally safety conscious as staff on other airlines.

EasyJet's telephone number is promoted widely. The company's telephone number, in bright orange, dominates the sides of the aircraft, where it has almost become part of the EasyJet corporate image. The organisation's approach to advertising has been described as "a guerrilla promotional approach", distinguished by attacks on the airline establishment and a series of PR stunts. Press and magazine advertising is widespread. Sales promotional activity has included joint promotions in national UK newspapers such as the Times and the Independent. The airline has also been the focus of a documentary series on UK television. The owner, Haji-Ioannou, has been featured in many business articles in the press, particularly for his high profile campaign against British Airways launch of its own low cost airline operation called 'GO'.

Question bank

EasyJet has also started targeting companies that wish to keep travel budgets under control. EasyJet emphasises that they do not offer a loyalty scheme where business customers can build up loyalty points and gain free flights. The suggestion is that although executives may like this perk the executive's company could be saving hundreds of pounds per trip by sending their staff on EasyJet flights.

The organisation's latest plan is to develop a family of companies with a common theme, beginning with the launch of a chain of cybercafes. Although the branding for this venture has yet to be decided, the working title is 'EasyCafe'. The company still has to make decisions, such as whether EasyJet's trademark bright orange colour is made a prominent feature of the cafes. Tony Anderson, who will oversee this new development, is quoted as saying that with these cafes 'We are targeting Joe Public, not the middle classes.'

This mini-case study has been prepared from secondary sources.

PART A

Question 1

(a) As a consultant you have been asked, as an initial step, to identify the core capabilities of EasyJet that can be used to grow the family of companies that Haji-Ioannou envisages. In particular you have been asked to use the value chain as part of this analysis. **(20 marks)**

(b) EasyJet have decided to develop a group of companies beginning with the cybercafe concept. You have been asked to provide advice on issues that need to be considered when making decisions on the organisation's branding strategy, for the group as a whole and for the 'Easycafe' concept in particular. **(20 marks)**

(40 marks)

Answer bank

Answer bank

1 TUTORIAL QUESTION: MARKETING AND CORPORATE PLANNING

Planning for the future, whether for the short, medium or long term, is a vital element of a manager's job. The future cannot be foreseen with certainty, of course, but while planning does not ensure success it does reduce the risks of failure and it does give the organisation direction and purpose.

In business, there is a standard, formal marketing planning process that operates at all management levels. Similarly we all get involved in planning activities in our non-professional lives. The general steps one would take when planning a house purchase, a holiday or a dinner party are the same.

Once you are clear about the level you are working at the rest is straightforward, because whoever you are and in whatever context you are working the principles of the planning process remain the same.

Where are we now?

The starting point must be a clear **assessment of the current position**. So for a house move you need to identify **resources and constraints**. Do you have a house to sell first? How much money can you afford to spend? In which geographic area must it be? What sort of house are you looking for? It is much the same when developing a corporate or marketing plan - both start with an **audit** and clarify the **mission statement.**

A **corporate audit** involves examining the strengths and weakness in each functional area: finance, production, personnel and marketing. Opportunities and threats of the corporate audit come predominantly from the marketing audit as it is here that the macro and micro environments (including PEST, customer and competitor analysis) are examined.

The **marketing audit** focuses on the external environment and the strengths and weaknesses of marketing strategy, functions, systems, structure and productivity. It is therefore less extensive than the corporate audit but in reality contributes greatly to this due to marketing's role as the customer/company interface.

Where are we going?

Planning can only have purpose if there is an agreed destination - an **objective** - what do you want to achieve from your plan? So for a holiday, do you want a relaxing holiday or an active holiday? Is it for one, two or three weeks? Will it be in Europe or elsewhere?

Corporate objectives are concerned with the whole firm and primary objectives relate to key financial factors for business success.

- Profitability (ROCE)
- Growth (sales)
- Reduction (increase in the product, customer, market base)
- Cash flow

All functions are deployed strategically towards achieving these objectives. For example, the production function can reduce costs, the finance function can manage funds more efficiently, the personnel function can recruit better people at less cost or increase their productivity and the marketing function can grow sales profitably. Because marketing's role is concerned with customers and products, marketing objectives are related to sales volume and market share and these are then translated down to tactical objectives for the marketing mix.

How do we get there?

Developing **strategies** involves making decisions about the best route to take. Without overall strategic direction everyone may set off from the same place but then veer off onto

Answer bank

their own preferred route. So for the dinner party it involves decisions about who to invite, what menu to develop, how much to spend and such like. Strategies should be devised after careful evaluation of the alternatives. The final choice should be the one that capitalises on the organisation's strengths and exploits opportunities identified at the first stage of planning.

Strategies are **how** you will achieve your objectives. Corporate strategy involves decisions regarding which businesses to be in. Portfolio analysis is employed to assess the attractiveness of the company business portfolio and decisions regarding what new business to enter, which to develop and which to harvest or divest are taken. Marketing strategy involves decisions concerned with what competitive advantage, positioning, customer segments and broad outline of the marketing mix to pursue in each target market.

How do we ensure arrival?

This involves **implementing the strategy** and checking that the objectives are being achieved.

The strategic statement is not a detailed route map. Its purpose is to put everyone on the same track. Action (tactical) plans are the responsibility of those further down the management ladder who provide the detail of how their department will achieve its part of the plan. Control information allows the manager to assess progress towards the objectives and to monitor any developments which require a change of plan. The tactics for the dinner party would be sending out the invitations and cooking the lasagne and pavlova - control would be checking that the lasagne doesn't burn (with a good contingency idea being buying a Vienetta in case the meringue goes wrong).

Corporate tactics are the strategies of each of the functional areas and control involves ensuring that the corporate turnover and profit objectives are met. Marketing tactics are the details of the marketing mix and control involves checking that sales volume and market share targets are achieved within budget.

So whilst the general principles of planning remain the same, the specific activities of corporate and marketing planning differ. However, of all the functional areas, marketing most closely relates to corporate planning because of the central importance of customers and products to corporate success.

2 MARKETING AND CORPORATE STRATEGY

Planning occurs at different management levels.

Level		Management	Time Scale
1	Corporate	Top	Long term
2	Business/Functional	Middle	Medium term
3	Operational/Action	Junior/staff	Short term

Clarifying the level of analysis within the overall framework of a business plan causes some students and managers alike difficulty. Confusion arises because there are a number of different terms used in the literature for the same thing.

To help understand these levels imagine you are on a staircase, as you move up from one level to another the strategy of the lower level is the tactics of the higher. So for example, marketing strategy is part of corporate tactics. Similarly, sales strategy is marketing tactics.

A strategic perspective centres around planning for the future, either planning for the whole organisation or just for the marketing aspects of the organisation.

Johnson and Scholes in *exploring corporate strategy* outline the characteristics associated with the word strategy and strategic decisions at the corporate or 'company wide' level.

(a) **The scope of an organisation's activities.** Does it focus on one area of activity or many? For example should BAe focus on defence?

(b) **The matching of the activities of an organisation to its environment.** In Europe, defence firms are seeking to collaborate to compete internationally, not just serve the home government.

(c) **The matching of an organisation's activities to its resource capability**: strategies need to be rooted in an adequate resource base.

(d) **The allocation of major resources** (often to do with major acquisitions or disposal of resources). BAe significantly rationalised its operations and workforce.

(e) **Affecting operational decisions.** Strategic decisions set off waves of lesser decisions. BAe's decision to rationalise the operation resulted in human resource issues for personnel, revised product and manufacturing plans which inevitably resulted in changes to the sorts of day-to-day problems faced by a production manager or a sales manager.

(f) **The values and expectations of those who have power.** Strategy can be thought of as a reflection of the attitudes and beliefs of those who have most influence in the organisation, this being related to the mission of the organisation. The expectations of the Government to maintain BAe as a major international competitor are influential in its mission.

(g) **The long term direction of the organisation.** The decision to privatise BAe affected its long-term future.

(h) **Implications for change and thus are likely to be complex in nature.** This arises for three reasons: strategic decisions usually involve a **high degree of uncertainty**, require **an integrated approach** to managing the organisation (including a cross-functional perspective) and thirdly, **involve change**, not only planning change but also in implementing it.

Marketing planning represents the strategic approach to marketing. Lancaster and Massingham (*Marketing Management* (1993)), outline three key reasons for what they see as an increasing need for a strategic approach to marketing.

(a) The pace of change and environmental complexity - environmental issues, technological change, social change etc.

(b) Increasing organisation size and complexity - a move from functionally structured to matrix and strategic business units, internationalisation.

(c) Increased competition (deregulation, globalisation, technology).

Kotler (in *Marketing Management*) highlights the characteristics of a strategic perspective in his definition of marketing management:

> 'The marketing management process consists of analysing market opportunities, researching and selecting target markets, designing marketing strategies, planning marketing programmes and organising, implementing and controlling the marketing effort.'

At the strategic level we see that marketing involves four processes.

(a) **Analysis**: the antecedent of decision making and plan formulation.

(b) **Planning**: analysis forms basis of plans, plans represent decision making.

(c) **Implementation**: having made plans they need to be put into action.

Answer bank

(d) **Control**: this completes the cycle of functional management as it feeds into the analysis and planning stages and the cycle starts again.

The tangible outcome of a strategic perspective to marketing is the marketing plan which outlines the current marketing situation, sets marketing objectives, strategies and tactics and outlines how the plan will be controlled.

Empirical research by Greenley (1987) and McDonald (1990) indicates that very few firms actually have formally written marketing plans, and this is particularly the case within the small business and not-for-profit sectors. Many organisations find it difficult to develop a strategic approach to marketing because of a lack of resources, marketing knowledge, skills, time and probably most importantly a lack of marketing orientation or culture.

Many prescriptive approaches have been developed, often as a checklist of activities needed to be done to write a marketing plan. However, changing an organisation's culture is not a simple or quick task. It requires top management support, internal communications and training on an on-going basis related to marketing skills and cross-function co-ordination.

However, the reality is that many organisations still do not adopt marketing planning practices at all. Therefore the first challenge for marketers working in these types of companies will be to introduce successfully a simple planning system which has the support of senior management.

3 MARKETING TASK

> **Examiner's comments: summary/extracts**. Better answers focused on a spectrum of issues accelerating the pace of change including demographics, global business and greater competition. Some candidates saw the words, 'product life cycle' and simply talked about the four stages of this model and consequently were awarded very few marks.

Marketers are facing a number of new **strategic challenges** as the environment changes. These include increasing pressure from governments to take a greater account of **'green', consumer and community relations** issues, the growing power of **global companies** and concentration of power within industries, changing social and cultural trends which bring about fragmentation of markets and innovation based on new technologies and emergent industries which stem from this. The focus of this question will be on the last two of these issues; **market fragmentation** and shorter/less predictable **life cycles**, the cause of these changes and how they affect the practice of marketing.

(a) **Market fragmentation**

People eat both health food and junk food and have a repertoire of brands depending upon the occasion. A few years ago, accessing daily news was something you did by listening to the BBC's 9 O'Clock News. Now you can listen to any of the hundreds of celestial, satellite and cable channels, read any one of hundreds of newspapers or magazines, listen to any of the myriad of radio stations or search for a particular topic on the internet.

(b) Shorter and less predictable product **life cycles** are a characteristic of high technology products and services. New technology and innovations have escalated over the last 30 years, with new products, concepts, channels and technology being launched at a massive rate. High technology products almost have a built in obsolescence, as technology development never stays still. Predicting the diffusion of innovation rate is very difficult.

Causes of market fragmentation and lack of predictability of life cycles

(a) **Social change**

The CIM/Henley Centre report, *'Metamorphosis in Marketing'* details how consumer behaviour and attitudes are changing. Traditional **consumer life stages** are changing. Wells and Guber's traditional family life cycle model which depicts a staged progression from youth to marriage and family to empty nesters is now a much less predictable path. A career for life is no longer the norm, redundancy and self-employment are rising, growing work and affluence of women, so too divorce, caring for elderly parents and middle age inheritances - all of these factors disrupt the pattern and lead to more consumer segments in many markets. The growth in 'minority' lifestyles is creating opportunities for niche brands aimed at consumers with very distinct purchasing habits.

(b) **Technological innovation**

This is bringing the ability to create large numbers of product variants without corresponding increases in resources. This is causing markets to become overcrowded. The fragmentation of the media to service ever more specialist and local audiences is denying mass media the ability to assure market dominance for major brand advertisers. This creates **space for niche players** and speeds up the diffusion of **innovation thus shortening life cycles**. The advance in information technology is enabling information about individual customers to be organised in ways that enable highly selective and personal communications. It also fuels **quicker 'me-too' product launches** which potentially shorten product life cycles.

How should the marketing manager respond to these challenges?

Finer segmentation, in response to market fragmentation, looks certain to play an even more crucial role in the marketing strategies in the years ahead. The move from traditional mass marketing to 'micro marketing' is rapidly gaining ground as marketers explore the incremental profit potential of niche markets.

Tyrrell from Henley, advises marketers to 'forget people' and think of **occasions** and, in a branding sense, to think about creating and 'owning' those occasions. An example of this leading edge approach to market segmentation is Bass Brewers' new product development focus. New alcoholic drinks categories are much more quickly being developed to satisfy different drinking occasions, Hooch as a punctuation, refreshing drink in the middle of a session, Red as a stimulant based drink to help ravers keep going, Snapshots to start the evening or help latecomers catch up.

Perhaps the most important response has to come in relation to **long-term marketing strategy**. With less predictable life cycles, marketing managers must redefine the guidelines provided by the traditional PLC. In order for PLC theory to be relevant, some kind of reliable method for **projecting lifespans** of the product is needed. With technology advancing so rapidly, historical data is no longer sufficient to be a useful predictive tool. Popper and Buskirk (1992) suggest that the concept of the Technology Life Cycle is superior to the PLC concept. A key difference in thinking is that high-tech firms must make a critical decision regarding focus. A company can attempt to follow a technology through its life cycle or specialise in one stage. Whichever is chosen, speed of response becomes vital.

Hooley and Saunders (1993) suggest that in fragmented markets, success depends on finding **niches** where particular product specifications are needed, as in the computer software market. As each niche provides little opportunity for growth, a firm needs to find a number of niches with some degree of commonality to allow economies to be achieved. In

Answer bank

contrast to niche players, brands such as Marks and Spencer and McDonald's over-arch social differences and appeal to standard needs on an international scale. As such marketers are having to stretch their vision to encompass the details and speed of micro-marketing and rapid new product development and the grand strategy of global branding, the cost pressures of tertiary brands and the image and service pressures of the differentiated offering.

As a recent article in Marketing Business concluded, marketers are having to become innovators, not only of brands and products, but of marketing itself.

4 DEVELOPING MARKETING ORIENTATION

Managers should not simply think of marketing as a department where people work or an activity that people do: they should appreciate that it is also a **management philosophy**. It represents an attitude adopted by the whole organisation and is characterised by the belief that if a business or service is to be successful then it has to ensure that the needs of its customers are satisfied.

The concepts which underpin marketing are not new. The economist Adam Smith wrote in 1760 that 'consumption is the sole end and purpose of production ...' Yet despite this early appreciation of the importance of the customer, marketing is still one of the newest business disciplines.

In the model below, it can be seen that management's attitude changes as the balance of power between supply and demand in the market place changes.

Demand/supply relationship	Orientation	Focus
Demand exceeds supply	Product orientation	Product and operational activities
Demand equals supply	Sales orientation	Promotion to ensure demand equals supply
Supply exceeds demand	Customer orientation	Identification of customer needs before committing resources

Three distinct phases in the evolution of the marketing concept can be recognised.

Product orientation

A product orientation featured in the early stages of the industrial revolution and still applies when a generic product is first introduced. Customers cannot afford to be choosy as there is no alternative choice. Dissatisfied customers can easily be replaced. In this situation, management's attention is focused on the production process: reducing costs and increasing output are the keys to increasing profitability.

Sales orientation

High profits attract other enterprises to enter the market. Eventually the volume of goods or services equals the amount demanded. Management's attention is now turned to ensuring that goods that **are** produced do in fact find a customer. Promotion is used to 'push' goods and services into the market.

In both product and sales orientated phases, the firm produces goods and services which it wants to make and then tries to sell them to the customers.

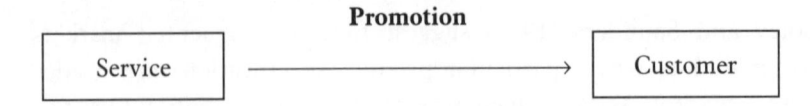

```
                        Promotion
        ┌─────────┐  ─────────────→  ┌──────────┐
        │ Service │                   │ Customer │
        └─────────┘                   └──────────┘
```

Customer orientation

When a buyer's market is established, managers are forced to change their approach and put the customer's needs first. Faced with a competitive environment, the strategy that ensures survival is the one that provides the services which customers want to use. This is done by researching customers' needs and problems before committing resources to production.

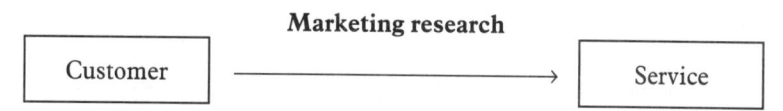

```
                    Marketing research
   ┌──────────┐    ─────────────────→    ┌──────────┐
   │ Customer │                          │ Service  │
   └──────────┘                          └──────────┘
```

To move from a customer orientation to a marketing orientation requires that customers, competition, company capabilities and changes in the environment are all considered when developing the marketing plan.

Wilson and Fook (*Marketing Business*, June 1990), define marketing orientation as the process by which an enterprise's target customer needs are effectively and efficiently satisfied within the resource limitations and long term survival requirements of that enterprise.

They use the McKinsey 7S model and link together:

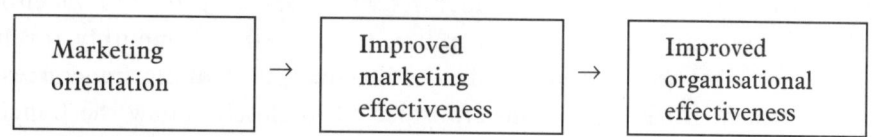

```
┌──────────────┐     ┌──────────────┐     ┌──────────────┐
│  Marketing   │ →   │   Improved   │ →   │   Improved   │
│ orientation  │     │  marketing   │     │organisational│
│              │     │effectiveness │     │effectiveness │
└──────────────┘     └──────────────┘     └──────────────┘
```

Developing a marketing orientation or culture is one side of the coin of **organisational effectiveness**, the other side is the development of functional marketing skills such as marketing planning. In this sense, a marketing orientation is vital for the effective development and implementation of a marketing plan. Without the focus on researching customer needs, the plan is likely to be poorly targeted. In relation to implementation, unless all employees are focused on customer satisfaction the plan is likely to fail.

The *McKinsey* Consultancy has worked on the issue of organisational effectiveness and a major statement of their findings is in Peters and Waterman's (1982) *In Search Of Excellence*. According to McKinsey, strategic planning and shared values are not enough. Strategy and shared values, however, are only two of seven elements that the best managed companies exhibit: strategy, structure, systems, staff, style, skills and shared values.

The McKinsey research showed that while the average and poorer performing companies tended to place most emphasis on the hard, tangible elements of strategy, structure and systems, the top performing companies placed emphasis on all seven elements in the framework including the behavioural elements of staff, skills, management style and shared values.

Christopher, Payne and Ballantyne in *Relationship Marketing* use the model as a framework for planning organisational change. The 'Seven S' model illustrates that organisational effectiveness and successful implementation of change comes about through careful consideration of all the elements. The model is also an excellent tool for judging the feasibility of a strategic implementation and strategic 'fit'.

There are three questions that should be asked in the context of checking strategic fit to achieve implementation:

- Given a proposed strategy, do the other S's support the strategy?
- How difficult is it to change each of the other S's?
- Does management have the will and patience to make these changes?

The examination of each of these elements should draw management attention to the need to focus on the **behavioural** aspects of implementing a marketing plan as well as the mechanistic ones.

Answer bank

To develop and implement any successful marketing plan, especially if it brings change, requires the organisation to be marketing orientated. This means a focus on 4Cs; customer needs, competitors, company capabilities and the changing environment. To be truly marketing orientated these shared values should be adopted through out the enterprise. In addition, marketing strategy and orientation also need to be supported by appropriate systems, structures, management style, staff and skills.

5 INFORMATION FOR FRANCHISING DECISION (12/98)

> **Examiner's comment: summary/extracts.** 'This was one of the least popular questions. The best answers concentrated on outlining the necessary information needed and the sources of this data. They also highlighted the importance of cultural issues. Poorer answers spent most of their time discussing the franchiser/franchisee relationship in general.'

Franchising

Compared to a company owned outlet, which is operated by salaried employees, a franchised store is operated by a franchisee who is an independent legal entity. **Franchisees** pay their respective franchisers an initial fee as well as a monthly royalty fee, which is usually specified as a percentage of sales revenue. In addition, franchisees are responsible for investment in the outlet and are expected to closely follow the franchiser's operating norms. Franchising's primary attributes (for example capital formation, motivated entrepreneurs, standard systems, brand recognition, and procedures to control operations) help to solve key challenges connected with services marketing firms (for example small size, intangibility of services, quality control) and, therefore, represent a 'practical business marriage' (Cross and Walker, 1987).

(a) **Information required**

As a Taiwan based organisation who has been approached by a UK clothing retailer with a view to franchising their operations in Taiwan certain information will be required before a decision can be made whether to take up this opportunity.

(i) **Marketing**

(1) How well recognised is the retail brand in its market and in our home market?

(2) What marketing support is provided by the franchiser; launch activity, on-going promotions, PR or advertising?

(3) What product range will be available and how much merchandising flexibility will be allowed?

(4) What happens in terms of stock ownership, returns, old stock and such like?

(5) What pricing policies are involved in the contract?

(6) How quick and effective are the current logistics?

(ii) **Finance**

(1) What are the costs of implementing and maintaining the operation?

(2) What are the forecasted sales?

(3) What are the forecasted profit implications?

(4) What historical sales, cash flow and profit figures are available from current franchisees?

(5) Are there capital borrowing implications?

Answer bank

      (6)   What financial consulting support is offered by franchiser?

(iii) **Human resources**

    (1)   Is there any recruitment, selection, appraisal and disciplinary support offered?

    (2)   What training guidelines and workshops are provided?

    (3)   Is any HRM software systems available for payroll?

    (4)   Are there any employment policy principles which will need to be adopted from franchiser's operating philosophy?

(iv) **Retail operations**

    (1)   What systems are required and/or provided (tills, EPOS, procurement)?

    (2)   What store location and design support is provided?

    (3)   What merchandising support/policies are stipulated?

    (4)   What information, monitoring and control procedures are required?

Acquiring this information

As with any research activity, the use of all the elements of a Marketing Information System should be utilised.

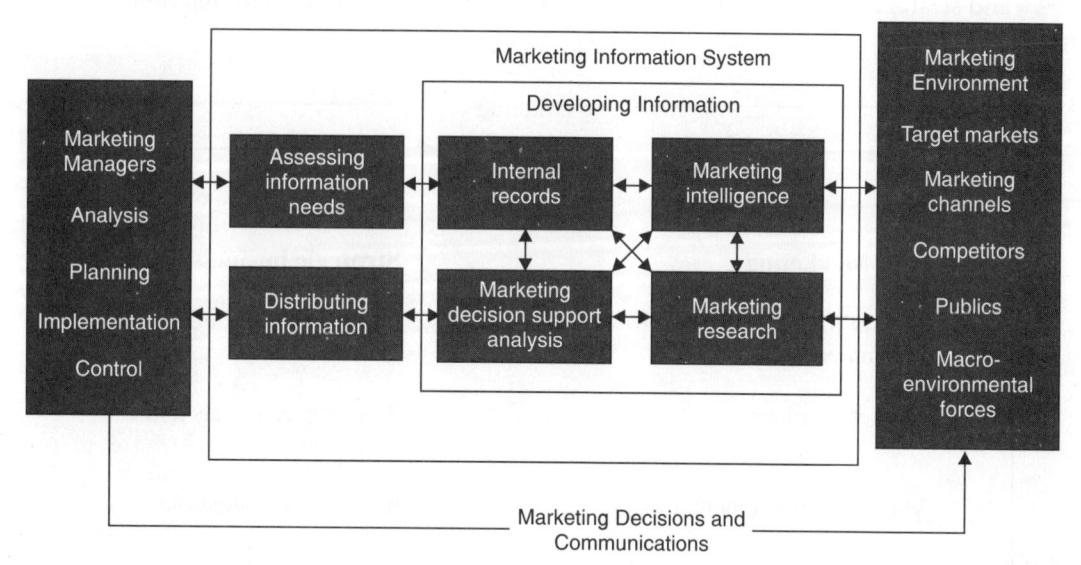

A lot of information can be gathered from **internal records** in the form of franchisee information provided by the UK retailer. Meetings to discuss the questions outlined above should provide a lot of background data. As the UK retailer has approached us, the firm should be receptive to our information requirements and make the relevant personnel in marketing, finance, HR and operations available to us, perhaps via email or a visit to the UK head office. On this visit, it would also be possible to conduct primary research in regard to a retail audit in UK principal town centres to see the retailer in operation in their home country. It would also be important to visit current franchisers in other countries around the world.

In addition, from market **intelligence sources**, reports would be available on retailing trends in both countries, financial performance of the retailer and reports on the retailer's franchising operations.

Meetings with our own **financial advisors** and lawyers would be required to assess the franchise agreement.

Answer bank

Finally, consumer research in Taiwan should be conducted to test the appeal of the new retail concept, store design, merchandise and pricing strategy. This would allow verification of sales forecast data provided by the franchiser.

Once these questions have answers with a reasonable degree of confidence a decision on whether to accept the franchise proposal could be taken.

6 EFFECTIVE MARKETING PLANNING (12/99)

> **Examiner's comments: summary/extracts.** This was a popular question but was generally poorly answered. The best answers discussed the stages in the planning process as a framework to structure their answer. These answers not only highlighted the problems associated with the planning process but went on to discuss the way in which these barriers can be overcome. Weaker answers ... failed to address the broader issues raised by the question.

Marketing planning is possibly the key activity in a customer orientated organisation. There is a significant relationship between marketing planning and other functions within the organisation.

The contribution of marketing planning to corporate planning

Kotler clearly expresses the interactive two-way relationship between marketing planning and strategic business planning. This is illustrated in the following diagram.

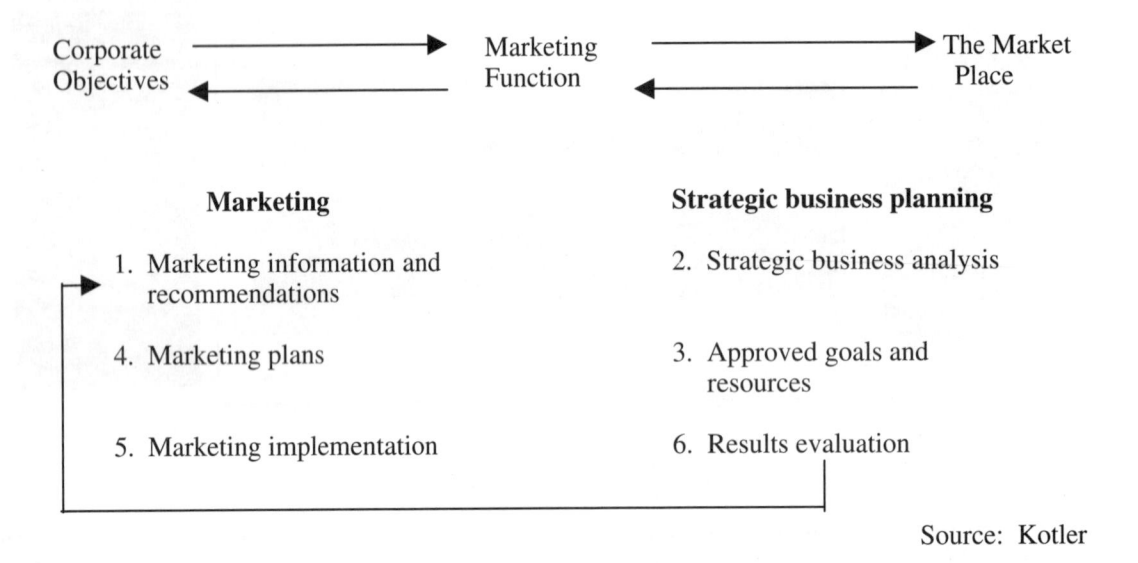

Corporate Objectives ⇄ Marketing Function ⇄ The Market Place

Marketing
1. Marketing information and recommendations
4. Marketing plans
5. Marketing implementation

Strategic business planning
2. Strategic business analysis
3. Approved goals and resources
6. Results evaluation

Source: Kotler

Marketing information is fed into the corporate planning process for analysis and formulation of the corporate plan, which directs the functional areas of the business, for example finance, operations and marketing. In particular it provides:

(a) **Information to enable the setting of corporate objectives, which provide focus for management**

This helps to achieve consistency between decisions made in different areas of the organisation about using skills and resources. This can lead to a focus on the core capabilities of the organisation and facilitates competitive advantage.

(b) **Effective control by which objectives can be assessed**

Corrective action may be taken when necessary, for example, contingency plans can be employed.

(c) **Motivation**

The set objectives can be used formally and informally to stimulate performance and create a culture which responds well to change.

Barriers to be overcome

(a) **Lack of information about events in the business environment**

An inefficient marketing information system affects knowledge about customers, markets, competition and social and economic change.

(b) **Lack of identification within the organisation's goals**

A formal, well defined organisational structure is necessary. Effective decision making must be communicated clearly to all levels and a two-way channel of information should be maintained.

Many managers are reluctant to make plans, and deal with problems only when they arise. This may be due to potential political conflicts for example over resource allocation. It might also be due to the manager disliking planning due to perceived extraneous effort. Similarly, a lack of knowledge may inhibit confidence in performing effectively and develop a fear of blame when planned targets are not achieved.

(c) **Opportunity costs**

Marketing may not always seem to be top priority when choices have to be made. Also, management may not be prepared to spend money on long term projects which will incur cost, even when the outcome would improve the organisation's capabilities and profits in the long run.

(d) **Insufficient marketing planning processes**

Inefficiency may arise because processes do not have sufficient 'ownership', or because no one takes responsibility for them. There may also be a lack of resources, or unrealistic allocation of resources (particularly time) for the achievement of the tasks involved.

Minimising potential problems

(a) **Develop a learning culture**

A culture should be developed where knowledge of markets, products, technologies and business processes are maintained. Simply investing for growth is insufficient.

There should be investment in staff development, training and effective reward systems. This can be linked to long term objectives which reward the 'defenders' and the 'harvesters'.

(b) **Create a well-defined organisational structure**

This would be characterised by effective decision making which is clearly communicated to staff of all levels. The communication channel should be two-way. This approach would allow all staff to be involved in the decision making and planning process. It could be described as a democratic leadership that is market orientated rather than a 'top down approach'.

(c) **Install an effective marketing information system**

A culture where marketing planning is not an annual event but a continuous process could be developed. This will be possible in an organisational structure which is flexible due to trained, skilled staff. They will be able to produce coherent marketing plans.

Answer bank

Management can commit to such a process by creating teams of people to manage key processes such as planning and actioning marketing efficiency reviews. They can create a culture where executives 'make it happen' and make adequate resources available to achieve this.

(d) **Use and development of enabling technology**

Links can be created within the existing organisational framework to enhance their value and improve the organisation's distribution, information and control.

Conclusion

A culture of change needs to be fostered so that the entire organisation include marketing planning as part of their strategic thinking. It is also important to encourage communications and internal marketing. Making marketing planning effective in an organisation is not just the role of the marketing department. It is something that needs to permeate the consciousness of the entire organisation.

7 TUTORIAL QUESTION: MARKETING AUDIT

A marketing audit answers the question, 'Where are we now?' and is needed in order to establish the current situation of an organisation:

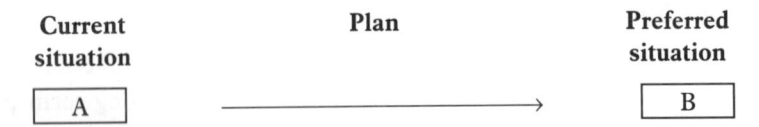

```
Current          Plan         Preferred
situation                     situation

   [A]        ─────────→         [B]
```

The marketing audit allows marketers to develop a Strengths, Weaknesses, Opportunities and Threats (SWOT) analysis and from there an achievable and realistic set of marketing objectives and strategies capable of moving the organisation towards the realisation of its objectives - situation B above.

A convenient way of modelling the areas of a marketing audit is as follows.

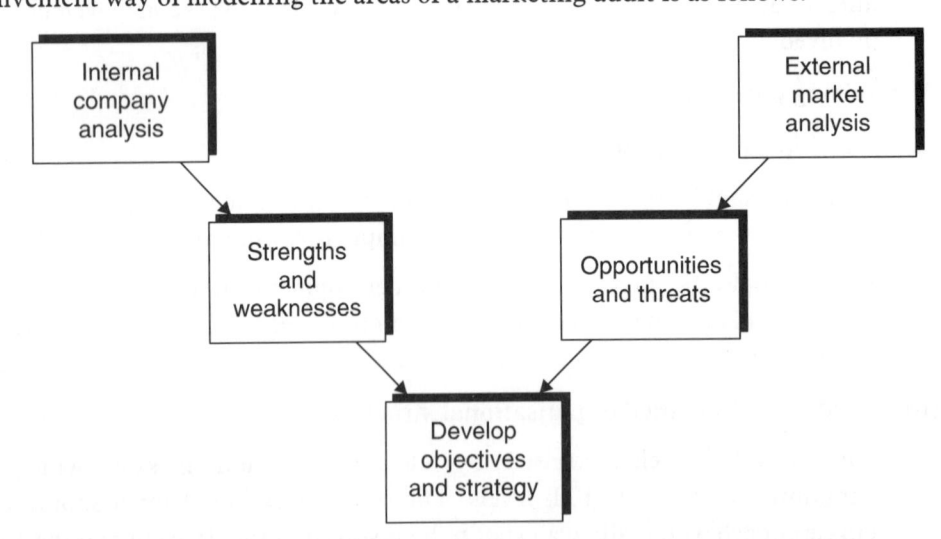

```
  Internal                           External
  company                             market
  analysis                           analysis
     │                                  │
     ▼                                  ▼
  Strengths                        Opportunities
     and                              and threats
  weaknesses
     │                                  │
     └──────────────┬───────────────────┘
                    ▼
                 Develop
                objectives
                and strategy
```

Kotler, Gregor and Rodger's article *The Marketing Audit Comes Of Age*, 1989, outlines six areas for a marketing audit; the marketing strategy audit, the marketing organisation audit, the marketing systems audit, the marketing productivity audit, the marketing functions audit and the marketing environment audit. The first five relate to an internal analysis of the marketing function and feed into the development of strengths and weaknesses for the SWOT analysis. The sixth audit is the external focus and whilst it may at first appear only to be a small part of the overall audit, factors in the macro and micro environment in fact require a great deal of analysis. The marketing environment audit is summarised by opportunities and threats in the SWOT analysis.

(a) **Internal company analysis**. Coverage should include strategy, organisation, systems, productivity and functions. This should highlight strengths and weaknesses through the posing and answering of certain questions.

(i) **The marketing strategy audit**: here a review of the organisation's marketing objectives and strategy should be conducted. The review should focus on how well suited these are to the realities of the external environment. For example, is the basis for market segmentation and positioning appropriate?

(ii) **The marketing organisation audit**: this aspect is concerned with an evaluation of the organisation's structural capability and suitability for implementing the strategy needed for the developing environment. For example, is the marketing function led by a person with appropriate experience and influence?

(iii) **The marketing systems audit**: this audit should consider the quality of systems for analysis, planning and control. For example, is there an appropriate MkIS providing timely and accurate information?

(iv) **The marketing productivity audit**: here the profitability of the marketing programme and cost effectiveness of marketing expenditure should be examined. For example, are there areas of marketing which appear to be experiencing rising costs?

(v) **The marketing functions audit**: this evaluates each of the elements of the marketing mix (4P'S or 7P'S). For example, how well managed is the product line? How appropriate are the pricing objectives? Is the distribution channel well motivated? Is the promotions budget well allocated?

(b) **External environmental analysis**. This should cover two levels of analysis; the more specific micro-environment and the broader macro environment.

The marketing environment audit: the micro or task environment includes an analysis of customers, competitors, suppliers, distributors and other parties in the immediate market place. Questions which should be posed include; what is the trend for market size and growth? Which customer segments show increasing demand? What scope exists for further market development? What are the major strengths and weaknesses of our competitors? What changes are taking place in the distributor and supplier networks?

The **macro-environment audit** should highlight key factors and trends in political, economic, social, technological forces. For example, what changes are taking place in product and process technology? How well placed is the organisation to exploit these changes? Are there likely to be any Government policies which will affect the organisation? What is likely to happen to inflation and interest rates in the short and medium term? Is the organisation keeping up with changes in consumer attitudes and tastes?

To do it properly, the marketing audit demands a large investment in resources; time, money, personnel and information. However the benefits outweigh the costs because the audit allows an organisation to be responsive to changes in the environment and to exploit its distinctive competencies most effectively.

8 MARKETING ANALYSIS: BUYER BEHAVIOUR

An understanding of who buys your product, how they buy it and what influences the buying process is fundamental to establishing marketing strategy for both consumer and industrial marketing managers. There is, however, general agreement that there are certain features in **organisational buying** that are not found in consumer markets and that these features have implications for sales strategy. As identified by Lancaster and Jobber (*Sales Technique and Strategy*) these are as follows.

(a) **Fewer potential organisational buyers**. Often 80% of output is sold to 10-15 organisations. In consumer selling, the presence of intermediaries (that is wholesalers/retailers) can mean there are relatively few direct buyers, although the **ultimate** number of end consumers can amount to millions.

(b) **Organisational buyers are more rational**. Although people buying for organisations are only human and may, as individuals, or prefer the colour of a particular product, on the whole the buying behaviour is more rational. Often economic criteria are used. Also, the buying decision has to be justified to other functions of the organisation.

(c) **Organisational buying may be to satisfy specific requirements**. Often buyers (especially industrial) determine product specifications and so the seller must tailor the product to meet them. In consumer marketing, products should be tailored to meet the needs of a segment, but these products are rarely geared to individual customers.

(d) **Reciprocal buying may be important**. For example, a company supplying business documentation (for example, invoices) to a chain of garages may only get the business if they have all their company cars serviced there.

(e) **Organisational buying can be more risky**. Often the contract is agreed before the product is made. Technical problems could arise later which could make the product uneconomic to produce. In additional very large sums of money are often involved as with the purchase of a new computer system.

(f) **Organisational buying is usually more complex than consumer buying**. Many people could potentially get involved - engineers, directors, marketing people. It may therefore be necessary to sell as a team.

The main way in which the decision making process varies is that a group of people, rather than an individual consumer, will normally be involved. This is known as the Decision Making Unit (DMU) (as termed by Webster in 1979). The DMU is usually made up of:

- Users (often initiators, for example production)
- Deciders (those with authority, for example directors)
- Influences (marketing, research and development, other managers)
- Buyers (who execute the purchase)
- Gatekeepers (for example, secretaries, receptionists)

The decision-making process itself is more complex than in consumer buying.

Answer bank

Organisational buying process

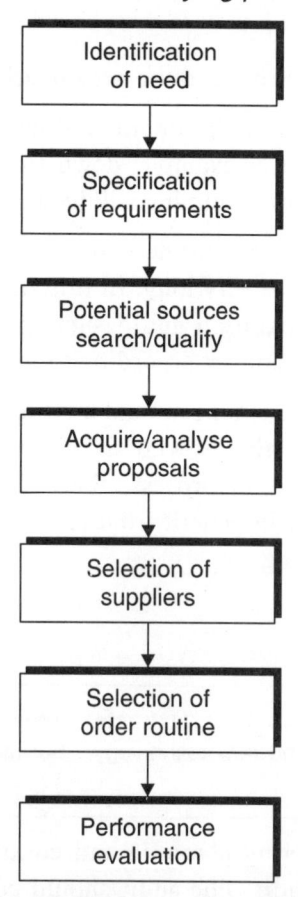

```
Identification
of need
     ↓
Specification
of requirements
     ↓
Potential sources
search/qualify
     ↓
Acquire/analyse
proposals
     ↓
Selection of
suppliers
     ↓
Selection of
order routine
     ↓
Performance
evaluation
```

One of the major differences between consumer and industrial buying is the buying motive or need. The former is usually for personal consumption whereas the latter is not. The development of formal specifications and the review of potential supplier proposals together with the development of an order routine make the process more formal and tangible.

In relation to sales strategy a number of factors affect the DMU, the process and criteria used by buyers to evaluate the product.

(a) **The buying situation/the buy class** (as noted by Robinson, Faris and Wind)

  (i) New buying situation: a lot of information is required.

  (ii) Modified: a regular requirement exists, but sufficient change has taken place to require some alteration to normal procedures.

  (iii) Straight rebuy: routine purchasing procedures set up.

  The DMU is likely to be more complex if the situation is new or modified, whereas on straight rebuys, it will probably be down to the purchasing officer to place an order. The salesperson needs to keep in regular contact with the organisation to be in at the start if a new purchase is to be made or to offer information where it is modified. Even if it is a straight rebuy, the company not supplying needs to be around to step in as soon as there's a problem with the other suppliers.

(b) **The product type**

  Products can be complex and expensive, such as plant and equipment. This is less so with materials (to be used in production process) or very simple and inexpensive items (for example, for MRO that is, maintenance, repair and operations, such as lubricants).

  The DMU is likely to contain different people, depending on the type of product. For example, directors are likely to be involved in purchase of plant and equipment, but

Answer bank

not in MROs. The sales strategy should highlight the members of the DMU to target for each product type.

(c) **Importance of the purchase to the organisation**

If the purchase involves large amounts of money and if the cost of making the wrong decision is very high (for example, down time), and if there is uncertainty about the outcome of the alternatives buying will be more complex.

It is deemed to be an important decision, many people will be involved, and the buying process will therefore be very long. In this situation it is necessary for the sales person to influence need recognition and design specification. It will be essential to present advantages to DMU members according to their own requirements.

So whilst research into organisational buying has pursued broadly similar questions as in the consumer field, (that is, who makes up the market, what is the process of buying and what influences this process, there are distinct differences), both sales and marketing managers will benefit from an understanding of the distinct characteristics of organisational buying.

9 SOCIAL CHANGE

> **Examiner's comments: summary/extracts.** Reasonable answers, with most candidates focusing on demography and new technology - but many ignored the implications for planning and control.

A key stage in the marketing planning and control process is an analysis of the current situation, or marketing audit. The audit should consist of an analysis of the wider macro environment, the more specific micro environment and an internal analysis of the organisation. The reason for conducting an audit is to ensure that the strategies, tactics and controls implemented are in line with the current needs, wants, behaviours and contexts of the target market. In this sense as societies change, so too should the way we market our products and services. Less than twenty years ago in the UK it was acceptable to market Supersoft shampoo with an image of a rather amused woman being forcibly taken away on the shoulder of a Viking. Equally the idea of a product designer being able to work together with a client hundreds of miles away via an Internet connection was not a possibility.

Societies constantly change. Doyle, in *Marketing Management and Strategy*, looks ahead to the year 2000 and offers ten environmental changes which appear to be accelerating:

(a) **Fashionisation:** goods affected by annual model changes, rapid obsolescence and unpredictable demand. New models and new services are becoming the key to enhancing margins.

(b) **Micro-markets**: customers expect customisation of goods to their specific needs. Technology permits ever-finer market segmentation and product range expansion.

(c) **Rising expectations**: brought about by higher quality products and services.

(d) **Technological change**: brought about both product and process improvements together with a society much more receptive to diffusion of technological innovation.

(e) **Competition**: market barriers have fallen with declining tariffs, lower transport costs and speed of information about market opportunities.

(f) **Globalisation**: rising incomes for travel and access to international media have created common demands and opportunities for common suppliers.

(g) **Service**: product advantages are difficult to gain and defend, often competition is based on service augmentation.

(h) **Commoditisation**: today's speciality products are tomorrow's commodities, unless companies can move the goalposts through faster innovation, profit margins decline.

(i) **Erosion of brands**: the fractionisation of previously homogenous markets, together with the growth in own label reliability is reducing the power of the big brands.

(j) **New constraints**: new regulations from the EU in terms of the environment and the raising of ethical standards brings offending companies under increasing scrutiny.

Mitchell, reporting in Marketing Business (1994), adds a number of additional ways in which society is changing: an ageing of the population in Europe; a growing social divide between relatively prosperous 'knowledge' workers and the rest; the fragmentation of traditional consumer lifestages due to fractured career paths, redundancy, self-employment, rising divorce, caring for parents, middle age inheritances and single parent families.

Of all these changes the two which will be selected for further discussion are **demographic change** and **technological change**.

Demography

At the beginning of the 1990s people aged over fifty were 17.8m or 31% of the UK population. By 2025 this will rise to 23m representing a significant increase in the proportion of old to young people, non-working to working people in the UK Currently, approximately 30% of the over fifties have no mortgage left to pay and they represent the inheritance generation with £10bn inherited in 1987 rising to £17bn in 1997. In the UK the over sixty-fives can be divided into three segments:

- 20% well-off
- 30% property rich but cash poor
- 50% state pension

Clearly with the growth in the older consumers and the related reduction in younger people, this brings significant implications for the planning and control for specific product groups. The demand for financial services, medical products, retirement housing and holidays is likely to increase whilst the demand for nightclubs, alcohol, starter homes and jeans is likely to fall. More specifically, the product manager of Thomson Holidays' 'Young at Heart' brand markets to 'JOLLies'; Jet-Setting Oldies with Loads of Loot, or the 20% well-off. At the beginning of the 1990s this represented 60,000 holidays. and the market is increasing. When marketing the brand a number of key points emerge.

(a) Good service is vital to repeat purchase.

(b) This segment is responsive to sales promotions which take time to redeem, involve collection and reward rather than competitions, free draws or lotteries.

(c) Media choice is skewed towards the Daily Telegraph and Daily Mail and retirement magazines such as Saga, Yours and Choice.

(d) This group watches a lot of TV. Good audience profiles include 'This Is Your Life' and 'Coronation Street'.

(e) This segment tend to identify with their children rather than with their parents and so think of themselves as 20 years younger.

For those organisations which find themselves in declining markets they will experience growing competition. Those that remain will need to more closely segment and position their products, consider expanding their product/market focus through market and product development strategies and closely control their cost and profit performance.

Technology

Perhaps even more significant than demographic changes is the influence exerted by changing technology on society. The convergence of computing and telecom technologies is significantly changing work, leisure and marketing planning practice. As the cost of IT falls and computer speeds increase the resultant information revolution is beginning to change how we learn and work. Consumers' acceptance of new technologically based products has also increased; the use of mobile telephones, faxes, home multi media systems, virtual shopping malls and interactive terminals is common. But what are the specific implications for marketing planning and control processes? Some examples of how technology is being applied will help to answer this question.

(a) **Sales**. The salesperson with a portable PC can run interactive sales demonstrations and automatic order processing.

(b) **Distribution**. The videobooth allows customers to talk directly to staff such as accounts personnel and forms can be signed and transmitted. Electronic data interchange has reduced the costs and speed of the grocery supply chain.

(c) **Product development**. The designer can have video clips of customers' reactions to prototypes from focus groups, designs can be viewed anywhere in the world, amended or approved in minutes rather than days through the post.

(d) **Market research**. Researchers can use software to tailor questions depending on the previous answer. Results can be downloaded for immediate analysis. Real time sales data can be merged, cut and presented in striking visual form and communicating direct to the marketing director.

(e) **Communications**. Companies can produce interactive infomercials such as Sainsburys recipe book and if linked to a home shopping system, purchases can be made. The logistics and costs of advertising are being re-worked due to the ability to send ads. from computer to computer down ISDN phone lines.

(f) **Control**. As the data gathering for the results of product launches moves from months to weeks this feedback is leading to more reactive, time-sensitive, accountable marketing strategies. Retailers can use scanning data to determine which lines should be delisted and which to carry.

Often changes in society are afforded too much significance in relation to the nature and speed of their affects on marketing practice. For example, many writers talked about how consumers would be prepared to pay vast extra amounts for environmentally friendly products. Then we all heard about the caring, sharing, stakeholding nineties. Whilst the ageing population, new technologies, environmentalism and a growing focus on social responsibility are all changes which are taking place, most marketers have kept their balance and not over responded, but adjusted gradually in-line with the pace of change. As Mitchell (1994) points out, the microwave, like the video recorder, patented just after world war two was not commercialised until the sixties and took twenty years to achieve wide scale consumer acceptance. That stated, those organisations which practises marketing planning and control successfully, will be those which anticipate and respond to changing societal needs.

10 OVERSEAS BUYER BEHAVIOUR

> **Examiner's comments: summary/extracts.** A popular question, but marks were lower than might have been expected. The main reason was that people did not relate their comments to the specific issues of fashion goods, for which cultural, social and personal factors are important influences on the buying decision.

A strong marketing manager has firm supports, one of which is a detailed understanding of buyers - how they buy, why they buy and their likely responses to the various elements of the marketing mix. Any company thinking of entering overseas markets with their current product range needs first to conduct a detailed analysis of the factors which affect buyer behaviour in each market.

Factors affecting buyer behaviour: cultural, social, personal, psychological

These factors apply equally to domestic and international markets. However the marketer will experience extra complexity due to the variable influences of these factors in different countries.

(a) **Cultural factors**

The factor with, arguably, the greatest impact upon the variability of buyer behaviour in relation to fashion products, is the buyer's cultural background. This factor includes culture, sub-culture and social class. Culture is said to be like an iceberg - you are not aware of nine tenths of it. Culture is transmitted by the family and other societal institutions and can be defined as 'the way we do things around here'. It is reflected in the values, preferences, perceptions and behaviour patterns of individuals, for example in the UK this will typically include freedom, individualism, competition and liberalism. This broad context will then be influenced by the buyer's sub-culture - his or her religion, race and geographic location for example. The influence of sub-culture is subsequently influenced by social class, even though the direct influence of this has come under question in recent years with income distribution between the classes become less clearly defined.

Taking the example of **female clothing**, the style of clothing between European countries differs with countries such as France and Italy placing greater importance on female grooming and haute couture. Jeans and casual clothing are demanded across Europe but would be unusual to see on women in India. Clothing for women in China was once very standard, reflecting the prevailing political values of the country. Religion has a pervasive influence on female clothing as clearly illustrated by women in many Islamic countries. In terms of social class retailers such as Laura Ashley and Country Casuals clearly use this as a positioning technique.

(b) **Social factors**

Against the background of cultural factors the marketer needs to consider social influences on buyer behaviour which include reference groups, the family, roles and status. Primary reference groups include family and friends with secondary groups including professional bodies for example. Buyers are often influenced by purchasing products which are used by groups to which they aspire and dissociating themselves from products synonymous with groups whose value and behaviour the individual rejects. The existence of 'status symbols' and the clearly defined social roles of 'breadwinner' and 'housekeeper' clearly affect what we purchase.

With regard to social factors and clothing, the influence of **reference groups** has typically proved to be significant. Many now exert regional if not global influence on fashion products such as designer clothes and international pop groups. However, each country is likely to have its own local reference groups which will need researching.

Answer bank

The use of aspirational appeals in sports clothing has resulted in whole groups of young people around the world wearing the same types of clothes and even killing for particular types of trainers! Often clothes are used by the young to dissociate themselves from the values of their parents hence the purchase of punk clothing in Europe and Western clothing in the for of jeans and T-shirts in Japan. The use of symbols such as designer labels, high heels and dock martins all make statements about each particular woman and the groups to which they belong or aspire.

(c) **Personal factors**

The personal circumstances of a customer represent a major influence on buyer behaviour and include age and life cycle stage, occupation, economic circumstances and lifestyle.

Personal circumstances will be influenced by social and cultural factors as well as the economic fortunes of the country concerned. Thus, in the US and some Western European countries individuals consume from twenty to forty times as many resources, during their lifetimes, as individuals in poorer developing countries. When marketing clothing in overseas markets it is likely that this will lead to widely different perceptions of value for money, attitudes to packaging and frequency of purchase.

(d) **Psychological factors**

Psychological factors include motivation, learning, perception and attitudes. Such factors plan an important part at all stages of the buying process, not least in interpreting the company's marketing communications. The issue of humour, for example, is a very sensitive area frequently used in British advertising. Humour is notoriously difficult to translate and will not, normally, cross international borders with ease. For example, Wranglers' use of parody with its **City Slickers** theme (where an attractive female model ridicules the men) would not be understood in many countries and certainly would go against masculine attitudes in Latin and Middle Eastern countries.

In both the selection of overseas markets and the subsequent development of the marketing mix it is important to consider all four factors and how they interact, together with the process used by buyers in the target market. With this information the total offering can be tailored to the needs and behaviour of the buyer more accurately.

The company may decide to market its range of fashion clothing to a global market segment, for example, the affluent, independent, young who purchase fashion products in a broadly similar way. Or it may find that due to cultural, social, personal and psychological factors that greater opportunities lie in adapting the marketing mix to the needs of distinct customer groups in different countries around the world.

11 COMPETITOR RESPONSE PROFILES

> **Examiner's comments: summary/extracts.** Although most candidates demonstrated the type of information about a competitor that might be needed, few went on to explain how this might be incorporated into competitive response profiles and how this might be used in developing a competitive strategy.

The first step in developing a competitive strategy involves gaining a detailed understanding of your opponents. Having a better understanding of competitors than they have of you will enable a business to retain the initiative both in defence and attack.

Porter (1980) provides a framework for competitor analysis comprising four diagnostic components; future goals, assumptions, current strategy and capabilities. This model indicates the sorts of information needed in order to develop a Competitive Response Profile.

What drives the competitor　　　　　**What the competitor is doing and can do**

FUTURE GOALS
At all levels of management and in multiple dimensions

CURRENT STRATEGY
How the business is currently competing

↓　　　　　　↓

COMPETITOR'S RESPONSE PROFILE

- Is the competitor satisfied with their current position?
- What moves is the competitor likely to make?
- In what segments is the competitor most vulnerable?
- What would provoke serious retaliation from this competitor?
- Where are we most vulnerable to attack from this competitor?
- What can we do to better defend ourselves?

↑　　　　　　↑

ASSUMPTIONS
Held about itself and the market

CAPABILITIES
Both strengths and weaknesses

This information can be collected from a variety of sources; secondary data such as annual reports, market intelligence reports (such as Mintel, Newspaper articles and Internet sites). Primary data can be gathered through observation at trade shows, copies of price lists and sales literature gathered by the sales force, employing competitors' employees and commissioning research projects.

Once collected it can then be used in the development of an organisation's marketing strategy. Defining future goals allows prediction to be made concerning likely future strategies and responses to an organisation's own strategic initiatives. The degree of response will vary in proportion to how threatening any move is to the competitor's central goals. Porter suggests that **analysis of your competitor's goals** is crucial because it helps firms avoid strategic moves that are likely to instigate aggressive competitive retaliation. Porter is clearly advocating indirect rather than direct strategy development (Kotler & Singh, 1981). When Laker Airlines tried to take British Airways head on it failed, however, Virgin's differentiated approach proved more successful. By determining a competitors' assumptions, 'blind spots' and areas of 'conventional wisdom' (Ohmae 1982) can be found and exploited.

Very often a successful new product launch, such as Kwikfit, or new distribution channel, such as First Direct, is based on 'changing the rules of the game'.

Understanding the competitor's current strategy and strengths and weaknesses can guide an organisation's development of competitive advantage, target marketing and approach to positioning. This information highlights gaps in the market and product and market development initiatives that would be hard to replicate quickly given the competitor's current resource base. Fuji identified Kodak's mass market position in the consumer photography marketplace and exploited the company's weakness in serving the enthusiast segment. From this niche strategy Fuji built up fighting potential to attack the larger mass market at a later date.

Ohmae suggests that business performance depends on three factors; the business's competitive position, the characteristics of the market in which the business operates and the strategy it pursues. In theory, the first two factors should dictate the third. Therefore

Answer bank

comprehensive competitive intelligence is part of the foundations upon which successful marketing strategy is developed.

12 INFORMATION ABOUT COMPETITORS

> **Examiner's comments: summary/extracts.** The better answers discussed the structure of a competitive information system, the nature of the inputs and how the outputs could then be fed into the strategic marketing process.

A competitive information system is an integral element of a marketing information system. The importance of this element is heightened when a company is faced with increasingly competitive market conditions. In this situation, information obtained from the system is invaluable when formulating competitive marketing strategy.

When establishing a competitive information system it is important to consider the operational set-up. Lancaster and Massingham (1993) suggest that the entire process should be considered in detail. The type of information required should be specified and sources of data and methods for collection considered. Procedures should then be formulated for gathering and reporting the information and responsibility for information gathering assigned. Finally, procedures for analysing and distributing the information are needed.

The nature of the inputs to the competitive information system would be as follows.

(a) **Marketing intelligence**

This constitutes information gathered on the marketplace on a day to day basis forming continual monitoring to identify trend, change and unexpected event data.

Sources

- Trade journals, publications and press articles
- Exhibitions and industry contacts
- Competitor promotional literature and price lists
- Competitors annual reports
- Industry reports such as Mintel and Euromonitor
- Trade Associations
- Sales representative reports
- Reports from marketing channels for example, distributors and retailers
- 'Off the peg' research data for example, AGB Superpanel

(b) **Marketing research**

Where information is needed on an 'ad-hoc' basis to make a specific marketing decision. Information of this type is obtained from two methods.

(i) **Secondary (desk) research**

Where data gathered for another purpose is applied to the problem at hand. A number of sources form the above list would be appropriate in this area, for example, Industry Reports.

(ii) **Primary (field) research**

Surveys, customer panels and observation research of this type could produce information on issues such as:

- Customer care
- Service/product quality

Answer bank

The **outputs from the system** need to be evaluated, analysed and disseminated to appropriate departments within the company. Information of this type can be used, for example, to build a profile on current and potential market competitors, their market positioning and comparative strengths and weaknesses. Strategically, this information would be invaluable when making decisions in areas such as segmentation and positioning, product and market development as well as building competitor response models. Overall, competitive information systems are invaluable to formulating marketing strategy, particularly in increasing competitive marketplaces.

13 INTERNAL CULTURAL BARRIERS

In 1990 Kohli and Jaworski interviewed 62 managers to gain an idea of what marketing meant to practitioners. In their article they state that the 2 pillars of all market orientation definitions are

1. Customer Focus
2. Coordinated Marketing

and that a market orientation refers to the organisation wide generation, dissemination, and responsiveness to market intelligence. Market-driven companies display a concern for customers throughout their business and recognition of the importance of marketing research to stay in touch with customer needs.

Whilst many organisations recognise the benefits of being customer focused, or market-orientated, many do little to actually change their orientation. This answer will focus on a suggested method (Payne 1988) to successfully develop a market-orientation with particular attention paid to internal cultural barriers which may arise.

Payne (1988) offers a three-stage process to guide any organisation in the pursuit of a greater market-orientation.

(a) **Understand existing orientation**

Any number of orientations are possible and have variously been termed as production, product, cost, capacity and sales orientated. Via workshops and questionnaires, employees' existing orientation(s) can be identified. This information can be used as a background to a discussion on the current mission and values of the organisation and what will be needed for a customer focussed mission.

(b) **Assess current level of marketing effectiveness via research**

The marketing effectiveness audit developed by Kotler (1977) should then be used to identify marketing strengths and weaknesses. The audit covers five areas and includes: customer philosophy, integrated marketing organisation, adequate marketing information, strategic orientation and operational efficiency.

(c) **Implement a plan to improve marketing orientation**

Once the current level of orientation and effectiveness has been established a plan is required to improve the organisation's market-orientation. Payne suggests five steps:

- Understand the organisational and cultural dimensions of the problem
- Identify a marketing champion
- Conduct a management development needs analysis
- Design a marketing training and development programme
- Organise key support activities

Answer bank

The McKinsey 7S diagram can be used to highlight the internal and cultural dimension of the problem. Market-orientated companies should display some, if not all, of the following characteristics.

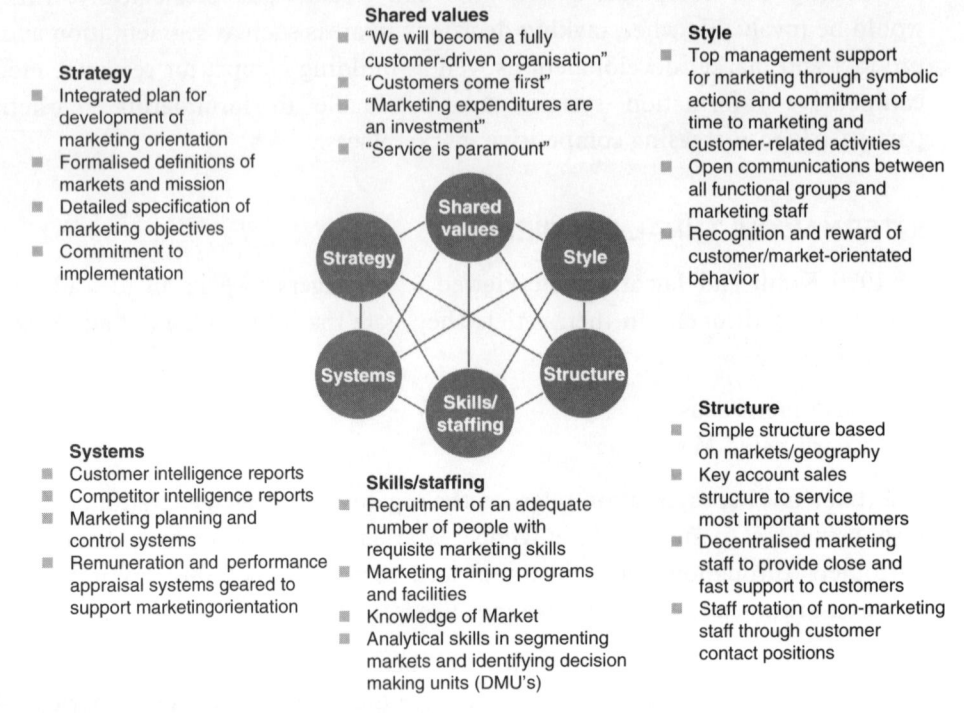

Strategy
- Integrated plan for development of marketing orientation
- Formalised definitions of markets and mission
- Detailed specification of marketing objectives
- Commitment to implementation

Shared values
- "We will become a fully customer-driven organisation"
- "Customers come first"
- "Marketing expenditures are an investment"
- "Service is paramount"

Style
- Top management support for marketing through symbolic actions and commitment of time to marketing and customer-related activities
- Open communications between all functional groups and marketing staff
- Recognition and reward of customer/market-orientated behavior

Systems
- Customer intelligence reports
- Competitor intelligence reports
- Marketing planning and control systems
- Remuneration and performance appraisal systems geared to support marketingorientation

Skills/staffing
- Recruitment of an adequate number of people with requisite marketing skills
- Marketing training programs and facilities
- Knowledge of Market
- Analytical skills in segmenting markets and identifying decision making units (DMU's)

Structure
- Simple structure based on markets/geography
- Key account sales structure to service most important customers
- Decentralised marketing staff to provide close and fast support to customers
- Staff rotation of non-marketing staff through customer contact positions

A champion for marketing is vital, preferably the CEO, or supported by him. A management development needs analysis is the third step with a marketing training programme the outcome. Finally a number of key support activities are vital.

- Establish a marketing task force
- Organise for marketing
- Acquire marketing talent
- Use external consultants/agencies
- Promote market-orientated executives
- Maximise the impact of management development
- Develop a marketing information system
- Install a marketing planning system
- Recognise the long term nature of the task
- Employ a committed champion/leader

As Payne states, the transition to a market orientation is a considerable challenge for management. Recognising and overcoming cultural barriers requires a focus on process issues and the recognition that commitment and ownership, softer behavioral issues, in the marketing planning process (Piercy, 1997) are vital to success.

14 POTENTIAL MARKET SEGMENTS

Report: Evaluating the Attractiveness of Market Segments

What is market segmentation?

Market segmentation has been defined as the process by which customers in markets with some heterogeneity can be grouped into smaller, more similar or homogenous segments (Kotler, 1997). What good marketers have realised for years is that customers' needs vary, companies have limited resources and in order to make the two parties meet it is necessary to aggregate customers, with similar needs, into groups.

Answer bank

The process of segmentation, as detailed by Dibb et al (1997), involves a series of stages.

(a) Market segmentation

    (i) Identify segmentation variables and segment market.
    (ii) Develop profiles of resulting segments.

(b) Market targeting

    (i) Evaluate the attractiveness of each segment.
    (ii) Select the target segment(s).

(c) Product positioning

    (i) Identify positioning concepts for each target segment.
    (ii) Select, develop and signal the chosen positioning concept.

The focus of this report is on stage b(i) within the hotel industry context.

Evaluating the attractiveness of each segment in the hotel industry

In the hotel industry segmentation is clearly applied. For example, each year more than 150 million people use one or more hotel or resort bearing one of Bass Hotels & Resorts international lodging brands. Around the globe, more than 2,600 hotels flying the Holiday Inn, Crowne Plaza Hotels and Resorts, Holiday Inn Express, and Inter-Continental Hotels and Resorts flags offer a variety of services, amenities and lodging experiences catering to different travel occasion and segment needs. Holiday Inn offers business and leisure travellers dependability, friendly service and modern attractive facilities at mid-market value. Crowne Plaza Hotels & Resorts are designed to meet the needs of today's traveller by offering enhanced services and amenities for the value conscious business traveller. Holiday Inn Express is the modern hotel for value-oriented travellers. Fresh, clean and uncomplicated, Express hotels offer very competitive rates for both business and leisure travellers. In contrast, Inter-Continental Hotels and Resorts serves the needs of the frequent international traveller offering a network of higher priced, first-class accommodation. A recent addition to the group is the Staybright brand, with a different hotel concept designed to accommodate the unique needs of travellers who require lodging for overnight stays of five consecutive nights or more. Staybright Suites offer studios and one and two-bedroom floorplans, which include a large well-lit work area, kitchen facilities with cooktop and full-size refrigerator and microwave, plus many other residential design features.

Bass plc would have selected these segments using an evaluation process based on criteria (Kotler, 1997) to assess attractiveness of each segment which includes

- Measurability
- Accessibility
- Substance
- Differentiable
- Actionable

Presuming segments are measurable and accessible, in choosing which segments to target, an overriding aim is going to be one of profitability (substance). This is influenced by segment size and growth and competitive activity. Through developing customer profiles in the first instance, the hotel will have an extremely good information base on which to make these decisions. Company objectives and resources affect actionability and, in the case of a small chain of independent hotels, perhaps one or two segments will be selected as compared to the five hotel concepts developed by Bass, being a large multinational. Company structures and processes should also be considered to ensure the segment(s) selected, fit in order to reduce any likely implementation barriers (Piercy & Morgan, 1993).

Answer bank

Conclusions

The process of market segmentation, targeting and positioning has a number of benefits which can be viewed at a number of different levels. At the customer level the hotel marketing manager will have a better understanding of customer characteristics and therefore should be able to better match their needs and wants. At the competitor level, a clearer picture of the competitive environment, which hotels compete where and where opportunities lie, should emerge. At the resource allocation level, the process offers more effective allocation of personnel, budgets and material resources. At the strategic marketing planning level, segmentation allows gaps to be identified. In a mature market such as the hotel industry, it promotes focus on those segments that are still in growth and it guides marketing actions and mix development in each target segment.

The dangers of not segmenting when competitors do so are great. Clearly large companies such as Bass plc, who own Holiday Inns, have developed different hotel offers to suit those segments identified as attractive business opportunities. A company practising a mass marketing strategy in a segmented market against competitors operating a focused strategy can find itself being the jack of all trades but the master of none.

15 TUTORIAL QUESTION: SWOT ANALYSIS

SWOT (Strengths, Weaknesses, Opportunities and Threats) analysis is a management technique used to clarify an organisation's current situation. SWOT is a popular tool, well recognised and easy to understand. The results of the analysis are typically shown as a four cell matrix with details on internal company strengths and weaknesses and external market opportunities and threats.

(a) **Strengths and weaknesses**

Strengths and weaknesses represent the internal aspects of an organisation over which management has control. Strengths are the factors about which the company feels confident that it is doing well, or at least as well if not better than competitors. A weakness is anything which is currently holding a company back or where there is room for improvement. In the marketing planning process the 4P's will typically be considered in all their aspects; 'how effective is our advertising?', 'what is happening with our new product development?' The strengths and weaknesses of marketing strategy, structures, organisation, systems and productivity should also be considered. Additionally, other areas of the organisation such as credit control or production may be included if these are having a significant effect on marketing activity.

(b) **Opportunities and threats**

Opportunities and threats represent those external factors over which management has little or no control, but which affect the business. All the macro environmental factors (social, legal, economic, political and technological) and the factors in the immediate market place (competitors, buyers, suppliers, publics, distributors) should be considered. For example, the impact of rapidly changing IT systems, the growth of global competition, environmental legislation and current acquisitions and strategic alliances are all likely to affect an organisation's current situation.

(c) **Marketing planning**

Marketing planning is the process by which an organisation formulates its customer and product activities for the forthcoming period. Whilst marketing plans take a variety of forms ranging from extensive written plans to verbal presentations a general marketing planning and control process can be outlined:

- Summary of the current situation
- Marketing objectives

- Marketing strategies
- Marketing programmes
- Action plans
- Marketing implementation

SWOT is most often used to assist in summarising the current situation. However a good SWOT analysis will have implications which are felt at all stages of the planning and control process. For example, a SWOT undertaken half way through the year can assist in the monitoring and control elements of implementation.

In contributing to strategy development, marketers must consider carefully whether an opportunity is really appropriate given an organisation's current size and resources. Factors should be ranked according to attractiveness and probability of success.

	Probability of success	
	High	Low
Attractiveness High	1	2
Attractiveness Low	3	4

If this is done correctly it will assist marketers in the establishment of strategy by directing them to focus resources on opportunities in cell 1 first, 2 and 3 with careful consideration and cell 4 last. Of course matrices for the other elements of the SWOT can be developed and appropriate matching and conversion strategies developed.

(d) **Criticisms of SWOT analysis**

This type of analysis is essentially subjective: one person's old production equipment (weakness) may be another's traditional production methods (strength). Under certain circumstances, a strength may become a weakness and vice versa. For example, a large sales force would normally be an asset, whereas the loss of a key customer or the movement to mass advertising as the most appropriate form of promotion can turn this large sales force into a drain on resources. It can be difficult to categorise factors, clearly new technology could be seen as either an opportunity or a threat. Perhaps most importantly, if SWOT analysis is undertaken flippantly or in too much detail it can loose its key attribute of identifying key issues to guide future strategy.

(e) **Advantages of SWOT analysis**

It is clear that an organisation's success is governed to a great extent by how well its distinctive competencies and competitive advantages match available opportunities. Sometimes this is down to luck - being in the right place at the right time. However a company's ability to change and respond to new opportunities and threats is more often the result of good planning and control and the use of SWOT analysis. SWOT is a useful tool as it promotes active thought and discussion and encourages marketers to look at every aspect of the business. It is easy to use and understand and as such makes a good communication tool within a company.

Answer bank

SWOT analysis is best used in conjunction with other management tools and techniques to gain a balanced picture. Finally marketers should involve others including suppliers and customers where ever possible in compiling the analysis and remember that effective analysis such as this can significantly contribute to all stages of the planning and control process.

16 TUTORIAL QUESTION: SALES FORECASTING

The annual sales forecast estimates the sales of an organisation's products and services in the next financial year. Annual forecasts are essentially used to assist the organisation's financial planning process as they are translated into expected income and thereafter into the budgets. It is only by estimating the following year's sales that senior management can estimate how much money is available to spend next year.

Sales forecasts, it must be remembered, are only estimates and it is very difficult to be accurate. In being pessimistic and **underestimating** the forecast, several problems can arise. This implies that actual demand is greater than supply. This can lead to:

(a) Backlogs of from customers who you cannot supply with goods because of out-of-stock situations. This puts additional pressure on customer service and warehouse personnel.

(b) Customer dissatisfaction due to delivery delay.

(c) Potential loss of custom to competitors in the short or possibly long term. Market share and profitability will therefore be affected.

(d) An increase the amount of overtime required and therefore higher salary costs, again affecting bottom-line profits.

(e) An increase in bonus payments to salespeople who exceed their targets.

In being optimistic and overestimating the sales forecast, several problems also arise. This implies that actual demand is less than supply which can lead to:

(a) High targets for the sales force will be demotivating as even with greater effort it will be unlikely for them to achieve their targets.

(b) Excess stocks as sales forecasts feed into production plans. Not only does this tie up capital, it also increases the likelihood of damage and waste.

(c) Extra staff in sales and production areas to cope with the expected level of sales. Redundancies may eventually be required which often has a negative affect on employee morale and is an additional expense against profits.

(d) A reduction in share price. If the organisation is quoted on the stock exchange, the effect on the City of overestimating the forecast may lead to a loss of confidence that could affect the share price.

As both under and over-estimating the sales forecast can lead to significant problems, it is clear that a balance is necessary. This entails having reliable, up-to-date internal records data and marketing intelligence. Sales statistics should be available in a suitable format and should be easily understood by the personnel involved in the forecasting process. Any assumptions made, such as rate of inflation, rate of adoption of the product, increase in competitor promotional activity etc, should be clearly stated so that if any of these change markedly, adjustments can be made easily. It therefore follows that it is important to review forecasts regularly and to take into account any such new information and adjust forecasts accordingly. In addition, appropriate methods of sales forecasting should be used, whether quantitative, such as time series analysis, or qualitative, such as the salesforce composite method, or ideally a mixture of the two.

Although totally accurate forecasts can never be guaranteed, at least the negative organisational implications of both underestimating and overestimating the expected level of sales can be minimised by adherence to the simple guidelines outlined above.

17 SWOT: NEED FOR RIGOUR

> **Examiner's comment: summary/extracts.** The better responses discussed the nature, source and significance of the weaknesses of SWOT analysis as a prelude to explaining how SWOTs can be conducted far more thoroughly than is typically the case.

SWOT analysis

Strengths **W**eaknesses **O**pportunities **T**hreats analysis is a management tool for organising information and for clarifying the current situation. For a SWOT analysis to be of use to a company it must be considered as part of an overall planning process. We are looking at the 'where are we now?' part of the process, which can be considered as a 'funnel', starting with a lot of information and through techniques such as SWOT we can identify a set of key issues.

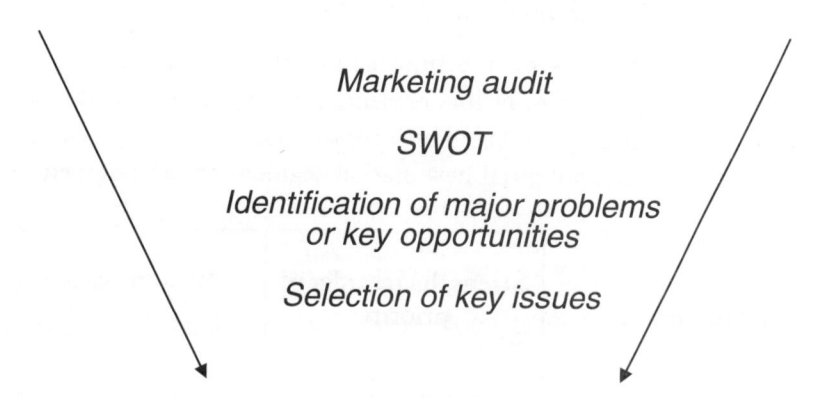

Marketing audit

SWOT

Identification of major problems or key opportunities

Selection of key issues

In order to complete a thorough SWOT analysis, there are four functional areas which need to be covered.

(a) **Financial**

The organisation's financial position, ratio analysis, gearing, profitability and liquidity.

(b) **Personnel**

Human resources which are available to the organisation. Time management, skills, training, management, philosophy, turnover and adaptability. Organisational structure and communication channels.

(c) **Production**

Materials, machines, production capabilities, fixed assets.

(d) **Marketing**

Marketing environment (both macro and micro). Marketing objectives and strategies. Marketing information systems evaluate and measure marketing effectiveness and the marketing mix.

The results of the SWOT would be displayed as a matrix of strengths, weaknesses, opportunities and threats.

The SWOT analysis tool is attractive due to its apparent simplicity. However if used unrigorously it can turn into descriptive lists of factors of little planning value to the organisation. In a critical review of the tool, Hill and Westbrook (1997) summarise the fundamental concerns about the intrinsic nature of SWOT analysis.

- The length of the lists
- No requirement to prioritise or weight the factors identified
- Unclear and ambiguous words and phrases
- No resolution of conflicts
- No obligation to verify statements and opinions with data or analysis
- Single level of analysis is all that is required
- No logical link with an implementation phase

Therefore to use the tool more rigorously, each of these criticisms should be addressed. An example used by the researchers was of a food company with a dominant customer taking more than 50% of the company's product sales. On their SWOT analysis strengths included, 'the value of our contract with company X', whilst amongst their weaknesses are, 'over-reliance on company X'. This contradiction should have been used as a spur to analytical debate and action. In what circumstances was it a strength? What conditions are needed for over-reliance to do harm? What was a sensible timescale for reduction of this dependence? Raising these questions would move analysis from a single level.

In order to assist decision making the information should give some indication of the relative importance of the different factors presented. Strengths and weaknesses are internal to the company such as strong cash based or internal conflict and opportunities and threats are external to the company, potential new market segment or development of a substitute product.

	Strengths in order of priority	**Weaknesses** in order of priority
Internal to the organisation		
External to the organisation	**Opportunities** in order of priority	**Threats** in order of priority

This matrix can assist strategy formulation through two options:

- Conversion
- Matching

Conversion strategies

- Convert weaknesses into strengths and be able to take advantage of an existing opportunity.
- Converting threats into opportunities, which can then be taken advantage of through existing strengths.

Matching strategies

- Match company strengths with market opportunities.

SWOT analysis can contribute to strategy planning by developing a match between the organisation's environment and its strategic direction. Whilst strong critics such as Mintzberg see the tool as being far too formal and offering false rationality, others such as Wheelen & Hunger (1995) and Weirich (1982) with his TOWS matrix support SWOT as a rigorous analytical tool. It can give initial ideas for strategy and objectives, used in conjunction with other analysis such as PLC, Ansoff and the BCG matrix. If used as the

Answer bank

basis for managerial debate, SWOT results in new information and ideas, from which the organisation can go on to make informed decisions on which strategy/ies would be most appropriate to follow.

Although SWOT analysis is a relatively simple model, if applied rigorously in similar manner to the one described it can be an extremely useful tool in organising information for the planning process.

18 PORTFOLIO ANALYSIS: BCG AND OTHERS (12/98)

> **Examiner's comment: summary/extracts.** 'This was a popular question and produced some competent answers. The best answers characterised the BCG and discussed its weaknesses. They went on to illustrate an alternative model, in most cases this was the GE model.'

(a) **Introduction**

The logic of product portfolio analysis is the same as that applied to share portfolios. Just as financial investors have different investments with varying risks and rates of return, firms should have a portfolio of products (and possibly strategic business units (SBU)) characterised by different market growth rates and relative market shares. A number of alternative models of portfolio analysis have been developed which include the BCG growth-share matrix, the General Electric multifactor portfolio model, the Shell directional policy matrix, Abell and Hammond's 3X3 matrix and Arthur D. Little strategic condition model (Wilson and Gilligan, 1998).

(b) **BCG Growth-Share Matrix**

The Boston Consulting Group in the mid 1960's developed the BCG matrix as a strategic planning tool with the rationale that relative market share and market growth rates are important for determining appropriate marketing strategies.

Market growth rate (20% – 10%)	**STARS** Moderate + or − cash flow	**QUESTION MARKS** Large Negative cash flow
Market growth rate (10% – 0%)	**CASH COWS** Large positive cash flow	**DOGS** Modest + or − cash flow
	x 10 x 5 x 1	x 0.5 x 0.1

Market share (relative to major competitor)

The logic of the matrix is based on four assumptions.

  (i) Margins and funds generated increase with market share as a result of experience and scale effects.

Answer bank

(ii) Sales growth demands cash to finance working capital and increases in capacity.

(iii) Increases in market share need cash to support share gaining tactics.

(iv) Market growth slows as the product reaches life cycle maturity and at this stage cash surpluses can be generated by high share players to support products still in the growth stages of their life cycle.

BCG stress the need to build a balanced portfolio to ensure sufficient positive net cash flow to ensure long term success. This means few or no dogs and enough cash cows to turn stars into cash cows as markets mature and to invest in question marks to build market share and hence become stars.

(c) **Weaknesses of the BCG Approach**

(i) Over simplification. More than two factors that affect cash flow.

(ii) Cash flow as the performance criteria: some argue return on investment is more important.

(iii) Ambiguity in classifications – it is difficult to separate SBU and product level analysis. In addition, what contributes a high and low share or growth rate? These factors make it difficult to plot positions accurately.

(iv) New products and negative growth situations are not dealt with.

(v) The **strategies** suggested by the model tend to be highly prescriptive in nature and there are situations where they may be inappropriate. Woo and Cooper point to the success of companies with low market share. Cash flow can be large from a small share player - when scale and experience effects are small, when a firm has a low cost source of raw material or if entry barriers are high. PIMS analysis also indicates that **quality** is a partial substitute for market share.

(vi) The questionable accuracy of data supplied and/or processing of the data.

(vii) Derivation of apparently reliable figures for a specific business from a generalist technique or model.

(viii) An initial over-optimism of its potential contribution.

(d) **General Electric's Multifactor Portfolio Model**

In an attempt to overcome some of the weaknesses of the BCG matrix, General Electric's Multifactor portfolio model takes into account more factors to determine market attractiveness and competitive position. Each company needs to determine the factors underlying each dimension in their particular market.

General Electric uses industry attractiveness split into high, medium and low and **business strength** split into strong, medium and weak. The nine cells fall into three distinct strategy and investment recommendations; **invest for growth**, manage selectively for **earnings** and **harvest/withdraw**.

A specific example for the Hydraulic Pumps market (Kotler, 1997) is provided below.

Market attractiveness	Weight	Rating (1-5)	Value
Market size	0.2	4	0.8
Market growth rate	0.2	5	1.0
Profit margin	0.15	4	0.6
Competitive intensity	0.15	2	0.3
Technological requirements	0.15	4	0.6
Inflationary vulnerability	0.05	3	0.15
Energy requirements	0.05	2	0.1
Environmental impact	0.05	3	0.15
			3.70

Business strength

Market share	0.1	4	0.4
Share growth	0.15	2	0.3
Product quality	0.1	4	0.3
Brand reputation	0.1	5	0.5
Distribution network	0.05	4	0.2
Promotional effectiveness	0.05	3	0.15
Productive capacity	0.05	3	0.15
Productive efficiency	0.05	2	0.1
Unit costs	0.15	3	0.45
Material supplies	0.05	5	0.25
R&D performance	0.1	3	0.3
Managerial personnel	0.05	4	0.2
			3.4

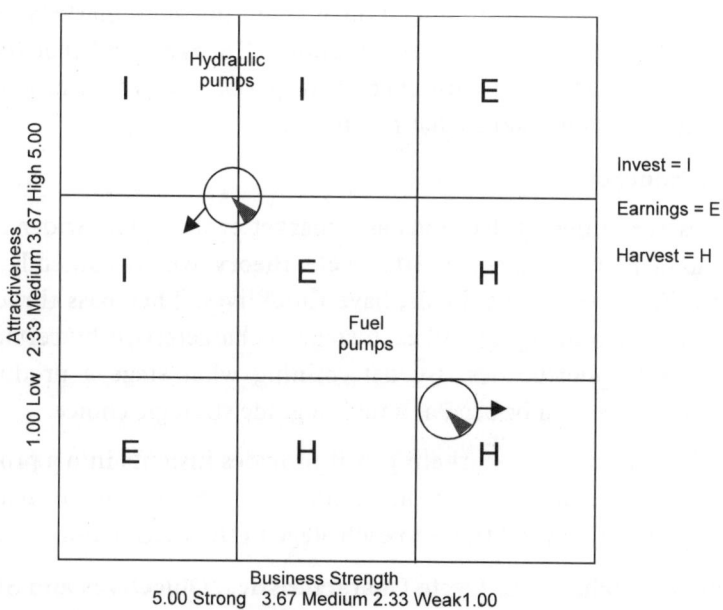

[GE matrix diagram: 3×3 grid with Attractiveness (1.00 Low, 2.33 Medium, 3.67 High, 5.00) on vertical axis and Business Strength (5.00 Strong, 3.67 Medium, 2.33 Weak, 1.00) on horizontal axis. Cells labelled top row: I, I, E; middle row: I, E, H; bottom row: E, H, H. Hydraulic pumps positioned in top-middle area with arrow pointing left-down; Fuel pumps positioned in bottom-right area with arrow pointing right. Legend: Invest = I, Earnings = E, Harvest = H.]

From the portfolio the two BCG factors are subsumed under the two major variables of the GE matrix, and thus the model leads planners to look at more factors in evaluating an actual business or product. In addition, the circle shows the **size** of the overall market and the **company's share** within the market plus the direction the business is likely to move in should no change in strategy occur. The hydraulic pumps business is in a fairly attractive part of the matrix whereas Fuel pumps are very unattractive. Overall, this portfolio matrix adds greater information into the decision making process.

Conclusion

Despite their limitations portfolio matrixes do prove useful in the **analysis** and **ideas generation** stage of strategy formulation. As there are a number of matrixes to choose from, the strategic planner should consider using more than one and adapt the model to their own organisational situation.

Answer bank

19 PRODUCT LIFE CYCLE (12/98)

> **Examiner's comment: summary/extracts.** 'This was a popular question. Those gaining marks actually discussed the weaknesses of the PLC. They also used examples from their own experience rather than the standard examples of internationally known brands.'

(a) **Introduction**

Every text advises managers to use tools such as Product Life Cycle (PLC), Portfolio Models and the **Profit Impact of Marketing Strategy (PIMS)** database to aid management decision-making, as marketing executives must operate in an age increasingly characterised by uncertainty and complexity. Decisions made now in companies can commit resources for many years into the future and often involve **high risk** and **high costs**. Furthermore, competition for customers is now intense and increasingly global in nature. Many companies have grown in size and often complexity by extending product ranges, entering new markets and acquiring new businesses. It is because of this **environmental background** that the strategic market planner must be equipped with every managerial tool which might make the task of analysis and decision-making that much easier.

(b) **The PLC concept**

Businesses face different decisions as a market evolves. The wider theory from which this forms a part is known as **life cycle theory** which contends that markets and products, like people and animals, have finite lives. They pass through distinct stages which makes up a life cycle and each stage is characterised by certain generally found problems and opportunities. By determining what stage a product or market has reached, the model can be used as a tool to guide strategic choice.

The PLC is important in marketing as it provides insights into a product's competitive dynamics because during a product's life, a company will normally reformulate its marketing strategy several times to each stage in the PLC as illustrated below:

Summary of Product Life-Cycle Characteristics, Objectives and Strategies

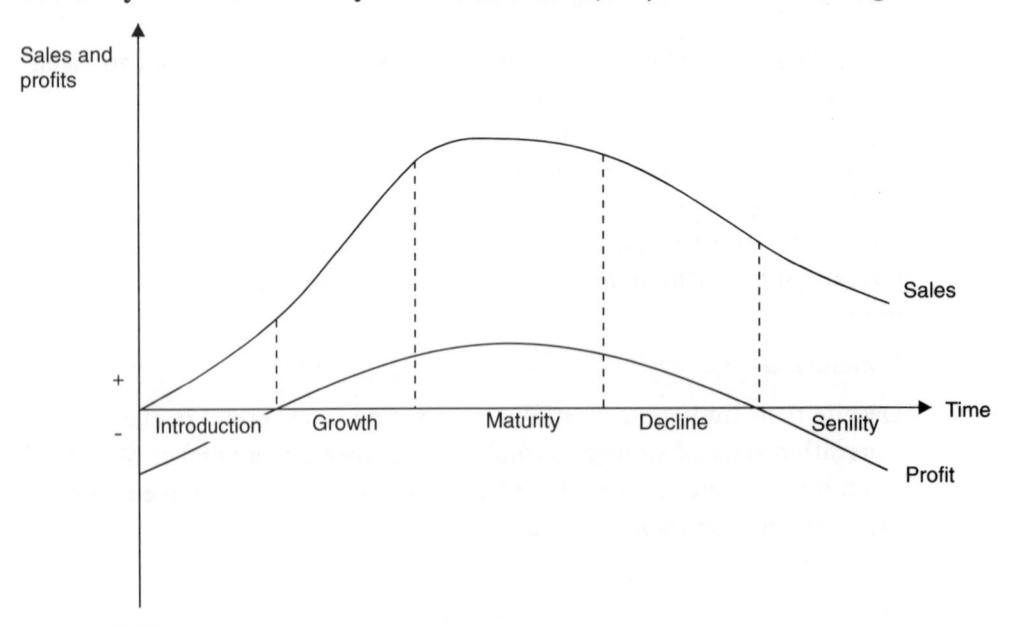

	Introduction	Growth	Maturity	Decline
Sales	Low sales	Rapidly rising sales	Peak sales	Declining sales
Costs	High cost per customer	Average cost per customer	Low cost per customer	Low cost per customer
Profits	Negative	Rising profits	High profits	Declining profits
Customers	Innovators	Early adopters	Middle majority	Laggards
Competitors	Few	Growing number	Stable number beginning to decline	Declining number
Marketing objectives	Create product awareness and trail	Maximise market share	Maximise profit while defending market share	Reduce expenditure and milk the brand

(c) **Criticisms of the PLC concept**

Tools such as the PLC are **aids** to management judgement, and not a substitute for management judgement. **Potential problems with all models** are these.

(i) Questionable accuracy of data supplied and/or processing of the data.

(ii) Depth and rigour of academic discipline applied to its use.

(iii) Derivation of apparently reliable figures for a **specific** business from a **generalist** technique or model.

Specific criticisms of the PLC

(i) No empirical evidence exists to support the idea that products follow distinct stages.

(ii) The stages vary, with one not necessarily following another.

(iii) It is dangerous to regard a decline in sales as a change from maturity to decline as this may just represent a plateau.

(iv) The life cycle is the **dependent** not the **independent** variable. Thanks to effective brand management techniques, products such as Kelloggs Corn Flakes, Bisto, Lloyds bank and Kodak Film have all been rejuvenated over the years and have not simply fallen into decline.

(v) The 'S' shaped curve is more applicable to product categories than brands.

(vi) Various alternative shapes have been determined which have different implications for planning and control as illustrated below.

Some Common Product Life-Cycle Patterns

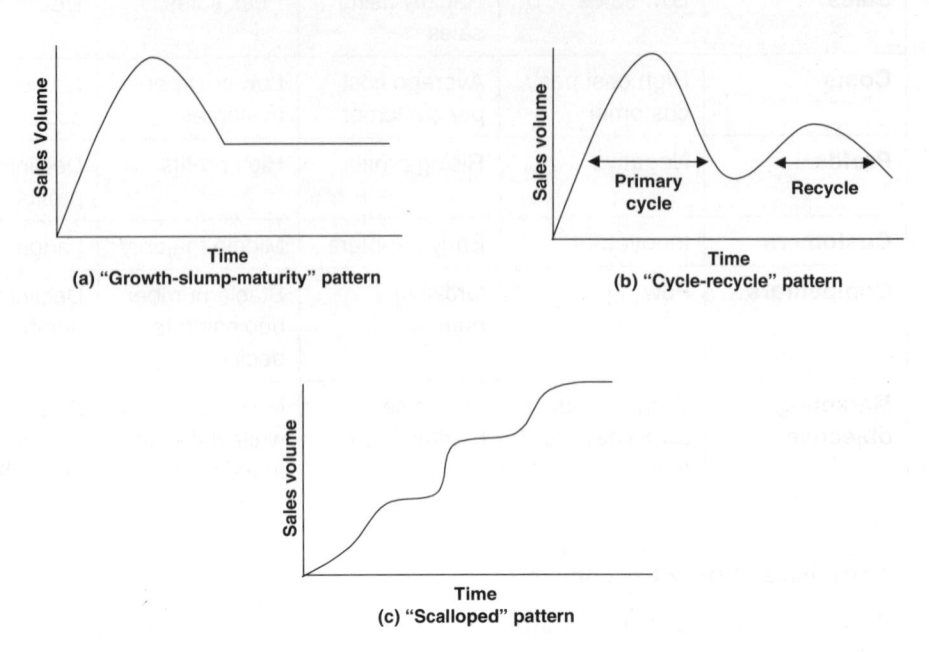

(a) "Growth-slump-maturity" pattern

(b) "Cycle-recycle" pattern — Primary cycle, Recycle

(c) "Scalloped" pattern

The growth-slump-maturity pattern can be applied to the Alcopops product category with an initial burst of sales, followed by a decline and a gradual levelling off, but with on-going demand. The cycle-recycle pattern is common for pharmaceutical products, where the company aggressively promotes a new drug as with Zovirax; sales then slow and a secondary promotional campaign lifts sales again. With the cold sore remedy, the second campaign urged users to apply the cream once the cold sore had arrived to speed recovery. The scalloped pattern is typical of products where new markets are found as with nylon for parachutes, then hosiery, shirts and carpeting.

Therefore, marketers, should not consider the S shaped curve or life cycle theory as a universal law but need to apply the concept with the kind of healthy perspective that O'Shaunessy in 'Competitive Marketing (1988) adopts:

'..market life stage conditions set semi-constraints on the strategy adopted, but they are just one input into our thinking about appropriate strategies. There is no one-to-one relationship between life stage and the marketing strategy to be adopted'.

The concept should also be adapted to the specific context of the marketing manager. For service firms, the **additional Ps of people**, process and physical evidence should be added and for high technology industries, for example, the life cycle is likely to be much faster as innovations are brought out very rapidly.

In **conclusion,** the concept that strategies and tactics need to be changed as the market evolves is valuable yet as a prescriptive tool the PLC is blunt. Marketing managers should monitor the real-life changes that are happening in their specific marketplace before setting precise objectives and strategies.

20 NEW PRODUCT POTENTIAL

> **Examiner's comments: summary/ extracts**. This was a popular question with many good answers. Strong candidates appreciated that market potential is capable of being influenced by marketing strategy and discussed a variety of methods that might be used to assess it.

As part of the new product development process, business analysis is required to evaluate the product's attractiveness in terms of estimating sales (market), cost and profit figures.

Business analysis comes fairly early on in the process; idea generation, screening, concept development and testing, marketing strategy, **business analysis**, product development, market testing, commercialisation. If these forecasts meet company objectives for the project then the product concept can move to the product development stage.

It is clearly an important stage of the process as organisations do not want to waste scarce resources in developing a product which will not show an acceptable return on investment. It is not, however, a simple stage because it involves forecasts which cannot be proved incorrect until after commercialisation, by which time large investments will have been made.

By definition, new products have no previous sales histories. The particularly innovative nature of the product will mean that comparisons with similar product sales histories may also prove difficult.

The forecaster will first need to refer to the marketing strategy document to see how many industrial markets the product is aimed at and within each market how many segments have been targeted.

(a) **Market potential forecasting: first time sales**

(i) **Comparison with similar innovatory product launches.** This is the simplest and quickest method. However it requires that the company has sales histories of product which could be considered similar in terms of attractiveness to the target markets. The diffusion of innovation cycle would need to be similar and it is likely that because of the innovatory nature of the product this may result in an inaccurate forecast.

(ii) **Panels of executive opinion.** Here a group of relevant managers with experience of the marketplace would be asked to come to a meeting with a prepared sales forecast and via discussion of alternative estimates a consensus figure would be reached.

A variation of this is where the project team would calculate a **sales forecast** based on **market knowledge.** For example, a medical equipment manufacturer who developed a new instrument for analysing blood specimens used this method. Three market segments were identified - hospitals, clinics and unaffiliated laboratories. For each segment the managers defined the smallest sized facility that would buy the product. Then they estimated the number of facilities in each segment and reduced this number further by estimating purchase probability. This resulted in a market potential figure. Market penetration was then estimated based on the planned marketing mix and forecasted competitive activity for the period. These two figures were then multiplied to estimate market potential.

(iii) **Sales force composite.** This would involve each industrial sales representative making a product forecast for his or her territory. These would then be agreed by the sales manager and aggregated. The problem here is if the salesperson believes the forecast will result in a later target to achieve which may affect their income.

(iv) **Product testing.** This technique is particularly suited to new products. Here a pre-production model is placed with a sample of potential buyers and they are asked to note their reactions to the product over a period of time. This information is then used to calculate the potential adoption rate, repeat purchase rate and replacement rate for the product. In terms of replacement rates, which will obviously affect long term market potential, this would only be possible for

Answer bank

industrial materials, parts and supplies rather than capital products which may not be replaced for years.

(v) **Diffusion models.** These models have been developed for the new product situation where previous sales figures can be used (unlike time series analysis). This technique for estimating sales comes from a body of theory called the **diffusion of innovation. Bass** has developed a diffusion model based on mathematical formula which takes into account the innovation, the communication of the innovation among individuals, the social system and time. Probability estimates are given by managers and put into the equation to come up with market potential. This method is similar to decision-tree analysis because of the need for management judgement in the first place.

Having estimated the product's market potential this information has implications for budget appropriation which in turn affects each element of the marketing mix. For example, a small market potential would preclude the use of a heavy advertising campaign and an intensive distribution strategy. A larger market potential would allow for greater research and development investment and so enhanced product functionality which would in turn affect the positioning strategy adopted. The sales force selling to the manufacturers would likely need less incentivising to sell through. Perhaps, most importantly, a larger market potential result would encourage the continuation of the new product development process from business analysis through to final commercialisation.

21 LASER DRILL LIFE CYCLE

> **Examiner's comments: summary/extracts.** This reasonably popular question proved problematic for many students as they failed to **evaluate** market potential. Some candidates merely described the PLC with no indication as to how it could be used for forecasting.

Introduction

Market potential and product life-cycle shapes are not independent variables. Rather both are partly dependent on the marketing strategy pursued, in this case by the laser drill product manager. That stated, a number of methods are available to help in forecasting market potential and a number of potential product life cycles are possible.

Evaluating market potential

Initially the organisation will need to identify:

- The potential **uses/needs** that the product could address.
- The potential **customer groups** that are seeking products to satisfy those needs and the dynamics of those market areas.
- The advantages and disadvantages of the products currently being used by customers to satisfy those needs.

The organisation is then in a position to establish a potential customer's perception of the benefits of their new product against products currently on the market. The information that allows this picture to be built up can come from several sources.

- Distributors
- Potential customers
- The sales force
- Industry experts

However, it is important to emphasise that there is no **definitive** market potential for this product. The **market potential** of this new product will depend in large part on the **marketing decisions** the organisation makes. They may choose to address a specific potential market segment or several. They may offer a range of products of different sizes and configurations or only one standardised product. The organisation's current position will also effect the market potential of this product.

- The current customer base.
- The organisation's reputation.
- The current distribution channels.
- How the product offerings are perceived.

All these factors will effect the potential of the laser drill.

Forecasting the Product Life Cycle (PLC)

It is debatable how useful it is to attempt to forecast the probable shape of the product life cycle. There is no evidence that most products follow the four stages of the PLC (Wilson and Gilligan 1995) nor is there any evidence that the point at which a product goes into the next stage is in anyway predictable. Part of the problem with the PLC is that studies haven't given 'Product' a clear definition. It has been used to mean:

- Total industry: Building industry.
- Product forms: 110 volt drills or pneumatic drills.
- Brands: Bosch.

This causes confusion. A brand may well be in growth when, at industry level, it is in maturity or decline. **Thus, as a forecasting tool it is of little use.** That stated a number of sales forecasting methods are available in order to provide forecasted sales and profits in the business analysis stage of the product development process.

Qualitative Forecasting Methods (judgmental, based on people's opinions)

(i) **Consumer/user survey method**

Customers are asked how much they are likely to buy in a certain time period. In industrial selling, the sales force can carry this out because of the small number of customers.

(ii) **Panels of executive opinion/jury method**

'Experts' in the industry, such as management consultants, economists, personnel from customers, are contacted. Usually each prepares a forecast in advance, which is debated and may be modified during discussion. An industry-wide forecast is then produced.

(iii) **Sales force composite**

Each salesperson forecasts sales for each product in his or her territory. These are combined to form area/region/company forecasts.

(iv) **Delphi method**

Similar to (ii), but the experts do not meet in committee as it is all done through a questionnaire. The responses to the questionnaire are aggregated and the results returned to the experts to elicit further opinions in light of the group's consensus view until no further changes in opinion are given.

(v) **Probability theory**

A mixture of qualitative & quantitative methods in reality. To use this method, it must be possible for the decision-maker to assign probabilities to different possible outcomes (and these should add up to 1). For example if there is a 75% probability of 'A' happening, or 0.75, the probability of it not happening is 25% or 0.25. Obviously the probabilities will be based on people's opinions and will be subjective. Having decided on the different probabilities of different sales turnover scenarios, a decision-tree model is developed and the probability of various sales levels considered.

Quantitative methods (mathematical, some rely on computers.)

(i) **Time series**

Relatively simple and fine where demand is stable. However, as a lot of emphasis is placed on past events to predict future sales, any changes in direction have to be introduced by the forecaster. For a new product similar product sales would have to be used.

(ii) **Causal techniques**

Leading indicators is based on finding a relationship or correlation between the sales of the product in question and data such as population statistics, construction output, highway statistics etc.

Simulation is a computer method, which allows the forecaster to look at lots of different alternatives and play around with many different variables.

Diffusion models are perhaps most useful in the case of the laser drill. As most techniques depend on past sales data as the basis of the forecast, this method has been developed for use with new products with minimal sales history.

Therefore we see that many methods to forecast sales are available to the planner, the choice of which method to use, dependant upon time, resources, skills and the product/market situation.

22 LIFE CYCLES AND HIGH-TECH PRODUCTS

> **Tutorial note: summary/extracts.** Strong candidates outlined the nature of the life cycle and then moved to a more detailed discussion of the problems associated with forecasting the length and shape of life cycles in fast moving high technology markets.

The product life cycle (PLC) was a model, which plotted sales, and profit over time developed some 30 years ago. The idea can be applied in a number of instances, products, markets, and channels the basis is that all follow a similar pattern of normal distribution from inception to eventual death.

The traditional thinking behind the Product Life Cycle (PLC) is that there four stages over time: introduction, growth, maturity and decline.

The Product lifecycle Phases

(a) **Introduction**

Sales growth low, high development and promotional costs.

(b) **Growth**

Faster sales and profits, fuelled by market acceptance and repeat purchases. Competitors enter the market place and profits begin to slow.

(c) **Maturity**

Sales have peaked and are flattening as saturation occurs. Weaker competitors cease production and drop out. The remaining companies strive for market share through, product improvements, advertising/promotions, price cutting, and dealer discounts.

Resulting in strained margins. There is a need for effective brand building as brand leaders are in the strongest position to be able to protect profit margins.

(d) **Decline**

Sales and profits fall as reduced demand for the product. Promotional and product development budgets may be slashed. The product may be 'milked' or dropped completely.

The PLC has been embraced by the marketing community for offering a simple guide to strategic activity over time. For the majority of markets and products the shape of the curve generally holds true over a long period of time. However it does have its critics and the usefulness of the PLC is a well documented debate.

The major problem of **high technology is the shortness of its lifecycle**. New technology and innovations have escalated over the last 30 years, with new products, concepts, channels and technology being launched at a massive rate. This phenomenon could not have been predicted when the PLC was conceived.

Another with using PLC especially for high-tech products is the **difficulty in predicting/identifying the exact shape of the curve**, the **position of the product** on the curve at any moment in time, and **the length of the cycle**.

(i) In 'new to the world' high technology products the introduction stage can be very long as consumers may be slow to adopt the product and traditionally introduction prices are very high to absorb high development costs. Then 'me too' products are introduced by competitors who have no development costs, and prices plummet and at this stage more consumers will try the products. High technology products almost have a built in obsolescence, as technology development never stays still.

For example if you buy a top of the range computer off the self today, you can almost guarantee that within the space of weeks it will become the entry-level specification.

(ii) Where the PLC is relevant is in introducing the idea that a product will live and die and probably that the overall market and distribution shape will be an S shape over its lifespan. At the beginning of its life a product is likely to have low sales volume, high margins and be a 'speciality' item. Through changes in process, markets and competition, sales volume should increase and should become high volume, low margin 'commodity product for example, CD players, TV's, CD's, PC's.

The major problem with PLC is predicting the lifespan. You can identify a comparitor product to use as a template (Cox '67), problem with this is that other factors inevitably do change, so at best can only be a vague guide, worst case could be misleading. This is particularly relevant in high technology with high competition and rapid technology developments.

In order for PLC theory to be relevant, some kind of reliable method for projecting lifespans of the product would be needed. With technology advancing so rapidly, historical data is no longer sufficient to be a useful predictive tool.

Certain researchers take a more extreme position than this on the usefulness of the PLC for forecasting in the high technology area. For example, Popper and Buskirk (1992) suggest that the concept of the **Technology Life Cycle** is superior to the PLC concept. They divide the TLC into six stages: **Cutting edge, state of the art, advanced, mainstream, mature** and **decline**.

Answer bank

(i) Cutting edge is really the R&D stage prior to marketplace applications. These firms tend to market their innovations to state of the art (SOTA) firms who specialise in adapting cutting-edge technologies to market needs and applications. Marketing plays a relatively minor role in these first two stages as markets tend to be small and sophisticated.

(ii) The transition to the advanced stage is characterised by a massive increase in market size and profits and engineering skills need to be replaced with marketing skills. As new players enter experience-curve pricing is common and the players with low marginal costs survive the inevitable shake-out. The alternative to price competition is market segmentation based on a defendable niche position which may be patent based.

(iii) At this point customers pressure manufacturers to standardise their products and when this happens the mainstream stage is reached. Now research moves from product development and application research to production research to achieve lowest cost position.

(iv) Mature and decline stages are when products become 'commodity' status and new technologies eventually displace the declined technology.

Popper and Buskirk state that not all technologies move through the entire TLC as with the case of **adding machines** being replaced by **electronic calculators**. Other technologies such as bicycles and trains have only been slightly diminished by new technologies such as supersonic jets. A key difference in thinking is that high-tech firms must make a critical decision regarding focus. A company can attempt to follow a technology through its life cycle or specialise in one stage. The authors state that the traditional PLC does nothing to help high-tech firms segment to these real market problems. By using the TLC, planners can examine the potential impact of new technologies as they develop.

23 DECLINE STAGE

> **Examiner's comments: summary/extracts.** In the past, candidates wrote all they knew about the product life cycle when faced with a question which concentrated only on one stage. However, most answers to this question did **not** fall into this trap. Too many candidates, unfortunately, 'failed then to go on to the second half of the question'.

(a) **The product life cycle concept**

The product life cycle (PLC) aims to show the progress of a typical product in terms of its sales from its introduction to the market to its decline and withdrawal.

The PLC can be applied to the following.

- Product family   Cosmetics
- Product class   Lipstick
- Product line   Tubes
- Product type   Matt
- Brand   Clinique
- Item   Clinique super peach

However it has a different degree of applicability in each case. The traditional S shaped curve, illustrated below, is more applicable to product classes than brand, which often demonstrate erratic life cycles:

Answer bank

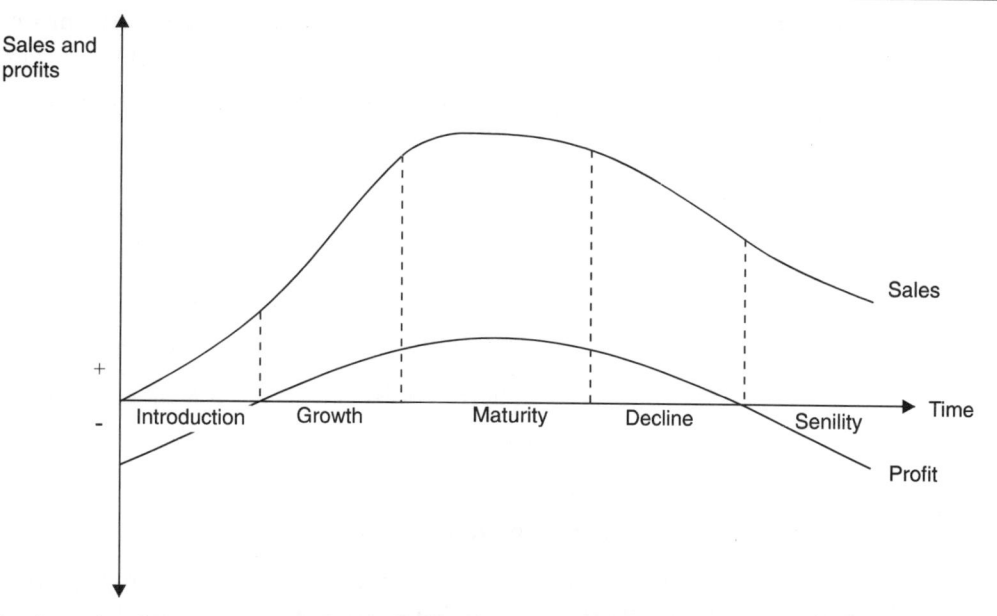

```
Sales and
profits
           ┌─────── Sales curve ───────┐
                                              ───── Sales
    +  ────┬────┬────┬────┬────┬────→ Time
    -    Introduction Growth Maturity Decline Senility
                                              ───── Profit
```

The length of a product's life and therefore the shape of the curve, is influenced by a number of factors; customers' response to the product, existence of substitutes, how much competition is experienced and how effectively it is countered and quality of product management in terms of strategy product development and other elements of the marketing mix. The PLC concept suggests that different strategies are appropriate at different stages in a product's life.

(b) **Strategic alternatives for decline stage**

When a product moves from maturity into the decline phase of the cycle the product manager is faced with two choices; either he/she manages the product into and through declines or he/she takes action to arrest the decline in sales through a rejuvenation strategy.

Managing decline

In the decline stage sales will be falling and profits will be low or non-existent. Suggested strategic actions include:

(i) Cutting prices to maintain sales/dealer loyalty. This requires cost reduction to allow the economic attractions of the product to outweigh its comparatively outmoded features. Advertising and sales promotion should be reduced to minimal levels and unprofitable items/lines and outlets will need to be phased out.

(ii) Promote a nostalgic loyalty amongst users and therefore niche the product and thereby maintain prices.

Rejuvenation strategy

Urban and Star define rejuvenation as, 'a pure marketing strategy. It entails finding new needs or uses for the product and fitting the product to them to produce a new spurt of sales'. Three groups of strategies can be used to increase the sales and profits of declining products.

(i) **Marketing mix modification**

- Reduce the price
- Increase promotion
- Expand distribution
- Refine the features of the product

(ii) **Product modification.** This is the production of new versions or derivatives of the product for the same customer base. For example, a chocolate biscuit manufacturer may decide to produce a snack bar or miniature version of the biscuit for adoption in different circumstances by loyal customers. This brand factoring enables the firm to capitalise on the goodwill attaching to its brand.

(iii) **Market modification.** This refers to increasing the demand for the product through increasing usage by present consumers and attracting new consumers. Examples include:

(1) Increase the pack size, build in multi-purchase promotions

(2) Suggest alternative uses (condensed soups for soup and as a base for sauces)

(3) Position the product for use by an additional customer group (a slimmers version or household version for an industrial good)

(c) **Criteria for deciding between alternatives**

The criteria used to decide between managing decline or attempting to rejuvenate the product needs to be both financial and non-financial in nature.

(i) What are the budget implications for the alternatives?

(ii) What is the estimated future profit stream for the alternatives?

(iii) What is the future market potential for the product/service?

(iv) What are the opportunity costs of executive time for the rejuvenation project, how much could be released b adopting the decline option?

(v) Is there evidence of demand for the product in other markets?

(vi) What are our distributors' expectations?

(vii) How much is the product/service likely to contribute to the sale of other products/services?

(viii) Is a replacement product available?

(ix) Will the decline of the product leave a gap in the market which a competitor might exploit?

(x) What is the likely success of rejuvenation in terms of organisational strengths and weaknesses, core competencies, consumer buying behaviour, competitive response and trends in the macro environment.

Taking into consideration the fact that the company has marketing this product for several years and the high costs of new product development, it is likely that the rejuvenation strategy may prove to be the best option.

24 PORTFOLIO REVIEW

> **Examiner's comment: summary/extracts.** A popular question with many candidates limiting their discussion to the BCG growth-share matrix. In reality any worthwhile portfolio evaluation would also involve examination of product, market and brand life cycles, financial measures and a series of operational measures. All of this conducted against a background of organisational objectives and competitive issues. The distinction between the good and less good script was therefore the breadth of the discussion.

Most companies have a number of products in their portfolio and these are often at different stages in their life-cycle and competing against different products in different markets. Marketing managers need to be able to make decision related to when to develop new products, when to invest in current products to promote growth in market share and when to delete products from the range. Marketing planning literature provides the marketing manager with a tool to conduct such an evaluation - the product portfolio matrix.

The **Boston Consulting Group** in the mid 1960's developed the BCG matrix which is perhaps the best known of a number of portfolio models which includes the GE multi-factor portfolio model and the A D Little's strategic condition matrix. The BCG model aids strategic planning and is based on the rationale that market growth rates and relative market shares are important for determining appropriate marketing strategies. The matrix results in four product categories: question marks which operate in high growth markets but do not have dominant market share. Stars also operate in high growth markets but do hold the market leadership position. Cash cows which operate in lower growth markets and have market leadership and dogs which do not enjoy either high market share or high growth markets.

As a newly appointed Marketing Manager the industrial equipment company has five products with the following sales and market characteristics:

Product	(£m)sales	£m sales Top 3	Market Growth rate	Relative Share
A	0.5	0.7, 0.7, 0.5★	15%	0.71
B	1.6	1.6, 1.6★ 1.0	18%	1.0
C	1.8	1.8★ 1.2, 1.0	7%	1.5
D	3.2	3.2★, 0.8, 0.7	4%	4.0
E	0.5	2.5, 1.8, 1.7	4%	0.2

★ Company sales within the market

This information can then be plotted on to the matrix where the circles indicate the contribution the product makes to overall turnover and the centre of circles indicates their position on the matrix:

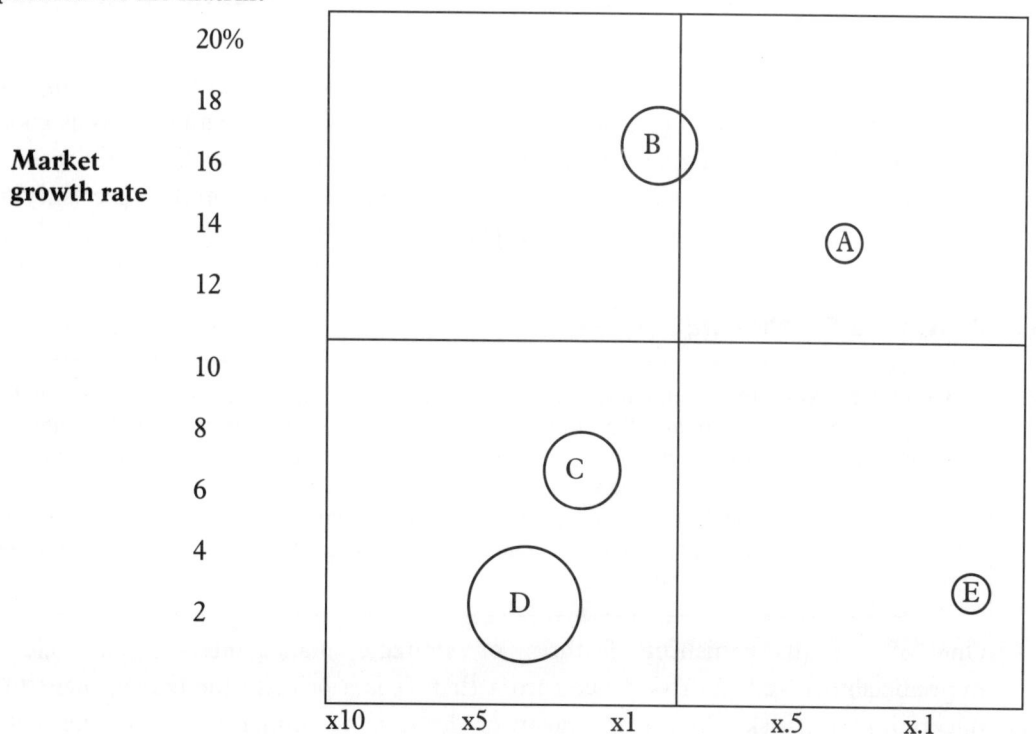

Market growth rate

```
20%
 18
 16           B
 14                    A
 12
 10
  8
  6        C
  4
  2     D              E

    x10   x5    x1   x.5   x.1
```
Market share (relative to major competitor)

To evaluate the matrix the marketing manager first needs to **establish the criteria** for evaluation. The appropriate criteria for the BCG matrix is based on the principles for cash generation and appropriate marketing strategy as advocated by such writers as Day in 1977.

Answer bank

BCG consultants stress the need to build a balanced portfolio to ensure sufficient positive net cash flow to ensure long term success. This means few or no dogs and enough cash cows to turn stars into cash cows as markets mature and to invest in question marks to build market share and hence become stars.

The evaluation and resultant strategic considerations for the industrial equipment company would be used to make the following type of conclusions for use in strategy setting stage of the marketing planning process:

(a) There are two cash cows thus the company should be in a cash-positive state.

(b) New products will be required to follow on from A.

(c) A is doing well (15%) but needs to gain market share to move from position 3 in the market - continued funding is essential (similar for B).

(d) C is a market leader in a maturing market - a strategy of consolidation is required.

(e) D is the major product which dominates its market; cash funds should be generated from this product.

(f) E is very small, but is it profitable? Maintenance funding or sell-off are the appropriate strategy.

Evaluation of any aspect of marketing activity involves considering 'which way is best' from a choice of alternatives. To evaluate effectively, the marketer needs to be explicit about the evaluation criteria to be used, be this financial or non-financial in nature, and about any additional information which will be required. Often the use of **multiple criteria** is better than using a single source. In the case of the BCG matrix information is only required about market share and market growth and this is a key weakness in the model. Multiple criteria is used in the GE matrix to evaluate the attractiveness of the firm's portfolio. In this way it is arguably a more reliable evaluation tool but of course it does increase the difficulty of application.

Portfolio models bridge the analysis and strategy setting stages of the marketing planning process, they are relatively **simple** in principle, the quality of the analysis is as good as the accuracy of the information provided. They can form the basis of in-depth strategy workshops, providing a more objective view of where the organisation is presently in terms of opportunities and threats of its current product portfolio.

25 ANALYSIS TECHNIQUES (12/99)

> **Examiner's comments: summary/extracts.** This was not a popular question and was the most poorly answered on the paper. Good answers had a clear focus on forecasting techniques and students clearly understood the difference between market research and market sensing. Weak candidates either discussed market research techniques in general or discussed tools such as portfolio models or the PLC. They also clearly demonstrated that they didn't understand the difference between market research and market sensing. The majority of candidates were relying on too narrow a base of reading.

One of the distinguishing features of strategic management is the element of unpredictability and the risk arising from that. It is a priority for management to reduce uncertainty and risk which can weaken or destroy the company. One of the methods of doing that is by forecasting. This has the effect of predicting things that will happen, which reduces unpredictability. No one can actually predict future events with certainty, but by using a series of tried and tested forecasting techniques a business can maintain a competitive edge in the long term over businesses that only react as situations arise.

Forecasting techniques

(a) **Trend extrapolation**

This is one of the simplest forms of forecasting. It involves analysing historical trends over time and extrapolating the information on a trend line to predict the future. This can offer a reasonable estimate of what might happen in some markets.

A problem with this technique is the accelerating rate of change that has taken place recently, particularly in technological markets and with the use of the Internet. Rapid change can make the predictions obsolete.

(b) **The Delphi technique**

This method is based on the theory that a group of experts is better than one. It attempts to make constructive and systematic use of informed intuitive judgements. This is achieved by setting a problem scenario in a given time frame and a questionnaire sent to each member of the group by the project leader. The answers are collected via the post or communicated over the telephone or e mail and the answers refined for the next round of questions. The objective is to focus the questions more tightly so that by the final round a consensus has been reached.

This information can be used to make marketing and production decisions. The advantages of this technique is that it provides a useful way of identifying the questions critical to change in areas where conventional methods may be inadequate and if basic data is lacking. The disadvantages are that good and bad estimates are given equal weight and certain questions are not asked which seem unimportant at the time but become more so in the future.

(c) **Jury method**

This is often referred to as the panel of experts. Unlike the Delphi method the experts meet as a committee. The experts are drawn from a wide spectrum of internal and external personnel including marketing, management consultants, investment analysts and professional forecasters.

The results are based on a majority decision. A problem is that this could be influenced by dominant people within the group who champion their own cause. The net result could be the wrong forecast. It can also be expensive in terms of manpower. It is a top down process, not making use of information from 'grass roots' staff.

(d) **Individual forecasting**

This method is often and well used by companies. An expert in a particular field can use that expertise to forecast the likely trends. A problem with this method is that it is subjective and, as often happens in a court of law under oath, experts can offer completely contrasting views on exactly the same subject.

(e) **Scenario planning**

This involves taking a set of important variable such as estimated levels of sales, reaction of competitors or impact of a new product and arriving at an agreed likely outcome. Around this desired outcome, two other sets of outcomes and conditions can be constructed. These will usually be a pessimistic and an optimistic view, based on competition, customers and market conditions. All three are assessed. From this assessment a refined forecast emerges which can be used by senior management in planning their future strategic course.

Difference between market research and market sensing

Piercy (1997) challenges the assumption that the production of precise information gathered by market research techniques in the form of research results are the hall marks of professional management. He argues the key factor for managers is market sensing or an understanding of events in the market.

An example of market research two decades ago, done by Sony, highlights his meaning. The research was conducted with young people to ascertain if a new small compact cassette player without recording facilities and very small headphones would be viable. The report showed a negative response, particularly as it could not record. The executives challenged the results as they sensed that the market would appreciate the product. They produced the Sony Walkman, which has been an extremely popular product.

A good way to understand the structure for market sensing is by using the model below.

Probability of events occurring

Effect of the event	High		Low
7 / 6	UTOPIA		FIELD OF DREAMS
5 / 4 / 3		THINGS TO WATCH	
2 / 1	DANGER		FUTURE RISKS

First the environment to be studied should be selected. The company should brainstorm potential events giving scores of 1 (disaster) to 7 (ideal) and assess the current view of the probability of the events happening, either low, medium or high. This can be re-evaluated later. Then each event can be plotted on the matrix under the following headings:

(i) **Utopia.** Events with a very good effect which are likely to occur.

(ii) **Field of dreams.** Events which are highly desirable but seem unlikely to happen the way that things are at the moment.

(iii) **Danger.** Events which are very threatening to the company and which are very likely to happen.

(iv) **Future risks**. Undesirable events which seem unlikely to happen but which we may want to monitor in case they become more likely.

(v) **Things to watch**. Events which are unlikely to happen and the impact would be fairly neutral.

This creates a model of the outside world on which to test market strategies, evaluate market attractiveness and identify information gaps. It can, however, be costly in terms of money, people and time.

Conclusion

Using the techniques highlighted singularly or in a combination helps companies reduce risk and is a step towards developing a strategy. The techniques are not perfect due to the inherent difficulties in predicting the future, but they are often a better method than only relying on instincts about future trends in the market place.

26 TUTORIAL QUESTION: MARKETING PLAN

The key requirement for any format for a marketing plan is that it should follow a logical structure, from historical and current analyses of the organisation and its market, on to a statement of objectives, then to the development of a strategy to approach that market, both in general terms and in terms of developing an appropriate marketing mix, and finally to an outline of the appropriate methods for plan implementation. The issues of implementation often appear briefly at the end of any discussion of marketing plans and yet arguably the process of monitoring and controlling marketing activities is the most crucial factor in determining whether a plan is successful or not.

The main function of the plan is to offer management a coherent set of clearly defined guidelines, but at the same time it must remain flexible enough to adapt to changing conditions within the organisation or its markets. In principle, the approaches to marketing planning which have been developed extensively in relation to products can be transferred to the marketing of services. Of course in practice, there are some features of services which necessarily add an additional dimension to the planning problem. In particular, we should recognise the dependence of services on the individuals (branch employees in the case of banks, sales staff) who deliver them, the difficulties associated with quality control and the problems associated with presenting essentially intangible services to a consumer.

Nine elements can be identified in a 'general purpose' marketing plan. These are dealt with in turn below. Inherent in this description is an analysis of the relationship of the marketing plan and the overall planning process.

(a) **Company mission**

The company mission is simple a statement of what an organisation is aiming to achieve through the conduct of its business; it can even be thought of as a statement of the organisation's reason for existence. The purpose of the mission statement is to provide the organisation with focus and direction. The precise nature of the corporate mission depends on a variety of factors. The commonest approach to determining the corporate mission is to rely on the product/market scope. The mission statement is then essentially based on customer groups, needs served and technology employed. This approach may be of particular use from the perspective of marketing since it forces managers to think of the customer groups and the particular set of needs/wants which the firm is looking to satisfy.

Answer bank

(b) **Statement of objectives**

Objectives enter into the planning process both at the corporate level and at the market level. Corporate objectives define specific goals for the organisation as a whole. These will feed down through the planning process and will be reflected in the stated objectives for marketing, branch and other functional plans. Clearly, the objectives specified for marketing will not be identical to those specified at the corporate level and an important component of the marketing planning process is the translation of corporate (often financial) objectives into market specific marketing objectives.

Once a clear statement of the corporate mission has been achieved and corporate objectives have been determined, this information, in conjunction with further detailed analysis of the environment, provides the input for the next stage in the planning process.

(c) **Situation analysis**

Although some understanding of the business environment will have provided an input to the mission statement and the identification of objectives, a much more comprehensive analysis is required for the development of overall and market specific strategies. Situation analysis requires a thorough study of the broad trends within economy and society as well as a detailed analysis of markets, consumers and competitors. In particular, it may involve some consideration of the nature and extent of market segmentation. It also requires an understanding of the organisation's internal environment and its particular strengths and weaknesses. Market research and external databases provide the main source of such information relating to the external environment while an audit of the organisation's marketing activities provides information on the internal environment. The marketing information system provides the ideal method for processing and analysing this type of data, while techniques such as SWOT analysis are of use in organising and presenting the results of such analysis.

(d) **Strategy development**

The process of strategy development is a key link between corporate level plans and market level plans. In developing strategy most large organisations will have important resource allocation decisions to make. With a variety of products (savings, lending, insurance) and divisions (international, corporate, personal), financial and human resources must be allocated in a manner consistent with the achievement of corporate objectives. Some areas will be designated for expansion, others perhaps for contraction. This process of resource allocation is a key component of corporate strategy and it indicates the direction in which specific markets or products are expected to develop. It therefore provides direction for the development of market level plans.

(e) **Market specific plans**

These indicate the organisation's intentions with respect to particular markets, or in some cases, particular products. They are closely tied to the corporate plan through the statement of objectives and the resource allocation component in strategy development. Situation analysis must continue at the market level to supply further information on patterns of competition, consumer behaviour and market segmentation. This will provide input to the development of marketing objectives and market specific strategies.

(f) **The marketing mix**

The market specific variables which are typically under the control of marketing are product, price, promotion and place. The development of the marketing mix is guided by the need to ensure that the service is appropriate to the market in terms of its features, its image, its perceived value and its availability.

(g) **Marketing expenditure**

The level of marketing expenditure will be determined largely by resource allocation decisions at corporate levels, but nevertheless a statement of the budget required and the way it is to be spent will be an important component of any marketing plan.

(h) **Implementation**

This requires an identification of the specific tasks which need to be performed, the allocation of those tasks to individuals and the establishment of a system for monitoring their implementation, identifying the nature of any short-term marketing research which needs to be undertaken to determine how appropriate the product is, the nature of customer reactions etc. The implementation procedure may also include some elements of contingency planning. However well thought out the marketing plan may be, the market is always changing. Consequently, certain planned activities may turn out to be inappropriate or ineffective; it is important to be aware of these and be in a position to respond - to modify the strategy as new information becomes available.

27 TUTORIAL QUESTION: COMPETITIVE STRATEGY

Competitive advantage is anything which gives an organisation an edge over its competitors - the reason why a customer would select that organisation's products or services over other competitive offerings. Once an advantage has been gained, competitors will try to copy or supersede it so continuous improvement is required unless the advantage can be protected through patents.

Porter suggests there are three broad generic competitive strategies which can be employed to achieve a competitive advantage.

(a) **Cost leadership**

This is essentially a manufacturing strategy which seeks to achieve the position of lowest cost producer in the industry. This enables the company to compete on price, if it so wishes, and earn the highest unit profits.

Skoda cars. Despite being the object of so many jokes, this company has sales of over 100,000 cars a year in the UK market by the simple competitive advantage of being cheaper than almost any other car. Low R&D budgets and wages facilitate this position which is attractive to less affluent purchasers who want to own a new car.

Overall cost leadership requires the following.

(i) Economies of scale via mass production, as with Vauxhall's multi-million car a year output.

(ii) Using the latest technology, as with Boot's EPOS system.

(iii) Concentration on productivity objectives, such as Tesco's sales per square metre of store.

(iv) Cost minimisation in variable costs such as distribution and marketing budgets, such as Kwik Save and Aldi.

(v) Low labour costs, such as Amstrad's manufacturing operations in Korea.

Market leadership as an objective follows from these characteristics or other significant advantages such as favourable access to sources of raw materials or unique lost cost production.

The implementation of this strategy calls for a large amount of 'up-front' capital expenditure on equipment and aggressive pricing and willingness to bear large losses initially in order to build up market share.

The risks of this strategy are the threat of competition from lower cost based countries, the vulnerability to a price-based attack, and the fragmentation of the market by competitors (based on high-price, high-quality brand image).

(b) **Differentiation**

This is a marketing strategy often based on raising the quality of the product and thus its costs and sale price. Quality improvements should be of more value to the customer than the price increase, which is referred to as 'perceived added value'. Loyalty is built up and because customers are not so price sensitive profits can be increased through higher prices.

McDonald's. Its competitive advantage is differentiation based on consistent quality and service. Whether in Reading or Rome, McDonald's is always quick and clean and, although **you** might not like it, the food always meets the quality criteria. This competitive advantage is sustained by having staff who are trained and motivated in the McDonald's philosophy.

Organisations following this strategy must continually innovate in order to stay ahead of competitors in quality thus necessitating larger R&D and promotional budgets. Competitive advantage can be achieved through quality products, service, technology and brand image.

The risks of this strategy are that customers will not want to pay the higher prices (the differentiation factor will not be valued, for example Sony and Betamax) and competitors will innovate faster and more successfully.

(c) **Focus**

Focus strategy is based on dividing the market into a number of market segments and concentrating attention on one or more particular segments or niches.

The strategy rests on the premise that the firm is thus able to serve its narrow strategic target more effectively or efficiently than competitors who are competing more broadly. As a result the firm achieves either differentiation from better meeting the needs of the particular target, or lower costs in serving this target, or both. For example, costs can be reduced by focusing on a small geographic area or increasing quality to a small group (for example, luxury goods).

Apple Computers' original competitive advantage came from focusing on a segment of the market and producing an operating system simpler than any other computer. Technology was used to build the ultimate user-friendly machine. They did not meet with the needs of computing 'experts' or people who want to play computer games. However they were ideal for people who want to write letters and produce desk top publishing easily and without any expertise or fuss.

However, a problem Apple faces is that it failed to recognise the direction of change in the industry. Its ground-breaking operating system has been successfully imitated by Microsoft.

Focus strategy is best suited to firms trying to enter the market for the first time or small firms who are flexible enough to respond quickly to changing customer needs.

The risks are that the segment might not be big enough to provide a profitable basis of operations, especially in recessions, for example, Sock Shop.

Without a specific generic strategy, a firm becomes what Porter refers to as 'stuck in the middle', which he says is a recipe for failure. However, against this view Wilson, Gilligan and Pearson comment that many firms compete on a combination of these principles, for example Marks and Spencer, with low costs due to retail experience but high quality and service.

28 TUTORIAL QUESTION: NEW PRODUCT DEVELOPMENT

Product development is of prime importance to companies, economies and consumers. A company's product choice determines the nature of its business, its competition and customer perception of the company. On a European and global scale, research by a number of writers (such as Dace and Baker) has indicated that innovation is a key to economic success. New products change consumer behaviour (for example, the 'pill' for birth control in the 1960s), therefore NPD is important as it has the potential to change our way of life.

This strategic importance and the high probability of failure has generated a considerable amount of research into the process of new product development. It is first necessary to outline the process of new product development and then go on to discuss the various ways in which this process can be organised.

Booz, Allen and Hamilton suggest that to develop a new product a number of stages of development are necessary.

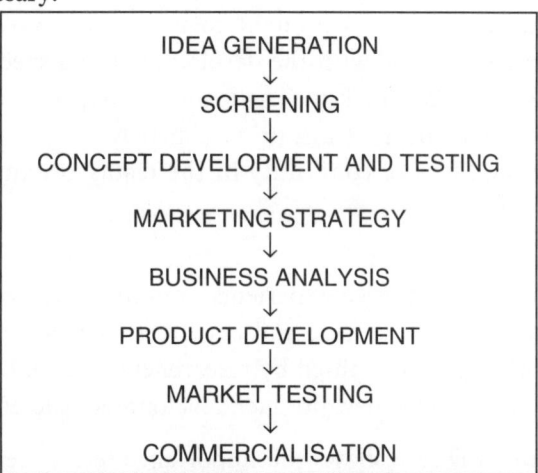

```
IDEA GENERATION
       ↓
   SCREENING
       ↓
CONCEPT DEVELOPMENT AND TESTING
       ↓
 MARKETING STRATEGY
       ↓
 BUSINESS ANALYSIS
       ↓
PRODUCT DEVELOPMENT
       ↓
  MARKET TESTING
       ↓
 COMMERCIALISATION
```

What is not indicated in this diagram is the need to establish **effective organisational structures** to handle this process. The traditional organisational approach to innovation is sequential in nature with the R&D department getting the idea which is then past on to engineering for design, over to production for manufacture and then to sales to sell. This causes many problems linked to a lack of teamwork and marketing orientation.

Five alternatives approaches can be highlighted.

(a) **Product managers**

   Often responsibility for the process is given to product or brand managers and their assistants. This has the advantage of the process being in the hands of executives who are close to the market but there are several problems with this form of organisation.

   (i) Firstly, lack of time due to a focus on day-to-day operational product management issues can mean little time and thought is given to the process.

   (ii) Secondly it is likely that product managers will lack the necessary specialist skills and knowledge needed to review and develop new products. They may be excellent at the marketing strategy stage but concept testing, for example, is better left to research experts.

(b) **New product managers**

Certain companies, especially blue chip fast moving consumer goods organisations, appoint specialist new product managers who report to group or senior product managers. This ensures focus and professionalism but is accused of promoting line extensions and existing product modifications rather than any 'newer' or 'innovative' ideas.

(c) **New product committees**

For approval of ideas, committees are often formed with some members having extensive cross-organisational experience. This form of organisation can, however, add bureaucracy to the process, slowing it up and political conflicts can emerge.

(d) **New product departments**

Where a large number of new products are developed each year, some companies establish a department given NPD as its sole responsibility. All eight steps are managed here, with liaison with the appropriate departments such as research and production. Such departments need strong strategic guidelines and, at operational level, good communications with product management teams to ensure the new product ideas fit within the corporate portfolio.

(e) **New product venture teams**

A venture team is a group brought together from various departments. This cross functional team is tasked with the development of a specific project and is established to encourage 'intrapreneurship'. The team is given time, budget and resources to focus on the project. Obviously it can prove expensive, especially if results are slight and it creates 'gaps' and lack of continuity in the teams' original jobs to which they have to return.

The choice of organisation for new product development should be based on a number of factors such as employee experience, number and type of new products required, organisational systems, culture and resources. It is a contingency based decision and one which has been highlighted by researchers such as Booz, Allen and Hamilton and Cooper as a key factor in new product development success.

(f) The high rate of failure shows the importance of a systematic NPD process along the following lines.

  (i) **Idea generation** requires the maximum number of new ideas to be generated. This necessitates an active search of the environment and for no suggestion to be rejected out of hand. Sources include employees, scientists, competitors, customers. Techniques include brainstorming, need/problem analysis, morphological analysis and attribute listing.

  (ii) **Screening** sorts the ideas for compatibility with organisational strategy, resources, distribution channels, competitive advantage and such like.

  (iii) **Concept development and testing** is focused on customer needs. Can we find a concept that wraps the idea up into a package that will be adopted by enough consumers? Conceptual positioning maps are often used with concept boards in a focus group situation.

  (iv) **Marketing strategy.** Having formalised the product concept and gained an understanding of probable consumer reactions, the next stage is to draft a marketing plan including short and long term sales, profit and market share objectives and the structure of the marketing mix.

(v) **Business analysis** is focused on determining whether the product will meet the plan's objectives. Sales forecasting is used with estimates firstly on the level and speed of first-time sales and secondly the level of replacement sales. Costs and profits are also estimated.

(vi) **Product development** involves the physical development of the product in the form of a prototype and a substantial increase in commitment and investment. Tests are then conducted (for example, food, for taste and shelf life).

(vii) **Market testing.** Test marketing is often used to arrive at a more reliable sales forecast and to pre-test marketing plans. Store tests are often used in consumer markets with product use tests and trade shows used more in industrial markets.

(viii) **Commercialisation.** Often, market testing is omitted and full scale product launch occurs. The questions to ask at this stage are: when to launch? where to launch? which groups should be targeted? How should the product be launched?

29 STRATEGIC OBJECTIVES TRADE OFF (12/99)

> **Examiner's comments: summary/extracts.** This was not a particularly popular question. Candidates' answers were polarised between good and weak with very few in the middle. Good answers discussed both the internal and external influences on an organisation's mission and objectives and went on to discuss a range of specific trade-offs that managers have to consider.
>
> Weak answers discussed the various influences on strategic planning in general often merely using the pest framework. They showed very little understanding of the trade-offs faced by managers when developing organisation's strategic objectives.

The strategic direction of an organisation is influenced by many factors.

Factors that influence strategic direction

(a) The nature of the business (products, customers, markets and technology)
(b) External factors (societal values, pressure groups, legal, political and economic factors)
(c) Competitors (activity and capability)
(d) Internal factors

There are many internal factors. Examples are, organisational culture, management style (for example, compare Lord King of British Airways with Richard Branson of Virgin), interests of different stakeholders, interest groups, trade unions, customers and employees within the organisation, suppliers, resources, competencies and the organisation's history and performance.

Management seek effective performance through organisational control. They have to attempt to maintain a balance between factors they can control and those that they cannot, for example, change of management (with associated organisational culture change) and economic recession or exchange rate changes.

Ideally, the strategic objectives of an organisation should be ranked, so that the least and most important objectives are identified. The objectives should be consistent and should reinforce each other. This should result in priorities being set. It is inevitable that trade-offs will occur in this decision making process.

Answer bank

Trade-offs to be considered by management when formulating strategic objectives.

(a) **Short term gains v long term profits**

Marketing strategies that maximise profits over the short run may be detrimental to achieving long term profits. For example, high prices in a new market attracts new entrants and therefore can reduce long term profitability. Similarly, it is easy to boost current earnings by reducing product development and investment but in the long term this is a form of asset stripping, which will not benefit the company in the long run.

In the past, Western companies have been orientated to profitability whereas the Japanese culture focused on market share. More recently there has been a trend for Western companies to invest in the future of the organisation. This has resulted in companies being more proactive, for example, focusing on innovation and new business opportunities to increase market share. Today, 3M expects each of its divisions to have a minimum of 25% of its profits from products introduced in the last five years.

(b) **Market penetration effort v market development effort**

Market penetration focuses growth in sales of the existing product range in current market segments by encouraging higher levels of take up among the existing target markets.

For example, a specialist tour operator wanting to accelerate growth in this way would try to sell more holidays, particularly by attracting customers from competitors. This strategy is attractive because the company is familiar with its products and customers.

Market development, in contrast, involves seeking new groups of customers for the company's existing product range. This could involve breaking into new geographical regions or attracting new customers from groups beyond its current age range or income segmentation.

A market development strategy is more risky than market penetration. The company may be confident in its core competencies of providing a product or service to its existing customers but would have to obtain knowledge of prospective buyer behaviour patterns.

An example of a company experiencing the problem of not knowing prospective buyer behaviour patterns when developing markets is Laura Ashley. They did not carry out market research before expanding to the USA. They assumed that American buyers would have the same needs and wants at British buyers and this was not the case.

(c) **Growth v stability**

Rapid growth can result in new challenges and organisational changes which can be difficult to manage. Excessive rates of growth often involve high levels of financial risk as a company takes on more financial responsibilities. This has been the case with some of the recent, fast growing Internet companies.

Incremental growth, sometimes called organic growth, provides value in the long term. The organisation grows organically by tackling one segment at a time, using its resources and knowledge. Sainsbury's grew organically by developing one region at a time, moving up from the south of England to the north. Organic growth requires consistent leadership which inspires commitment from the rest of the organisation. The knowledge and skill of everyone at the organisation will assist in the growth of the company.

(d) **Market share v profit**

A company only has a certain quantity of resources and thus has to focus these in the most appropriate manner, for example through the products in its portfolio. In the terminology of the Boston Consulting Group Matrix, these may be Dogs, Stars, Problem Children or Cash Cows. The manager has to decide which is best to invest in.

The manager also has to decide how to grow. Ansoff's matrix suggests four methods of growth: market penetration, market development, product development or even diversification.

New Markets	Market development	Diversification
Existing Markets	Market penetration	Product development
	New Products	Existing products

Ansoff matrix

This is not a comprehensive list of trade-offs, management in reality face many more.

Conclusion

In conclusion, none of these trade-offs should be considered in isolation. Broad objectives need to be refined into definite goals with specific measures of attainment in order to provide clear incentives for performance. For most businesses, diverse objectives can be incorporated into four perspectives which result in a balanced score card. These perspectives are:

- Financial perspective: meeting the objectives of shareholders
- Customer perspective: meeting the needs of customers
- Operational perspective: high achievement on the key drivers, for example productivity or benchmarking
- Internal perspective: meeting the expectations and developing the capabilities of employees

> **Tutorial note.** There were several other trade-offs that you could have outlined. Other examples are:
> - Profit margins v competitive position
> - Related v non-related growth opportunities
> - Profit v non profit objectives
> - Risk avoidance v risk taking

30 STRATEGIC WEAROUT (12/99)

> **Examiner's comments: summary/extracts.** This was another popular question and again generally handled well. Good answers addressed both aspects of the question and provided appropriate examples to support their arguments. Weaker candidates discussed this as just an issue of poor marketing planning and failed to address the second half of the question.

Answer bank

Report

To: Managing director
From: Marketing manager
Date: December 1999
Subject: Strategic wear-out and its implications for an organisation.

Introduction

Strategic wear-out is when an organisation adheres to a particular strategy or tactics for too long without any review or consideration of change. All strategies have a limited life, even the most successful ones, and failing to refocus or respond to changes in the market can result in failure to achieve company objectives.

It is essential to regularly monitor company strategy in order to be able to adapt to the changing environment and maintain effectiveness.

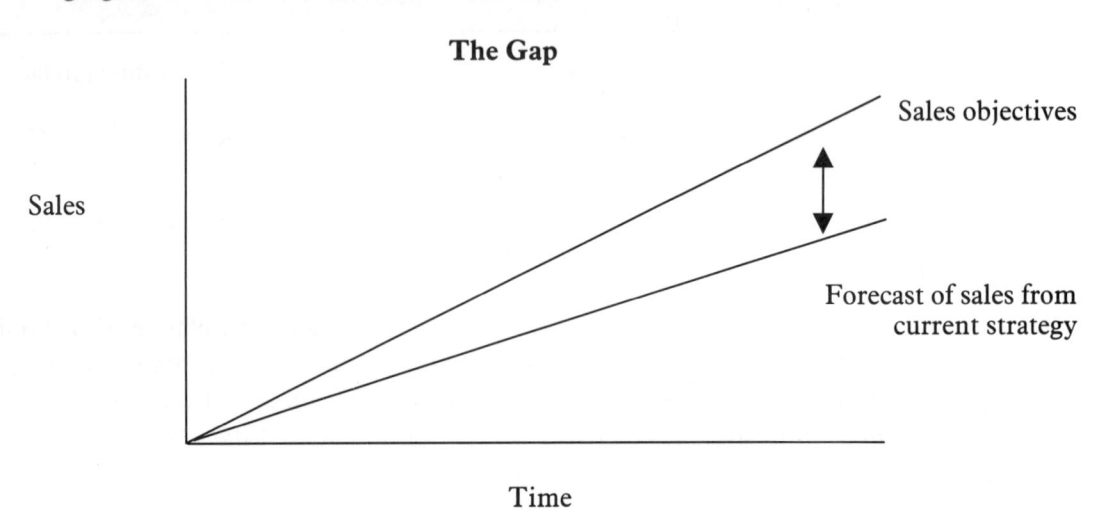

The Gap

[Graph: Sales (y-axis) vs Time (x-axis) showing two diverging lines from origin — upper line labelled "Sales objectives" and lower line labelled "Forecast of sales from current strategy", with a double-headed arrow indicating the gap between them.]

The gap between what the company is doing and what it should be doing increases to a point at which performance and prospects begin to suffer.

Reasons for strategic wear out

There are many reasons for strategic wear-out. Examples are:

(a) **Changes in technology.** Encyclopaedia Britannica failed to identify the development of the CD Rom in the 1990s and consequently lost market share.

(b) **Distribution changes.** Coats Viyella (and many others) did not anticipate Marks and Spencer's change in policy to source outside of the UK.

(c) **Lack of internal investment.** This has been the case in the textile industry in the UK.

(d) **Changing capabilities within the organisation.** Both IBM and British Telecom did not recognise the need for investment in the upgrade of their technologies in an increasingly competitive market.

(e) **Competitive innovators.** Marconi, known for technological innovation, has to balance its skill sets within the organisation between technology and human resources.

(f) **Changes in consumers' expectations.** Iridium found that there products were to high tech for their customers and they had to dismantle their mobile phone satellites.

Similarly, Marks and Spencer pursued a low profile marketing strategy with emphasis on quality at reasonable prices. However, they lost sight of what their customers wanted just as their competitors were answering their customers' needs.

The experiences of some of the above organisations highlights the dangers of strategic wear-out which are:

- Market share is lost
- Customer confidence is damaged
- Supplier and distributor confidence is damaged
- Profits fall

Causes of strategic wear-out

(a) **Failure to look.** Some organisations do not have environmental monitoring and strategic review procedures at the heart of their marketing planning systems.

(b) **Change is becoming harder to forecast.** Many organisations opt to stay with what is familiar. If they have had a successful strategy they can be reluctant to change it.

An organisation needs to be proactive. It needs to review what it has been doing and what it should do. If it does not, then its competitors will. They will adapt what they are doing to current market trends and will take some market share. For example, Bodyshop has remained static and its image has become old-fashioned. Its competitors Bath and Body Works continue to change and move forward responding to customer needs.

Avoiding strategic wear out

A company needs to develop a combination of strategic, organisational and cultural change in which the following criteria are met.

- Coherence of direction, actions and timing
- Environmental assessment of competitors, customers and regulatory climate
- Leading change by creating the correct climate
- Linking strategic and operational change (communication/reward systems)
- Treating people as assets and investments rather than costs

The main purpose is to identify areas in which scope exists for marketing improvement by identifying strengths and weaknesses. Revised plans can then be drawn up and the organisation can then benchmark itself against its main competitors and prepare accurate budgets.

31 MISSION AND OBJECTIVES

Wilson, Gilligan and Pearson suggest that to be effective, a strategic planning system must be goal driven. The setting of a mission statement and objectives is therefore a key step in the marketing planning process, since unless it is carried out effectively, everything that follows will lack cohesion and focus.

In the authors' model of the strategic planning process, the development of the mission statement is the second stage after the initial environmental and business analysis.

The **mission statement** comes at the start of both corporate and marketing planning as it represents a vision of what the company is or should attempt to become. Brooksbank (in *Marketing Planning: A Seven Stage Process*) also considers it to come at stage two, after establishing a marketing orientation. He outlines three components of the mission statement.

(a) The firm's basic business in terms of products and/or services to provide and markets to serve.

(b) The identification of future directions to be pursued by the firm.

(c) The establishment of business values, attitudes and beliefs (that is, how the firm should conduct its affairs).

The basis for deciding on the mission is the firm's response to two fundamental questions:

- 'Where is our business now?'
- 'Where should our business go in the future?'

In reality, formulating a mission is more complicated and difficult than the above two questions make it sound. Most aspects of a company's strategic situation will require analysis first before such long term and strategically significant decisions can be taken.

Once clarified, the business mission should ideally take the form of a concisely written statement, which should then remain the focus of the firm's energies for a considerable time period. In theory at least, the benefit of a well chosen mission statement is that it can provide a powerful source of motivation for all company personnel - based on a shared purpose, opportunity and direction.

As with 'aims', **policy** is somewhere between missions and objectives. Policy can come from legislation, economics or the culture of the organisation. In essence policy comprises the operating decisions which individual managers are not free to make, as they have been made for the organisation as a whole. For example 'It is our policy to prosecute shoplifters', 'It is our policy for staff to spend no more than £55 on one nights hotel accommodation'. Whilst policies and mission are corporate in nature (that is, they affect the whole organisation), the key distinction is the **level** at which they operate. The mission has long term strategic implications whereas policy is operational in nature and unlikely to affect significantly the organisation's long term direction.

Aims are general statements of intention which focus attention and lead to the need for certain, definitive action. For example, 'Our aim is to be the best employer in town', 'Our aim is to produce the highest quality products'. These are not objectives because they are not performance specific or time related. Very often managers believe they are setting objectives but strictly speaking objectives need to be capable of measurement otherwise they are aims. In this sense, aims are more general statements than objectives. (Sometimes aims are called non-operational goals.)

Objectives are clear statements of what the business or function intends to achieve. Objectives should be hierarchical, measurable, realistic and consistent.

Corporate objectives are concerned with the whole firm and primary objectives relate to key financial factors for business success:

- Profitability - ROCE increase
- Growth - sales, market share
- Risk reduction - increase product, customer, market base
- Cash flow

All functions are deployed strategically towards achieving these objectives. For example, the production function can reduce costs, the finance function can manage funds more efficiently, the personnel function can recruit better people at less cost or increase their productivity and the marketing function can grow sales profitably.

In other words, all functions need to work together to achieve the most common primary corporate objective of profitable growth.

There are often also secondary objectives related to social and ethical obligations (responsibilities or constraints). Most companies seek a good public image and have objectives stating their attempts:

- To be good employers
- To contribute to the local community
- To safeguard the environment

These are often hard to quantify and so strictly speaking should be considered aims for example, 'to become a more environmentally conscious organisation'. Often these 'objectives' can be seen to clearly derive from the core values in the mission statement.

Once corporate objectives have been established and translated into a co-ordinated corporate strategy the various functions can develop their own objectives.

Marketing objectives are usually expressed in sales terms, for example:

- Market share
- Sales revenue
- Sales volume

and are then translated down into tactical objectives for product, pricing, promotion and distribution.

The key feature distinguishing missions, policies, aims and objectives are the time scale and the degree of specificity. Missions are very broad, corporate and long term in nature whereas objectives are specific, quantifiable and shorter term in nature.

32 IMPORTANCE OF MARKET SHARE

> **Examiner's comment: summary/extracts.** Some reasonably strong answers. Although the first part of the question was well answered, few discussed when market share increases may not be appropriate.

Why is market share typically seen as important?

The importance of market share to modern marketing is widely accepted and, in fact, reflected in many of the marketing planning tools used in analysis and strategic development. Tools such as the product life cycle and the BCG matrix are underpinned by the relationship between market share, cash flow and profitability. In addition, in terms of marketing control, a key marketing objective is that of market share.

Perhaps the strongest support for the importance of market share comes from PIMS. PIMS is a business consultancy which began in 1971 at the Harvard Business School and is based on a database of strategic information from over 3000 business units. The research identified 37 factors that explained more than 80% of variability in profit performance. The top two were **market share** and product quality. Buzzell, Gale and Sultan (1975) found that a difference of 10% points in market share was accompanied by around 5% points increase in pre-tax return on investment.

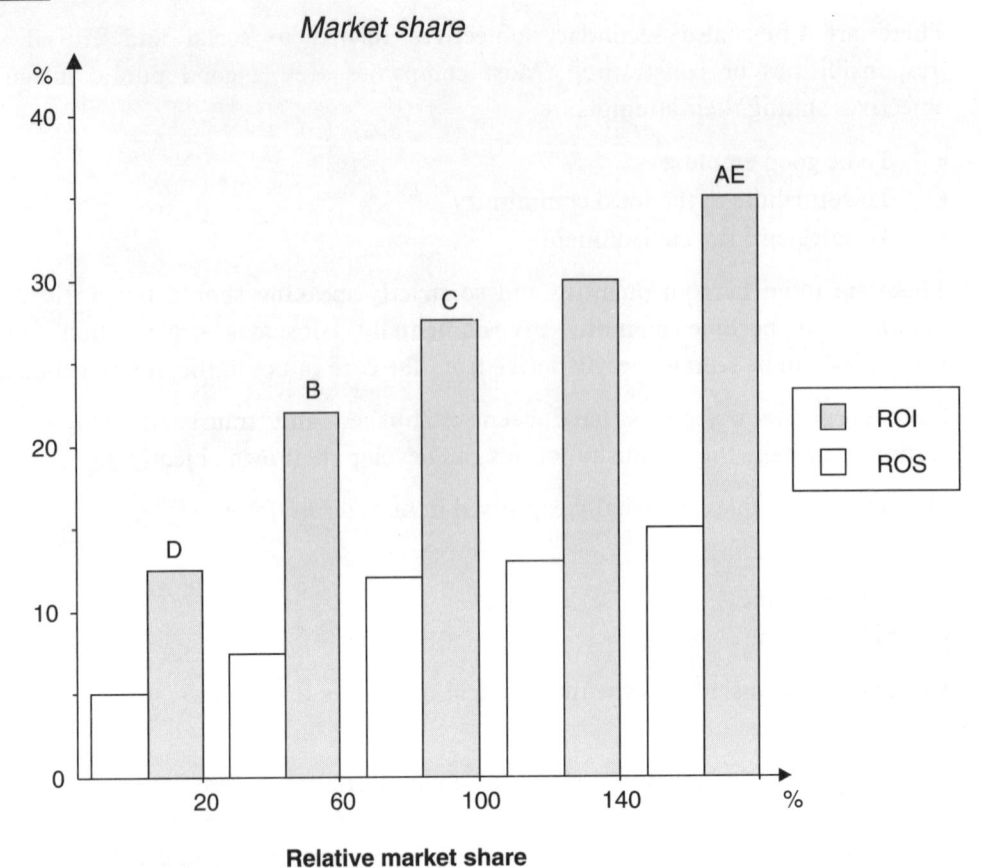

Answer bank

Market share

[Bar chart showing ROI and ROS against Relative market share (%), with data points labeled D, B, C, A, E at relative market shares of approximately 20, 60, 100, 140, and 180%. ROI bars: D≈12, B≈22, C≈28, A≈30, E≈35. ROS bars: D≈5, B≈7, C≈12, A≈13, E≈15.]

Relative market share
= Your share ÷ share of top three competitors

In addition, the Boston Consulting Group in the mid 1960's developed the BCG matrix as a strategic planning tool with the rationale that two factors, market growth and **market share,** are important for determining appropriate marketing strategies:

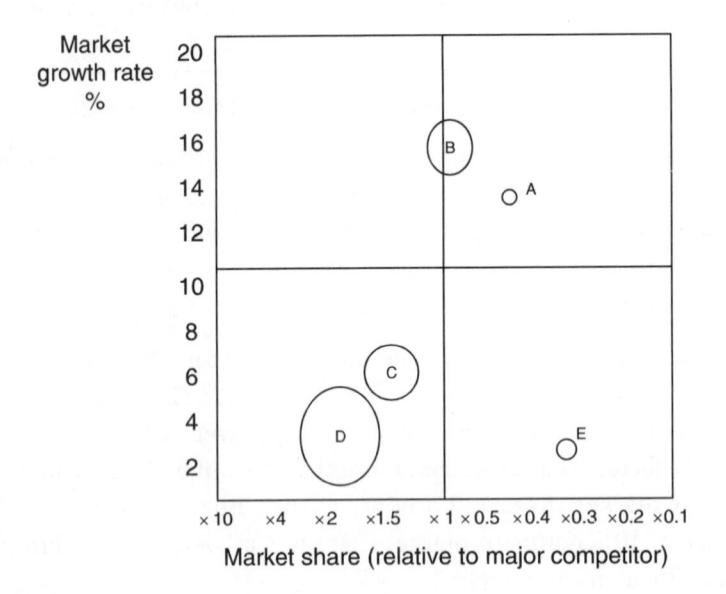

[BCG matrix showing Market growth rate % (vertical axis, 2-20) vs Market share relative to major competitor (horizontal axis, ×10 to ×0.1). Products plotted: B at (×1.5, 16), A at (×0.5, 14), C at (×2, 6), D at (×4, 3) as a large circle, E at (×0.3, 3).]

Market share (relative to major competitor)

Part of the logic of the matrix is based on the assumption that margins and funds generated increase with market share as a result of experience and scale effects. BCG stress the need to build a **balanced portfolio** to ensure sufficient positive net cash flow to ensure long term success. This means few or no dogs and enough cash cows to turn stars into cash cows as markets mature and to invest in question marks to build market share and hence become stars. The basic message to marketers is that it is better for products, brands and businesses to have high relative market share.

In addition to the advice of many academics and planning tools, many practitioners pursue market share growth as a **symbol of success** and in order to exert greater market influence. It is often the case that many companies simply 'follow' the market leader rather than 'challenge' their position.

When market share is less important

The importance of market share in the sense of its relationship to profitability has, however, been brought into question by a number of researchers. Jacobson and Aaker (1985) concluded that the direct impact of market share on ROI was substantially less than commonly assumed. In their study, a 1% change in market share was associated with only a 0.1% change in ROI. They argue that a large proportion of the association between ROI and market share was incorrect because both are the joint outcome of other factors such as marketing strategy. In addition, PIMS own findings highlight situations where market share is more and less important.

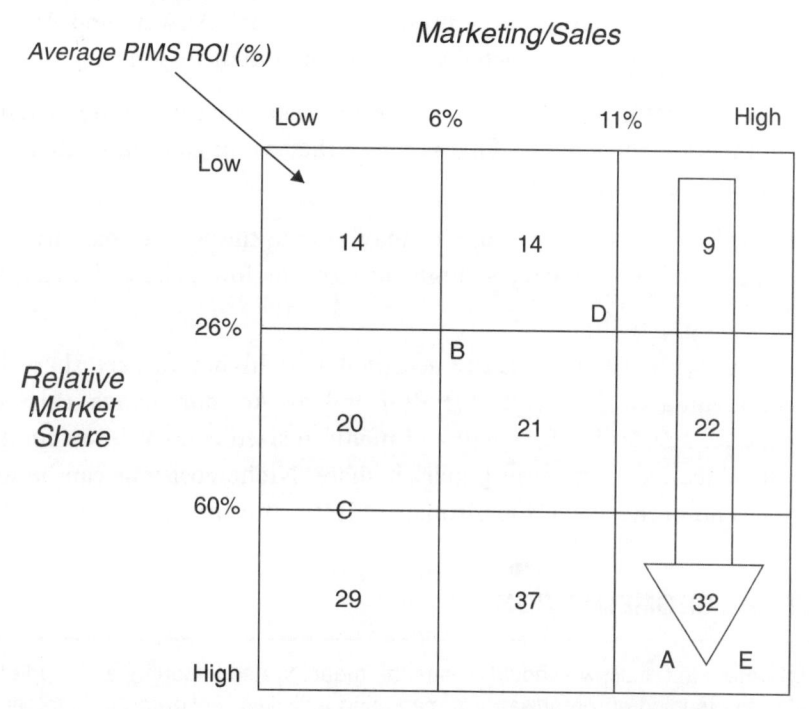

Average PIMS ROI (%) — Marketing/Sales

	Low	6%	11%	High
Low	14	14		9
26%		B (D)		
	20	21		22
60%	C			
	29	37		32
High				A E

Relative Market Share

Buzzell & Gale in 'The PIMS Principles' state that high marketing expenditures are negatively correlated to ROI but when spend is low market share matters less. In addition, market share matters less when R&D intensity is low - only high share players benefit from higher expenditure on R&D. PIMS Associates do highlight that some high share businesses fail to achieve ROI's greater than 15% and that some low share businesses do achieve ROI's greater than 25% but it should be said that these are the exceptions to the rule.

BCG's assumption that market share reflects relative costs and profitability can also be criticised because this presupposes a host of assumptions, for example that competitors have the same technology and marketing spend. If a company invested heavily in communications their market share would be higher than rivals spending much less; however **experience curve** effects may not compensate for the higher marketing expenditure.

As Woo and Cooper showed (1982), low market share and profitability are not incompatible. The researchers point out that PIMS can mislead marketers into thinking increasing market share is the only option. They studied 126 low share companies which demonstrated superior performance. The key characteristics were industries with high value-added with slow growth and few product changes that produced frequently bought items. The firm's strategies were differentiation focus with a reputation for high quality (PIMS second factor), medium to low prices, low total costs by concentrating on a narrow line of standardised products and distinctive strategies not imitative of the market leader.

When increasing market share is an inappropriate objective

Market share gains can also be an inappropriate objective for **market leaders**. Kotler (1995) highlights that firms should not think that increased market share will necessarily increase their profits and should consider three factors.

(a) The first factor, and probably the most important, is the possibility of attracting antitrust action. The Monopolies and Mergers Commission has had dramatic effects on market leaders in industries ranging from brewing to airlines in the UK. Bass Brewers was ordered to sell-off a significant proportion of its tied houses because it was seen to be controlling the distribution of beers to the detriment of competition. British Airways has been taken to court by Virgin in America for monopolising the slots at Heathrow. Whilst Virgin are unlikely to win the law suit it is still an expensive battle to have to fight. In addition the proposal for British Airways and American Airlines to go into partnership has attracted attention for similar reasons.

(b) The second factor is economic costs in the sense that profitability falls after a certain level of market share gains. That is to say the cost of gaining further market share will eventually exceed the value.

(c) The third factor is that companies may pursue the wrong marketing mix strategy in their bid for higher share, ie high quality but low prices, thereby reducing overall profits.

In conclusion, whilst it is generally accepted that higher market share brings with it a number of advantages such as higher ROI and market dominance, this is not always the case. It is perfectly possible for small and medium sized companies to compete successfully without the objective of increasing market share. Niche positions can be highly profitable, which at the end of the day, is the ultimate objective for the market share advocates.

33 INDUSTRIAL SEGMENTATION

> **Tutorial note.** First of all, we should outline the meaning and importance of market segmentation in relation to planning an organisation's marketing activities. Following this, traditional and more recent developments in thinking about the way consumer and industrial firms should segment their markets will be presented. Conclusions will be drawn that it is not so much a gap in knowledge between how to segment consumer and industrial markets, rather our knowledge is lacking in how managers actually apply theoretical segmentation issues in practice.

(a) **Meaning and importance of market segmentation**

Market segmentation is the first step in the process of **target marketing** (which involves market segmentation, market targeting and market positioning). Market segmentation is the process whereby the market is divided into distinct groups of buyers on the basis of similar needs.

Customers' needs and wants are identified using various bases but because of the diversity of needs in nearly every market, it is unlikely that a single company can satisfy all of them.

Segmentation allows a company to decide which groups of customers it can service most effectively and to design marketing mix programmes so that the needs of these targeted groups are then more closely met.

The bases used to segment the total market should result in a group of buyers with the following characteristics.

Answer bank

(i) **Measurability.** Information on buyer characteristics should be obtainable cost effectively so that the marketer knows who is in the segment and therefore the size of the segment.

(ii) **Accessibility.** It should be possible to communicate effectively with the chosen segment using marketing methods.

(iii) **Substance.** Large enough to consider for separate marketing activity.

(iv) **Meaning.** Buyers who have different preferences and vary in market behaviour/response to marketing efforts.

A base which results in a 'meaningful' segment is the most important because without this, tailoring the offering would be pointless. In recent years much more has been written about new bases for segmenting consumer markets than has been written about segmenting industrial markets.

(b) **Bases for segmenting consumer markets**

(i) More traditional bases have revolved around geographic variables and demographic variables such as age, sex and social class. In recent years the combination of these variables and the increasing power of computer technology has resulted in geodemographic bases for segmentation.

(ii) ACORN is a system which uses computer databases and census data to link geographic location with the economic status indicator of housing. By linking this to postcode data Webber identified 38 separate neighbourhood types. These were linked to the British Market Research Bureau's Target Group Index consumer database and it was found that consumers in different neighbourhood groups bought significantly different products and services. From here various geodemographic systems have been developed.

(iii) **Behavioural segmentation** has been used for years. Bases here include readiness stage, usage rate, benefits sought and occasions. A recent development of occasion-related segmentation has been the use of critical events to segment buyers. Typical examples are marriage, birth and retirement. Many car manufacturers such as Rover, are now using direct marketing and communicating with potential buyers in the critical new car purchasing period.

(iv) The final set of bases can be grouped under the psychographic heading. Personality was first used as a differentiation of product choice but largely because of difficulties in using this as a base attention in recent years has switched to lifestyle as with the PERSONA database.

(c) **Bases for segmenting industrial markets**

Industrial markets can be segmented with many of the bases used in consumer markets such as geography, usage rate and benefits sought. Additional, more traditional bases include customer type, product/technology, customer size and purchasing procedures. Research (by both Bonoma and Shapiro in 1983 and Doyle and Saunders in 1985) highlighted the fact that less research has been done into market segmentation in industrial markets.

However Wind and Cardozo developed a two-stage framework. Stage 1 calls for the formation of macro-segments based on organisational characteristics such as size, SIC code and product applications. Stage 2 involves dividing these into micro-segments based on the distinguishing characteristics of decision making units. This approach of successively combining bases to achieve more meaningful segments has been taken further by Shapiro and Bonama. Their 'nested' approach identifies five general segmentation bases moving from the outer nest towards the inner in the following sequence: demographic, operating variables, purchasing approaches, situational factors and personal characteristics of the buyer.

(d) **Is there a difference in knowledge?**

Less research has been carried out in industrial markets as compared with consumer markets. Consumer goods companies have generally more consciously and rigorously applied marketing theory in practice.

However recent research by Jenkins and McDonald indicates that knowledge is more clearly lagging behind in terms of understanding how organisations actually arrive at and sustain particular market definitions and segments. One of the few empirical studies into market segmentation practices of industrial marketers (by Abratt in 1993) also noted that marketers know much more about the theoretical and methodological issues of segmentation rather than about how this is translated into the strategy process in practice.

So whilst the proposition can be supported, it is not so much the fact that our knowledge of how to segment industrial markets lags behind, rather what is greater is a lack of knowledge about how practitioners use the market segmentation concept in practice in both consumer and industrial markets.

34 INFORMATION FOR SEGMENTATION AND POSITIONING

> **Examiner's comment: summary/extracts.** Another popular question - but many candidates only covered segmentation and positioning in general terms, rather than on the problems of the sector.

Introduction

A key element of launching any new product is the segmentation, targeting and positioning decisions taken. Such strategic decisions should be made against a sound understanding of the market in which the product will be launched. Answers to questions such as, 'what products do our competitors offer?', 'on what basis do they differentiate their offering?' and, 'what are the key purchase criteria of the various buyers in the market?', are vital.

Market Information Required

In the case of computer software package targeted at specialist distribution companies, the information that is needed before developing a segmentation and positioning strategy can be divided into two categories (Gilligan, 1995).

Market Information

- Size of the market and likely development over next few years
- Structure of the market and areas of growth and decline, geographic and sector spread
- Competition, their strategies and future directions, strengths and weaknesses, product portfolios and positioning approaches, pricing and distribution tactics
- Customers' buyer behaviour, levels of loyalty, demographics, ratings of service quality and perceptions of all players in the market

Given this information we can begin to develop a market map to identify areas for development and growth, competitive vulnerability and market attractiveness. Against this background we can then move to the second category of information that is needed.

Company information

- Current approach to segmentation and positioning

- Overall marketing strategy and vision
- Corporate image
- Distribution approach
- Pricing approach
- Promotional mix
- Resource availability
- Systems capability
- Organisation's financial and sales targets
- Management expectations, perceptions and skills regarding segmentation and positioning
- Very importantly, current product range, breadth, depth and performance

Developing a Segmentation and positioning policy

Having gathered this information the organisation can then begin to use it to identify customer segments. To do this they will need to identify variables they can use to break down the market into discreet groupings. In this case the customers are in industrial/organisational markets and therefore the following variables could be used.

- Demographic: the size of company; geographic location, type of industry/consumer market served.
- Operating variables: heavy, medium or light users; customer capabilities.
- Purchasing approaches: buying criteria used; current buying relationships; buying policies in force.
- Situational factors: urgency of orders, size of order.
- Personal characteristics: levels of loyalty, attitudes to risk.

This process will have identified customer segments by using the information initially identified. The information will also help in making positioning decisions.

A **products/services position** is defined by the way consumers perceive the offering relative to competing options. Therefore it is essential to have information relating to customers perceptions of current products and suppliers as well as information relating to their current perception of our organisation. Specifically the information can be used to build perceptual maps to help identify positioning opportunities. An effective position should combine both functional and emotional brand values and be translated into an effective customer proposition statement, for example, 'Tracker Software: professionally designed to give you the gist in logistics' (this can be improved!).

35 LIFESTYLE SEGMENTATION (12/99)

> **Examiner's comment: summary/extracts.** 'Good answers illustrated the advantages of lifestyle segmentation and then went on to discuss the problems of using this technique by a company operating internationally. Poorer candidates discussed segmentation techniques in general rather than lifestyle segmentation's advantages over other methods.'

The market is not a homogeneous mass, but is made up of individual consumers or organisations, each with a unique set of needs. Dealing with each customer individually would be the ultimate in customer orientation. Whilst this may be possible in the personal service markets like bespoke tailoring, and it may be a future development in consumer durable markets (for example, where cars can be 'finished' to specific requirements), for most manufacturers segmentation of the market is an acceptable middle ground.

Segmentation is the process of dividing the market into different groups of buyers, as smaller groups have broadly similar patterns of need and so are more easily managed at a strategic level. These groups can then be targeted and their needs are more likely to be satisfied. The logic of this approach is straightforward. The critical factor in putting it into practice lies in the way in which the market is segmented.

Segments have to be significant enough to be worthwhile, easily identifiable so their members can be isolated from the rest of the population, and accessible so they can be reached. Over twenty years or so, writers and practitioners have invented suitable methods of segmenting different markets. This practical task has been made both easier and more sophisticated by improvements in technology and the growth of databases. Over the years all sorts of variables have been used for segmentation, sometimes in isolation, more usually together.

- Demographic
- Geographical
- Behavioural
- Psychographic

Life style segmentation fits into the **psychographic** category and it is increasingly popular. Work undertaken in the 1950's by Reisman is responsible for the linking of lifestyle segmentation with progression through Maslow's hierarchy of needs.

(a) Reisman identified three distinct types of social characterisation and behaviour.

    (i) **Tradition directed behaviour** seldom changes over time, and is easy to predict.

    (ii) **Other directedness** can be recognised when individuals adapt their behaviour to mirror their peer groups eg the beer drinker who switches to gin and tonic when he joins the golf club or the student whose trousers change for jeans on entry to college.

    (iii) **Inner directedness** is where individuals are concerned not with others but themselves, a stage which could be reflected in the self-actualisation level of Maslow's need hierarchy. The successful business person who swaps the corporate limousine for a small car, which is easier to park, is an example.

As people in advanced economies move past the point of satisfying just their basic needs ie traditional behaviour, which is easy to predict, their needs and aspirations become complex and fragmented. Lifestyle techniques consider more than income or social class and more than personality. They try to develop group profiles as to how people relate with, and respond to, the world.

(b) A number of models of categorising lifestyle have been developed over the years. One of the best known is Young and Rubicam's Cross Cultural Consumer Classification, developed to help with targeting marketing and advertising campaigns. It identifies three groups.

- The constrained of resigned and struggling poor
- The middle majority of mainstreamers, aspirers and succeeders
- The innovators of reformers and transitionals

Lifestyle analysis has proved to be significant in marketing terms. 'Yuppies' of the 80's might have provided plenty of material for comedians, but also led to massive new product developments for items like filofax and car phones. Recognition of lesser known lifestyle groups like '**Glams**' (greying leisured affluent middle aged) have been of great importance to the marketing strategists of the 1990s looking for high potential growth market opportunities. As a firm's ability to pinpoint such specific groups improves, so its targeting and use of marketing resources becomes more effective.

A company operating internationally would need to take into account the different values and lifestyles of the consumers in the **country** being targeted. Wolfe (1991) and Treadgold (1990) discount the idea of a Euro-consumer for the foreseeable future, stressing that pan-European differences are more compelling than any similarities. Likewise, Reichel (1989) maintains that EU consumers' preferences have not been internationalized. These arguments have recently been supported by the findings of a 'European lifestyles 1993' study published by Mintel, based on research conducted in seven major European countries. The study highlights differences rather than similarities in spending and consumption patterns and concludes that a typical Euro-consumer is unlikely to emerge for some time.

Despite these problems a number of international lifestyle segmentation approaches have been developed (Schmidt 1996). The majority of national as well as European-based typologies of this nature are in essence variations of the US Value Lifestyle (VALS) typology developed in the late 1970s and early 1980s. An example of this is the German 'My Life' Euro-typology which maps lifestyles along the axes of materialism - spiritualism and dynamic - reactive (Reynolds, 1994). However psychographic analysis hardly ever starts from an existing database. This means that due to the resource implications involved in any attempt at a pan-European psychographic consumer typology, this work has largely been restricted to a few large commercial agencies.

One well-known psychographic classification is the result of the work of the International **Research Institute on Social Change** (RISC). Experian distributes RISC in the UK which uses a longitudinal approach examining consumer response to change within Europe. Based on three central dimensions of change (individualism, hedonism and flexibility) three key groups are identified and monitored. This establishes the basic framework for analysis, within which further segmentation is possible. RISC has ten lifestyle groups.

1		Explorers
2G		Moral Guides
2L		Care Givers
3G		Mobile Networkers
3L		High Energy Pleasure Seekers
4G		Guardians
4L		Rooted Traditionalists
5G		Social Climbers
5L		Avid Consumers
6		Survivors

Social climbers, for example, are described as living on the surface and in the present. They have a short term vision of instant gratification and pleasure. Aspirations centre more on 'having' than 'achieving'. They like to impress, or even to shock, with a casual, easy going self image, short term focus, enjoying celebrity and visibility.

In addition to European-wide attempts at consumer typologies, a multitude of national lifestyle segmentation systems exist. The issue is further complicated by the diverse range of customer typologies developed for particular products and services, ranging from pubs to garden products.

If the central task of the marketing-led business is to satisfy the needs of its (international) customers, then this is still hindered by the many differences in standards, technical norms and legal procedures, which make it impossible to arrive at a truly pan-European, let alone global, segmentation system. In terms of the search for the elusive Euro-consumer this means that the striving for ever more sophisticated segmentation will continue. Global, and as a subset pan-European, marketing will expand attempts to segment from a national base to world- or European-wide proportions. However the problems of cultural comparability, international information sources and the need to 'think global, act local' will all create problems for the international marketer.

36 GEODEMOGRAPHICAL SEGMENTATION (12/99)

> **Examiner's comments: summary/extracts.** This was a popular question and was answered particularly well in general. Good answers demonstrated a clear understanding of geodemographic segmentation and were able to link this to direct marketing as well as relating their answer to the financial services sector. Weaker answers tended to answer only one aspect of the question and found it difficult to relate geodemographical segmentation and direct marketing to the financial services sector.

Introduction

Geodemographical segmentation is an extension of geographical techniques. It recognises that people who live within the same geographical area share similar characteristics in tastes, purchasing habits, lifestyles and financial means and these can be mapped according to their post code.

The most popular example of geodemographical segmentation is ACORN but more sophisticated approaches have been developed including Experian's MOSIAC, which has 52 distinct lifestyle types.

In MOSIAC, each group has been given a descriptive name like 'Clever Capitalists' or 'Nestmaking families' based on their socio-economic and socio-cultural behaviour. These are further aggregated into twelve groups like 'Suburban semis' or 'Blue collar owners'. Experian have refined their model to include Financial MOSIAC to meet the increasing demand for specific service classification. This will be highlighted under advantages.

Advantages of geodemographical segmentation

A financial MOSIAC collects information on the financial holdings, behaviour and intentions of consumers, gathered through 48,000 interviews a year. This information, coupled with the more general MOSIAC profile will enable the financial services company to pinpoint more accurately the most attractive segments to target for their expansion into the insurance market.

An example of this is mortgage protection and redundancy packages being targeted at those who are at greater risk, that is, over forty with high outgoings. This is because the state no longer pays mortgage costs in the case of redundancy, and insurance is required to cover the cost of a mortgage in such an event.

For more general insurance products such as motor, home contents, building, holiday or car insurance, the information can be used to target broader segments throughout the country. Examples are people who have more than one holiday a year or have more than one car. Further research into the desired segments will enable the company to customise their data and give them a competitive advantage over their competitors.

This will be a step towards creating a specific insurance customer database, which is essential in differentiating the customer list from competitors who have purchased standard information. A customer database can be used to focus on prime prospects and evaluate new ones. It can also be used to build customer loyalty.

Disadvantages of geodemographical segmentation

The biggest practical disadvantage of geodemographical segmentation is that the data purchased is not always accurate and up to date. Census information linked to postal codes is not always accurate. The list can be devalued by the modern tendency for people to move frequently. This results in companies having to update their own database frequently by direct marketing techniques to make it up to date.

Direct Marketing

Direct marketing allows companies to develop communication with identified market segments. The message can be tailored in a way that is not possible with other forms of the media. Through techniques like direct mail, telemarketing and personal selling a financial services company can directly target the individuals most suitable to buy new products.

Direct marketing is usually more expensive per person than other forms of marketing, but response rates are often higher. It also has the added advantage of using the information from respondents to update the current database, cut out waste and improve customer service and new product development.

Conclusion

Geodemographical segmentation will assist a financial services company to specifically tailor its products to the most appropriate segments. This may also maximise the response rate of customers in the most cost efficient way.

However, regional trends brought about by economic factors can alter the characteristics of these segments. Response from too much competitor activity can also change the features of the segments. These issues need to be scrutinised regularly so that the company's message or products can be adapted so that they are more suitable.

37 CUSTOMER PROFILES AND SOFTWARE

To: Marketing Director
From: Marketing Manager
Date: June 1997
Subject: Report Identifying Customer Information Required

This report aims to identify the information needed to develop customer profiles and how these profiles might then be used to develop the segmentation, targeting and positioning strategy.

Who are our Customers?

Our key customers are likely to be Airlines, Travel Agencies and any business involved in booking holidays and flights. Within those markets there are several people who will be **using** the systems. They are also our customers, so they will likely to affect the choice of software bought. The airlines and hotels are also likely to exert pressure on the choice of software bought in terms of how the information is presented to them and software compatibility.

Organisational buying has distinct characteristics (Kotler, 1994).

(a) Organisations buy goods and services to satisfy a variety of goals: making profits, reducing costs, meeting employee needs, and meeting social and legal obligations.

(b) More persons are typically involved in organisational buying decisions, especially in procuring major items. The decision group often will have different job titles and apply different criteria to the purchase decision.

(c) There may be formalised structures and policies that they must follow.

Although no two companies are likely to buy in the same way, it is possible that there is enough similarity in the way that buyers of the DMU approach the task to be of strategic significance.

Information Required

The kinds of customer profiling information that we would be interested in compiling would be as follows.

(a) **Demographic**
- Industry
- Company
- Location

(b) **Operating variables**
- Technology
- User status
- Customer capabilities

(c) **Purchasing approaches**
- Buying criteria
- Buying policies
- Current relationships

(d) **Situational factors**
- Urgency
- Size of order
- Applications

(e) **Personal characteristics**
- Loyalty
- Attitudes to risk

This information will give us alternative variables for segmenting our market. For example, we could concentrate on companies which buy large orders (situational factor), companies that use a specific operating system (operating variable) or segments which combine a number of similar characteristics in different areas.

Targeting

Once we have segmented the markets we need to assess the attractiveness of each of the segments. These need to be assessed in terms of the following.

- Measurability
- Accessibility
- Substance
- Meaning

In choosing which segments to target, of course our overriding aim is going to be **profitability**. This is influenced by competitive activity as illustrated by Porter.

Through developing our customer profiles, in the first instance we will have an extremely good information base on which to make these decisions for example the number of purchases they make, the length of time they take over decision making and geographical spread.

Positioning

Once we have made the decisions on how to segment and which segments we are going to target we can position our product and company in the best possible position to meet the different needs of the segment.

From the customer profiling, it may be the case that a segment emerges which uses a specific kind of technology at the moment; we can present our products unique compatibility as being a USP. This would be extremely attractive to those companies and we know that no other software is available to do this so easily.

Answer bank

Conclusion

It is only through such detailed customer profiling that we can identify and target the most lucrative segments. Using the information that we have complied about them, we know what their needs are and can present them with the best/most appropriate solution/package.

The time and expense involved in the initial profiling stage will be offset with the efficiency in which we will be able to target the most lucrative markets and present our software package in the most attractive manner.

38 MARKETING STRATEGY DEVELOPMENT

> **Tutorial note.** This question is identical to question 3 in the June 1996 exam, which is question 39 below in this Kit. Rather than repeat the solution we suggest you consult the answer to question 39 below.
>
> **Examiner's comments: summary/extracts.** The answers proved to be very variable with weaker candidates writing in very general terms about either the structure of the planning process or using SWOT and portfolio models. What was required was a discussion of all the factors in an extensive marketing audit - both internal and external- that typically influence strategy.

39 DEVELOPING A STRATEGY

> **Examiner's comments: summary/extracts.** This question produced some good answers, but 'a significant number of candidates produced an outline of a marketing plan' which was not asked for.

The development of marketing strategy is one stage in the overall marketing planning process. It is therefore necessary to first outline the overall managerial process and explain what elements make up a marketing strategy before we can fully understand what factors should be considered.

Stages in strategic marketing planning

Marketing is a company-wide commitment to providing customer satisfaction. According to Brooksbank (1990), it is also a managerial process involving the regular analysis of the firm's competitive situation, leading to the development of marketing objectives, and the formulation and implementation of strategies, tactics, organisation, measures and controls for their achievement. There is general consensus in the literature that marketing planning is made up of several steps or stages, Brooksbank suggests there are seven.

Answer bank

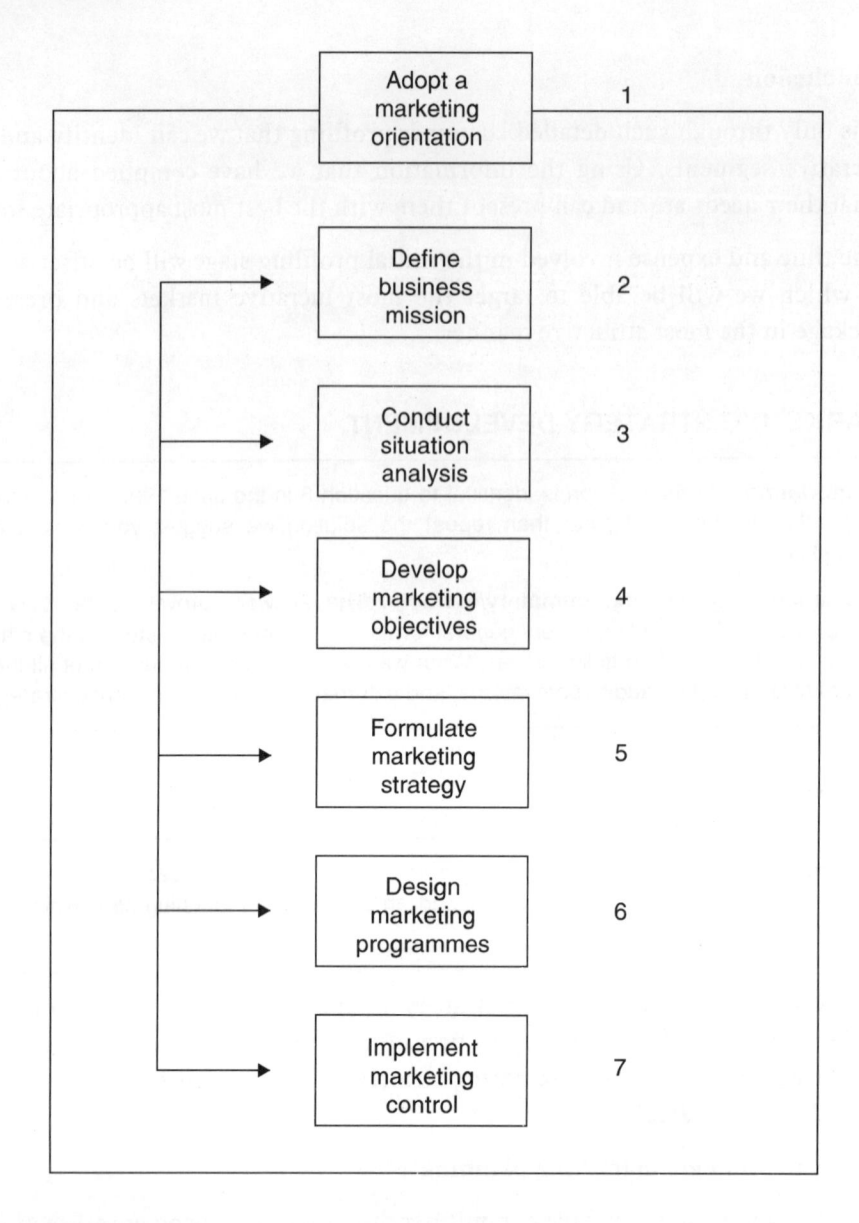

```
1. Adopt a marketing orientation
2. Define business mission
3. Conduct situation analysis
4. Develop marketing objectives
5. Formulate marketing strategy
6. Design marketing programmes
7. Implement marketing control
```

Wilson, Gilligan & Pearson's five stages mirror steps 3-7 above, with marketing orientation and business mission being subsumed into these steps. Whilst a number of different models exist they all follow the basic logic illustrated above. What we can see from this model is that consideration of marketing strategy should come some way into the process of developing the marketing plan.

Developing marketing strategy - what are the components?

(a) **Setting strategic focus**. Profitability can be improved by either raising volume or improving productivity.

(b) **Defining competitive advantage:** is a company's chosen route to distinguishing its offering from the competition and should be based on something of value to the target market. It can be derived from any of the firm's strengths relative to competition. It is embodied in the company's positioning strategy which, according to Brooksbank, is the amalgam of the following two components ((c) and (d)).

(c) **Selecting customer targets:** emphasises the role of marketing segmentation and target marketing in the development of marketing strategy.

(d) **Selecting competitor targets:** emphasises the role of competitor intelligence and analysis in the development of marketing strategy.

(e) **Assembling the marketing mix:** translates the segmentation and positioning plan into action in the marketplace and is, in fact, the tangible elements of strategy as far as customers are concerned. Each target market will require a separate mix of product, price, promotion and distribution offering which should be superior to that offered by the competition.

Dibb, Simkin and Bradley (1996) offer a similar list of components for marketing strategy but also include business mission and marketing objectives. It is certainly true that these factors are vital considerations when deciding which strategy is the best to pursue.

Factors to be considered in marketing strategy development

A business must determine its core target markets and how it expects to be perceived within these markets in relation to its rivals on the basis of marketing intelligence. Marketing strategy must maximise the business's strengths and differential advantages whenever possible and should relate to the organisation's mission statement, objectives and resource base. Therefore all the factors in a full marketing audit should be considered in the development of a marketing strategy. This includes the following.

(a) **Macro environmental factors**: political/legal, economic, socio-cultural, technological trends.

Various longer term opportunities and threats to the organisation can then be identified and taken into consideration when developing strategy. For example with the trend toward greater environmental awareness, many companies such as The Cooperative Bank have recently begun to target 'green' consumer groups.

(b) **Micro environmental factors**: suppliers, competitors, customers.

Clearly without an understanding of these factors target markets and differential advantage cannot be identified. Unilever's research of customers and competitors in the low suds detergent market identified that odour removal was an unsatisfied need hence it launched Radion onto the UK market.

(c) **Internal factors**: marketing strategy, programmes, systems, structure and productivity. Strengths and weaknesses in other functional areas such as finance, production and personnel.

Direct Line has exploited its operational strength of a low cost base and strong brand image in care insurance to develop a number of new financial products such as pensions and personal equity plans in order to cross sell and attract new customer groups.

By considering external market and internal company factors a SWOT analysis can be developed together with the identification of distinctive competencies and key factors for success in the market place. All of this information is therefore vital in the development of an effective marketing strategy.

40 COMPETITIVE ADVANTAGES

> **Examiner's comments: summary/extracts.**
>
> 6/95. This question was not popular; those who did it answered it well.
>
> 12/96. A patchy response, showing lack of breadth. The second part of the question was ignored or treated superficially.

Creating and sustaining a competitive advantage, something of value you can offer the target market that competition cannot, is at the heart of a successful marketing strategy. There are a number of ways of creating a competitive advantage. However, many

Answer bank

organisations try to operate without a clear advantage and instead try to imitate the market leader.

A competitive advantage can be created out of any of the company's strengths or distinctive competences, relative to the competition. In choosing the advantage, the key decision criteria is that it must be valued by the customer. Porter (1980) has argued that a competitive advantage can be created in two main ways; either through cost leadership or differentiation.

Cost leadership aims to develop the lowest cost base of any organisation in the industry. A low-cost structure with comparative products and prices to competition does allow higher than average returns to be generated. Cost leadership requires continuous attention to costs through achieving scale economies, experience effects, tight overhead control and minimisation in R&D and marketing budgets. For example, the strengths of efficient production processes and access to superior technology, or backward integration giving favourable access to raw materials could all be converted into a competitive advantage. This strategy is particularly suited to commodity industries where product differentiation is very difficult. The idea of **cost leadership** has been criticised by marketers (such as Hooley and Saunders (1994)) as it **is not market orientated** (that is, low costs are not a reason for a customer to buy the firm's products). This could be translated into lower prices, but strictly this would then be a form of differentiation based on price.

Differentiation is creating something which is seen as unique by target customers. Each element of the marketing mix should be considered as a potential base of competitive advantage. Product differentiation can be achieved through augmenting the generic and expected product. So for example Shell sells petrol (generic product) in easily accessible forecourts (expected product) and has sought to augment and thereby differentiate its product by adding **Shell shops** with various convenience products and by introducing loyalty schemes. The problem with these advantages is that they are easily copied. The potential product is only bounded by the imagination and resource capability of the company.

(a) **Promotional differentiation** can be achieved through using different types, content and intensity of promotion. For example, Branson and Virgin have used PR effectively; and Boddingtons used innovative advertising based on the product truth of creaminess to create a distinctive campaign.

(b) **Distribution differentiation** comes from using different outlets, having a different network or coverage of the market. For example direct marketing has created a new channel in a number of markets (for example, First Direct in banking who attract customers based on the convenience that this form of banking delivers).

(c) **Price differentiation** can be based on lower or higher prices. For example Aldi competes on low price in food retailing whereas Stella Artois seeks to differentiate itself on high price in the beer market with its claim to being 'reassuringly expensive'. The additional P of people can also create and advantage through excellent customer service delivered by responsive and trustworthy employees. The development of a positive relationship and history between a buyer and supplier can also held a company distinguish itself from the competition.

Risks associated with each strategy

(a) Cost leadership may be impossible to sustain due to **competitor imitation** through using the same technology and processes. Alternatively a company may be overtaken and its advantage wiped out if a competitor finds and exploits better way of reducing costs. Cost leadership may not convert into an advantage where **differentiation** is valued above price.

(b) **Differentiation** can also be wiped out where imitation is simple as in the petrol example above. The current differentiating factors may become less important to customer than new ones. For both approaches which seek to appeal industry-wide there is the added risk that focusers or nichers in the market may achieve lower costs or differentiation in specific segments.

Many marketing campaigns reflect a 'me-too' approach and are never based on a competitive advantage. These are the ones most likely to fail and can be attributed to managerial complacency, lack of professional marketing training, lack of information systems which results in little understanding of the environment, competition, customers or internal capabilities. In addition, these companies lack planning systems, effective new product development processes or the appropriate organisational structure which promotes the cross functional team work needed. Briefly, competitive advantage is difficult to develop in organisations with cultures which foster a desire to avoid confrontation, hard work and results and, of course, where a market orientation is not the driving force.

41 DEFENDING POSITION (12/98)

> **Examiner's comment: summary/extracts.** 'This was a popular question. Candidates doing well on this question related their answer directly to the factors that a direct insurer would need to consider when deciding how to responds to a new discount orientated competitor. The answer was also in the form of a briefing paper. Poorer candidates outlined alternative strategies without fully addressing the issue of how to respond to a discount operator.'

Introduction

Price competition is a factor in many markets ranging from industrial air conditioning to FMCGs such as cat food to the specific case of this question, financial services and motor insurance. In fact the advent of direct insures such as Direct Line changed the competitive forces in this market by rapidly increasing the direct writers share of the market at the expense of higher priced insurance brokers.

(a) **Issues to consider in response to a price-based attack**

    (i) **Service criteria**

        (1) Is your service significantly different from the competitor initiating the price attack?

        (2) Do you have a strong brand?

        (3) Can you supply a different range of insurance packages?

        (4) Can you add services to your current range?

    (ii) **Demand criteria**

        (1) Is the price cut significant enough to attract consumer attention?

        (2) Are there a number of market segments with different insurance requirements and price sensitivities?

        (3) Do you have strong customer loyalty?

    (iii) **Competition criteria**

        (1) Why did the competitor change the price?

            • Take market share

Answer bank

- Utilise excess capacity
- Meet changing cost conditions
- Lead an industry-wide price change

(2) Is it likely to be a permanent price cut?

(3) What is the likely affect of the price cut on your market share?

(4) What are other competitors likely to do?

(iv) **Cost criteria**

(1) What is the likely affect of the price cut on your profitability?

(2) Will the price cut take your price below your costs?

(3) Will a price cut increase demand and produce economies of scale effects?

(v) **Strategy criteria**

(1) How will a change in price affect overall marketing strategy?

(b) **Options available**

If the decision is taken, after considering the answers to the above questions, that the competitor is offering superior value to our customers and taking business away from us, we have several options to consider.

(i) **Maintain price:** if it is decided that by dropping prices the company would lose too much margin, or the insurer would not loose much market share, or it could regain share when necessary, or it would retain the more profitable customers.

The Radio Times in the TV listings price war maintained its price at 50p when all others dropped theirs in response to price based attacks. At the end of six months a number of the new entrants left the market, unable to sustain an acceptable margin, and the prices stabilised. The Radio Times, whilst losing some market share, came out of the war maintaining higher levels of profitability.

(ii) **Raise perceived quality:** if it is cheaper to maintain price but improve the actual or perceived quality of the insurance package. Improving the product, service and communications could do this.

(iii) **Reduce price:** if the insurer's costs fall with volume, the market is price sensitive, it would be difficult to rebuild share once lost to the new entrant.

However, engaging in price wars can be very costly. When the price wars began in the supermarkets in the early 1990s, Sainsbury's responded to the price cutters such as Kwik Save and Aldi by trying to draw more customers in with their Essentials campaign which cut the price of hundreds of own-label products. This wiped more than £850 million off the stock market value of Sainsburys and sales showed an underlying fall of 1%.

(i) **Increase price and improve quality:** if a target segment can be identified which values quality and is substantial enough to offset the reduction in volumes.

(ii) **Launch lower-price insurance package:** if the company has the resources to have a deeper product line, one higher priced, one the same as the competitors and one lower, this will signal a strong competitive reaction and may dissuade further price erosions or force the competitor to exit the market.

The right decision will be partly dependent on the reactions of the other players in the market. However, by considering the questions outlined above, the chances of making the wrong decision should be greatly reduced.

42 CRITICAL FACTORS FOR SUCCESS

What are critical factors for success? Other words are also used interchangeably which may help to clarify the term: critical success factors (CSF), key factors for success (KFS), key variables and key result areas. CFS is also the application of Pareto's Law or the 80/20 rule. In sales terms, Pareto's law means that 80% of sales are likely to come from 20% of customers. In the same way, but more broadly, 80% of a company's success is likely to result from 20% of factors - these being the 'critical factors for success'.

An understanding of CSF can be used at each of the stages of the planning and control cycle.

(a) **CSF and strategic analysis**

A vital aspect of strategic analysis is the identification of competitors' likely response profiles. Henderson argues that competitive response is effected by the competitive equilibrium.

(i) If competitors are nearly identical and make their living in the same way, then their competitive equilibrium is unstable. In commodity industries, CSFs are difficult to find and price wars often result.

(ii) If a single major factor is the critical factor, then competitive equilibrium is unstable. This describes industries were cost advantages exist. Again price wars break out as cost advantages are converted into lower prices.

(iii) If many factors are critical, then it is possible for each competitor to have some advantage and be differentially attractive to some customers. The more the multiple factors that may provide an advantage, the more the number of competitors who can coexist. This describes industries where opportunities exist for differentiating quality, service, convenience, style etc.

(iv) The fewer the number of competitive variables that are critical, the fewer the number of competitors. Where global, standardised opportunities exist these industries are often dominated by a few massive organisations.

Competitive equilibrium is therefore affected by the number and nature of CSF in the specific industry.

(b) **CSF and strategic alternatives**

The business strategist Kenichi Ohmae believes strategy is all about altering a company's strengths relative to those of its competitors. One strategic alternative he recommends is to identify the key factors for success or KFS in the industry or business concerned and then to inject a concentration of resources into a particular area where the company sees an opportunity to gain the most significant strategic advantage over its competition.

Competing in existing markets via intensifying functional differentiation can lead to superior positioning,

> 'If you can identify the areas which really hold the key to success in your industry and apply the right mix of resources to them, you may be able to put yourself into a position of real competitive superiority.' *(The Mind of The Strategist)*

(c) **CSF and criteria for choice at the strategic level**

Wilson, Gilligan and Pearson state that in choosing between alternative strategies it is desirable to choose the best; but how is the 'best' to be recognised? The best from the viewpoint of one stakeholder may not be the best from another stakeholder's viewpoint. Similarly, what is best in the short term may not be best in the long term.

Specifying the criteria, or CFS, by which choices are made among competing alternatives is a crucial step in working towards improved marketing planning and control. There exists five generally applicable CSFs which cover both financial and non-financial criteria.

Sphere of activity	Critical factors
Environment	Economic - interest rates - inflation rates - concentration Political stability
Marketing	Sales volume Market share Gross margins
Production	Capacity utilisation Quality Standards
Logistics	Capacity utilisation Level of service
Asset management	Return on Investment Accounts receivable balance

Using multiple criteria is better, as it offers a broader perspective. In addition, CSFs specific to the particular industry in question are required, for example in the food processing industry, new product development, good distribution and effective advertising are vital. Thus an understanding of CSFs can translate into criteria for choosing among competing strategies.

(d) **CSF and criteria for choice at the marketing mix level**

It is harder to apply CSFs to individual elements of the marketing mix because it is difficult to separate out the impact of price or distribution say on advertising success. However Wilson, Gilligan and Pearson outline criteria which are regularly used in choosing between alternative plans for specific elements of the mix.

Activity	Criteria
New product development	Trial rate Repurchase rate
Sales programmes	Contribution by region, salesman Controllable margin as percentage of sales Number of new accounts Travel costs
Advertising programmes	Awareness levels Attribute ratings Cost levels
Pricing programmes	Price relative to industry average Price elasticity of demand
Distribution programmes	Number of distributors carrying the product

(e) **CSF and management control**

Identification of CSFs can also be used in the control process. Essentially the control plan should instruct management on what should be monitored and indicate variance levels beyond which action will have to be taken. In this way, CSFs represent the most important factors to be monitored and reported upon. In the example of food processing above, a company such as Mars would need to monitor the number and success of its new product development programmes and specifically, the adoption rate and repurchase rate of each new product.

An understanding of critical factors for success in any sphere of activity is clearly going to prove invaluable to the success of that specific enterprise. In relation to planning and control, CSFs are useful at all stages in the process.

43 PRICE-BASED STRATEGIES

> **Examiner's comments: summary/extracts.** Stronger candidates made reference to a variety of marketing and financial criteria that should be used in deciding whether to use an aggressive price-based attack and gave full recognition to the dangers of so doing. Many candidates ignored the second part of the question and so scored poorly even if they provided a strong answer initially.

Increasing competition in any market brings into stark relief the need to establish a **defendable competitive advantage**. One route to achieving this is via the **marketing mix element of price**. In reality this does not necessarily have to mean the lowest price; the highest price point in any market can also be an advantage where prestige is a key brand value (Rolex watches for example). Also advantage can be obtained through innovative trade discounting and credit terms. However, the focus of this question is on the option of developing advantage through an aggressive cut-price based strategy, the criteria to use in deciding if this is a logical option and how marketing directors can forecast the probable effects of price cuts upon demand.

Jobber (1995) provides a useful table which summarises the factors which should be considered when initiating price changes:

	Increases	Cuts
Circumstances	Value greater than price	Value less than price
	Rising costs	Excess supply
	Excess demand	Build objective
	Harvest objective	Price war unlikely
		Pre-empt competitive entry
Tactics	Price jump	Price fall
	Staged price increases	Stages price reductions
	Escalator clauses	Fighter brands
	Price unbundling	Price bundling
	Lower discounts	Higher discounts
Estimating competitor reaction	Strategic objectives	
	Self-interest	
	Competitive situation	
	Past experience	

In evaluating the option of a reduced price strategy, relevant although not exhaustive criteria are as follows.

Demand based criteria

- Is price high compared to the value customers place on the product?
- Do we have strong customer loyalty?
- Can we cut prices enough to attract consumer attention?
- Are there a number of market segments with different product requirements and price sensitivities?

- Is the price sensitive segment attractive?

Cost based criteria

- Are we experiencing excess supply leading to spare capacity?
- Will the price cut take our price below our costs?
- Will the resultant increase in demand bring significant economies of scale?
- Are we enjoying falling costs?

Competition based criteria

- Price war likely?
- Will this pre-empt competitive entry?
- Is our product significantly different from competition in areas other than price?
- What are our other competitors likely to do?

Strategy-based criteria

- Do we have a build objective in terms of sales and market share?
- What is the likely affect of the price cut on our market share?
- What is the likely affect of the price cut on our profitability?

Product-based criteria

- Do we have a strong brand?
- Can we source a different range of products?
- Can we easily add value to our current product range?

Forecasting probable effects of price cuts on demand

If the decision is taken, after considering the answers to the above criteria, to cut prices there are a number of marketing research methods available to enable the Marketing Director to forecast the effect of the price cuts on demand.

To make an effective pricing decision the director needs to know, as a minimum, the **level of demand** to be expected in the future and how demand changes with price. To the economist, this translates as the shape and slope of the demand curve. To the researcher it is the forecast of demand and the price sensitivity of the market. A real problem when forecasting is the dimension of time. It is not sufficient to establish the demand curve today as it will be constantly influenced by competitive activity, product life cycle stages and marketing strategy. Research needs to provide a moving picture of demand, both now and in the future via the following methods (Churchill, 1995).

Historical data

Historical sales data can provide broad indications of the reactions of demand to previous price rises and cuts. Care must be taken to take account of the effect of *other* factors on demand at the time.

Statistical analysis

Statistical techniques which can be used include regression analysis, time series forecasting and Bayesian decision techniques. These require sophisticated computer packages, interviewing skills in extracting the decision-maker's judgements and translating these into probability statements.

Surveys

Customer surveys are of limited value as little reliable data comes from direct questioning along the lines of, 'How much would you buy if the price was £X or £Y?'

Test marketing

The market place provides the best method to forecast price sensitivity. Test markets can be set up with a different price in each and the resulting variations in demand assessed. Sales promotions based on price can also be tested. But again extraneous factors such as regional competitive activity can affect the results

Setting the right price is an inherently difficult task due to the wide number of variables that affect the results of any decision. Yet despite this inherent difficulty, the penalties for getting it wrong can be serious. If price is too high this can result in lost customers, market share decline and inadequate revenue to cover costs. If prices are set too low this can result in damaged customer perceptions of quality, total costs remaining uncovered and a price war. By applying explicit criteria to the decision and researching the resultant effects the risks associated with making a poor decision will be greatly reduced.

44 EVALUATION CRITERIA

In order to evaluate performance the company needs to clarify, first of all, its overall objectives and if they are clear, the evaluation and control process will need to monitor the achievement of these various objectives in the product and market sectors in which the company operates.

Effectiveness is concerned with 'doing the right things' and it the marketing manager's job to ensure that the financial and non-financial criteria focuses management attention on the right things. The sorts of criteria to which reference might be made include the following.

Financial	Non-financial
Liquidity	Sales volume
Cash generation	Market share
Value-added	Growth rate
Earnings per share	Competitive position
Shareholders value	Consumer franchise
Share price	Risk exposure
Profit	Reliance on new products
Profitability	Customer satisfaction
Cost leadership	Sustainable competitive advantage

Let us take an example from each side to explore this issue in more detail.

(a) **Financial criteria: profitability**

This can be defined as the rate at which profit is generated. Companies clearly need to measure the profitability of their various products and markets and also more desegregated areas such as customer groups, trade channels and order sizes. This information should help in the decisions concerning expansion, reduction or elimination.

The profit measure is valuable for the following reasons.

(i) It provides a simple criteria.

(ii) It permits a quantitative analysis in which performance can be directly compared with costs.

(iii) It provides a single broad measure which subsumes many other aspects of performance.

(iv) It permits the comparison of performance over time, or comparisons of a group of products or markets at any particular point in time.

(v) Profit measures typically focus on current rather than long run performance.

This last point is important for multinational products and markets because lower profits are likely when building up market presence. In addition, the quality of profits from a product in the growth stage of its life cycle are more valuable than profits from a product in decline since the former has a more promising future.

(b) **Non-financial criteria: customer satisfaction**

This provides a qualitative measure of performance which is, by definition, the most marketing orientated. This provides an early warning of impending market share changes. Monitoring the attitudes and satisfaction of customers, dealers and other stakeholders allows corrective action to be taken before sales are greatly affected. Systems which could be used include suggestion/complaint schemes, mystery shoppers and extensive customer surveys.

When establishing criteria to measure performance it is necessary to consider the level at which performance is being measured, its purpose and therefore at which point it feeds into the planning and control process:

Type of control	Purpose	Approach/ performance measure
Strategic control	To examine whether the firm is pursuing its best opportunities	Marketing effectiveness rating instrument Marketing audit Marketing excellence review
Annual plan control	To examine whether the planned objectives are being achieved	Sales analysis Market share analysis Sales to expense ratios Financial analysis Attitude tracking Customer satisfaction
Profitability control	To examine where the firm is making and losing money	Profitability by: product, territory, customer, trade channel
Efficiency control	To evaluate and improve the efficiency and impact of marketing expenditures	Efficiency of : sales force, advertising, sales promotion, distribution

Essentially this table outlines a control plan which should instruct management on what should be monitored and indicate variance levels beyond which action will have to be taken.

Future performance would be particularly highlighted by the approaches outlined under **strategic control**. This operates at the marketing and corporate strategy interface and would be the responsibility of senior management - board of directors. Annual plan control and profitability control monitor the performance of marketing objective achievement and would be the responsibility of the senior and middle management - marketing director and marketing manager. Efficiency control would monitor the performance of the middle and junior management responsible for each element of the marketing mix.

The right hand side of the table represents a very comprehensive list of both financial and non-financial measures of performance which could be used to develop a clear picture of past and probable future performance in all our product and market sectors.

45 EFFECT OF TECHNOLOGY ON CUSTOMERS

> **Examiner's comments: summary/extracts.** Weaker answers concentrated on the technology itself rather than the *uses* to which it could be put.

The benefits of the Internet as a marketing medium have been much hyped, with hundreds of companies leaping on the bandwagon as essentially an act of faith. But has the Web delivered on all its promises? Keeler (1995) states that the marketing uses of the Internet are fivefold.

- Sending messages via e-mail thereby eradicating location issues.
- Transferring files thus quickly and cheaply connecting customers and suppliers.
- Monitoring news and opinion thus very useful for marketing research.
- Searching and browsing.
- Posting, hosting and presenting information which facilitates brand building and sales generation.

Effects on marketing strategy

Companies operating through the Internet are likely to build databases of customers who have visited or used their site as the basis for further activity. Both approaches lead to the development of a more direct relationship being built with the individual customer over time. The areas of marketing strategy the Internet is likely to effect are:

(a) **Markets:** markets can be exploited that are not related to geographic nearness or physical contact (ie face to face activity). Customers' needs can be serviced remotely using the new technologies. However, investment would be needed in the IT infrastructure of an organisation. The cost of a web-site can range from a few thousand pounds to many hundred of thousands. Rank Xerox's web-site reinforces the company's brand values, as it documents its history of innovation but it also leads the user on a sales journey that aims to stimulate and capture a response. Over £2m has been generated from sales leads in one year.

(b) **Brands.** In the service sector the Internet may allow customers access to service providers anywhere in the world, where previously the customer has been restricted to local providers. This could lead to the globalisation of service brands. (For instance why study an MBA at your local university when you could study via the Internet at a major international business school?)

(c) **Products.** A whole new generation of information based products/services can be developed. Feedback from customers can facilitate more tailor-made offerings.

(d) **Promotion.** The Internet creates a new approach to promotion, as it creates a new mass communication medium for marketers to use and one which promotes far greater two-way communication. It allows customers to 'enter' an advert, providing involvement and direct response.

(e) **Distribution channels.** The Internet enables an organisation to operate in the world market from a small and centralised base. It could change the whole nature of distribution in the service sector in particular as a result.

(f) **Service.** The Internet can deliver economies via providing service 24 hours a day, seven days a week, without prohibitive cost implications.

Answer bank

Managing Customers

The Internet allows for a customer relationship to be built without direct face-to-face contact. In order to do this successfully, companies will need to develop sophisticated databases that allow companies to develop tailor made products and offers for customer groupings within their database. It also helps in securing their loyalty through the greater convenience it delivers. For example, Marketing Business (June 1997) provides an interesting case study. Transport company **TNT Express Worldwide** is in fierce competition with its rivals. It hopes that its new web site will encourage its customers to ship parcels with it again and again. Central to the site is a facility that delivers improved customer service - Web Tracker. While tracking parcels from a web site is not new TNT wanted to make it easier. So instead of having to cut and paste individual parcel consignment numbers into Web tracker, TNT engineered its site to accept up to 500 consignment numbers at one time and users didn't have to enter date or destination details either. Customers like it - 5% of TNT parcels are now tracked on-line - and a number are working to integrate Web Tracker into their Intranets.

Conclusions

Use of the Internet in marketing is here to stay. Like all developments the extreme positive and negative forecasts are likely to be exaggerated. Whilst it offers new ways of reaching your customer, servicing them and encouraging their loyalty there are a number of pitfalls which O'Commor and Galvin (1997) highlight.

- Poor targeting capabilities
- Cost
- Incompatible marketing messages
- Immaturity of the medium and its users
- Communication speed

That stated the Internet should certainly be on every marketing manager's agenda.

46 BRAND STRETCHING

> **Examiner's comments: summary/extracts.** Not a popular question, and whilst many candidates identified brand strategy, they did not extend this to cover the specific issue of brand stretching.

Introduction

Experts now view **brands** as the **link** between a company's marketing activities and consumers' perceptions of these activities. In the 1990s this brand revolution is particularly relevant to sectors such as financial services. The difficulties consumers have in understanding intangible products and the extent to which the service **becomes** the brand, both present marketing challenges together with the need to exploit brand equity through brand **stretching activities.**

Elements of Brand Strategy

Arnold (1992) in The Handbook of Brand Management, outlines a five stage brand management process.

1. **Market analysis:** Market definition, Market segmentation, Competitor positions, Trends: PEST and Micro factors.

2. **Brand situation analysis:** Brand personality, Individual attributes. Internal analysis = is advertising projecting the right image? Is the packaging too aggressive? Does the product need updating? Fundamental evaluation of the brand's character.

Answer bank

3. **Targeting future positions:** Future developments. Brand strategy: any brand strategy should incorporate what has been learnt in steps 1 and 2 into a view of how the market will evolve and what strategic response is most appropriate. Target markets, brand positions and brand scope are the elements of brand strategy.

4. **Testing new offers:** Individual elements of mix and test marketing the total offer.

5. **Planning and evaluating performance:** Level of expenditure. Type of support activity. Measurement against objectives: awareness and availability, attitudes. Information on tracking of performance feeds into step 1 on analysis.

From this we see that brand strategy involves decision on three issues: target market(s), brand positioning and brand stretching.

Brand Stretching

Brand stretching refers specifically to the use of an existing, successful brand being used to launch products in an unrelated market. (Note: a brand extension is the use of an established brand name on a new product within the same broad market.)

The starting point for this activity is to identify the current brand's core values. Brands should only be **stretched** in these cases.

(a) The **core values of the brand have relevance** to the new market into which it is to be launched. Marks & Spencer with its retail operations has established a strong brand image for quality, value and integrity. All these values are also important in the financial services market. This has allowed Marks & Spencer to stretch their brand successfully into the financial services sector.

(b) The **new market area will not effect the value of the brand in its core market**. Virgin's brand name has been successfully stretched into a number of markets including financial services. However the brand may now be affected by the problems it is experiencing operating train services in the UK.

There is a school of thought that states that it may be easier for service companies to stretch umbrella brands across markets. Financial services companies using umbrella brands can also run into database marketing programmes across their whole service range, American Express being a good example. In general though, most financial service brands are currently too weak to support much brand stretching activity.

47 BRAND STRATEGY

> **Examiner's comments: summary/extracts.** As brand strategy issues have come to the fore recently, the examiner was surprised that few attempted the question. Answers varied 'from a detailed treatment of the ways in which a brand strategy might be developed, through to a simple and mechanistic rehearsal of corporate umbrella branding, range branding and individual branding'.

To: Marketing director
From: Marketing analyst
Subject: Key elements of a brand strategy

(a) **What is a brand?**

Drawing on the ideas of John Murphy, (Group Chairman, Interbrand), 'a brand is a simple thing, it is in effect a trade mark which through careful management, skilful promotion and wide use, comes in the minds of consumers to embrace a particular set of values and attributes both tangible and intangible'. Professor Doyle suggests that brands that reach their potential have five key characteristics.

Answer bank

- A quality product
- Being first to market
- Unique positioning concept
- Strong communications
- Time and consistency

(b) **The brand planning process**

Brand strategy is one of the steps in the brand planning process just as **marketing strategy** is one step in the marketing planning process.

Arnold (1992) in *The Handbook of Brand Management* offers a five stage brand planning process.

(i) **Market analysis:** requires an overview of trends in the macro and micro environment and so includes customer and competitor analysis and the identification of any PEST factors which may affect our brand. For soft drinks, the explosion of competitive activity, particularly by own label, and new product introductions, such as Fruitopia, will be important.

(ii) **Brand situation analysis:** requires analysis of the brand's personality and individual attributes. This represents the internal audit and questions such as, 'Is advertising projecting the right image?', 'is the packaging too aggressive?', 'Does the product need updating?' need asking. This is a fundamental evaluation of the brand's character.

(iii) **Targeting future positions.** This is the core of brand strategy. Any brand strategy should incorporate what has been learnt in steps (i) and (ii) into a view of how the market will evolve and what strategic response is most appropriate. Brand strategy can be considered under three headings.

　　(1) Target markets
　　(2) Brand positions
　　(3) Brand scope

(iv) **Testing new offers.** Once the strategy has been decided the next step is to develop individual elements of the marketing mix and test the brand concept for clarity, credibility and competitiveness with the target market.

(v) **Planning and evaluating performance.** This requires the setting of the brand budget, establishing the type of support activity needed and measurement of results against objectives. Information on tracking of performance feeds into step (i) of the brand management process.

(c) **Brand strategy**

The elements of brand strategy can perhaps best be illustrated by way of a case study example. Unilever recently launched a new low suds detergent brand, Radion, on to a mature and saturated market. In 1980 Lever held 61% of the market by value but by 1988 this had fallen to below 40% with Procter & Gamble and own label taking the majority of the share. In the US the company increased the share of its Surf brand by positioning it as the 'fights dirt and odours' brand. This was not possible in the UK as Surf's brand values were based on the 'Square Deal Surf' proposition. Therefore the company had to introduce a new brand - enter Radion. The first year objective was 35% penetration and 24% repeat purchase. The key strategic questions were these.

(i) How could **Radion** attract consumers away from long established brands?

(ii) How could Lever ensure that Radion sales were not gained at the expense of its other brands?

The solution in brand strategy terms is outlined below.

(i) **Target market**

Housewives owning front-loading automatic washing machines, who were attracted to functional cleaning promise and who were responsive to an authoritarian tone in advertising.

(ii) **Position**

Radion was positioned as a superior alternative to competitor brands based on two functional (tangible) brand values: odour removal and cleaning effectiveness and supported with the emotional (intangible) brand values of modern, vigorous, uncompromising and challenging.

(iii) **Brand scope**

Radion was launched in same formats as current brands: powders and liquids, biological and non-biological, various pack sizes.

(iv) **Promoted differently to other Lever brands**

Radion advertising included TV, posters, radio, 'day-glo' orange packaging, all with a modern, vigorous, uncompromising and challenging tone of voice. The advertising proportion was, 'New Radion is as good as any other brand at cleaning and removes lingering odours that they sometimes leave behind' with the strapline of, 'Removes dirt **and** odours'.

(v) **Competitive pricing parity with other premium brands**

Radion was launched in October 1989 and by March 1990 Lever's share had increased from 41.7% to 44.8%. This excellent brand strategy, supported by a £8.98m spend, resulted in a 7% market share increase in just six months.

(d) **Conclusions**

As a company we should ensure that each brand has a clear strategy and annual brand plan. We should then assess our portfolio of brands and in this way allocate the marketing budget according to their position on the portfolio.

48 INNOVATION: IMPLEMENTATION ISSUES (12/98)

> **Examiner's comment: summary/extracts.** 'This was a reasonably popular question. The better candidates answered in report format and illustrated how structures, processes, organisational culture and people are all important elements in accelerating the pace of innovation.'

(a) **Faster NPD – the benefits**

The consistent introduction of **new products** and development of **existing products** that customers value are important criteria for corporate growth and sustained competitive advantage. Booz, Allen & Hamilton (1982) stated that only 10 per cent of all products introduced over the last five years were new, while the latter 90 per cent were incremental in nature. Hardaker, Pervaiz & Graham (1998) suggest that the slow time to market of product innovations by many organisations in Western nations inhibits competitiveness and aids the rise of Far Eastern organisations in global markets.

The NPD process can be characterised by such factors as turbulent domestic and global competition; continuous development of new technologies that quickly enter the market; changing market needs and requirements which directly alter existing and new product development; higher new product development costs; and increased need

Answer bank

for organisational alliances, with customers, suppliers, strategic partners, government bodies, in the NPD process (Kotler, 1997). Such characteristics point to the need for the domestic appliance manufacturer to consider how it can increase the pace of its innovation processes.

Benefits of faster NPD

- The imperative of shorter product life cycles (PLCs)
- The opportunity for cost reductions
- Gaining a price premium
- More frequent/fresher innovations
- Better product quality
- Greater product-line variety
- Improved market feedback

(b) **How to speed up the NPD process**

The processes of NPD are affected by organisational management style, attention to detail in the processes of NPD, support for product innovation by top management, organisational strategic thinking, and manufacturing facilities to support NPD. **Product innovation** is second only to corporate strategy in the way it involves **all aspects and all functions** of management. This emphasises the importance of **integration** for improving the speed of NPD. As NPD is clearly multi-functional in nature, developing effective technological and organisational integration mechanisms is of fundamental importance.

The overall timescale for the innovation process can be considered as a series of 'contributory' elements. Optimising and integrating them all can produce very significant time and money benefits. Getting one wrong can prejudice the success of the domestic appliance in the market or even the future of the company.

Eight contributory elements to NPD

1. The time to harness appropriate technologies
2. The time to understand the market needs
3. The time to establish a concept that is technically and commercially sound
4. The time to develop concepts to a functioning and producible design
5. The time to mobilise the manufacturing facilities and processes
6. The time to ramp-up to production volumes
7. The time to deliver and fulfil orders
8. The time to maintain or service a product.

Implementation issues

The changes suggested to reduce the time and cost of each of these elements could be summarised as a combination of people, processes and systems changes which are the key issues in implementing a faster NPD process (Brooks and Schofield 1995).

(i) The use of multidisciplinary, co-located teams

(ii) An emphasis on process rather than function

(iii) Senior management actively creates an environment in which parallel working can flourish

(iv) Clearly defined roles and responsibilities with empowered individuals

(v) Increased emphasis on understanding and meeting real customer needs

(vi) Involvement of suppliers and customers as part of the team

(vii) Routine use of appropriate process modelling and development tools

(viii) Positive use of relevant measurements to encourage continual process improvement

(ix) A significant increase in parallel processing of activities and information pull

(x) A common information system with easy access to relevant information

Achieving time and cost reductions involves a **combination** of changes to the people, processes and systems aspects of the domestic appliance manufacturing company. These are the enablers – or the 'things you have to do' - if the organisation is to bring about an increase in its pace of innovation.

The starting-point is likely to be some form of **process re-engineering** where the current process of working is established together with a series of change issues. These issues are often derived by **challenging the current process and performance** using time and cost metrics established through benchmarking. A 'to be' process model is then developed, representing the planned way of working in the future.

People need to understand how to work together more effectively in teams that focus on using the new processes. In this way, the risks associated with parallel working can be assessed and decisions taken to balance the risks against the potential time and cost savings. More frequent changes may well be involved, and making them in a controlled way that is visible to all the team will be a crucial ingredient in developing products successfully, in less time and with reduced rework. The technology and information management aspects of this way of working are addressed by the systems dimension such as **Effective Engineering Data Management** (EDM) and CAD tools will enable project team members to better communicate and share information.

In conclusion, the company needs to split down its current innovation process and calculate the time of each stage. Then by considering new integrated processes with team working and supporting systems, speed to market should be increased.

49 LOYALTY MARKETING

> **Examiner's comments: summary/extracts.** This question was popular and many candidates produced strong answers in which they discussed the nature of loyalty, the dimensions of a loyalty campaign and how it might be developed. Poorer answers confused loyalty marketing with internal marketing.

Current marketing literature has developed in recent year beyond '4P', transaction or customer attraction marketing to include activities which deliver the objective of customer retention, loosely termed **relationship marketing** (Coviello et al. 1997).

Loyalty marketing is a sub-set of this new approach and is employed by companies with a relationship-building view of their customers. Such companies create and sponsor programmes to keep their customers coming back, buying more and staying loyal. According to Kotler (1996), the challenge is to develop a special relationship with the company's 'best customers' in which they experience good two-way communication and see themselves as benefiting from special privileges and awards.

Customer loyalty programmes have been in existence for some time. Most people will remember collecting cigarettes cards, Green Shield stamps or Co-operative stamps and sticking them into specially designed books. But licking and sticking stamps is an activity of the past. Technology has now caught up for most people, making **computerised loyalty systems** one of the new issues of marketing management today.

Answer bank

True customer loyalty is not about achieving short-term sales increases through the use of incentives and promotions. It is about building a long-term relationship with customers to increase profitability. Jacobs, in an article in **Admap** in June 1996, outlines the main benefits to marketers of loyalty schemes. Statistics about loyal customers include:

- They spend 30-50% more per transaction
- They visit three times the average
- They spend four times more a year
- They account for over 50% of sales

The author reports on a scheme by a petrol company that increased turnover by 25%, increases of 20-30% a week for a fast food chain and a variety store where spending from its loyal customers increased by 30%. It is not just retailers implementing these schemes. Manufacturers look to maintain and improve loyalty among their trade customers by installing terminals in distributor outlets to introduce reward schemes for the end-user of their products.

American Express is a good case study of an organisation trying to encourage loyalty from both its distribution channel and card holders. Relationship billing involves providing benefits to users through the distribution channel. For example, a card holder who frequently uses a restaurant may not just get the bill for visits on the monthly statement but an offer to have a free bottle of wine at their next visit to the restaurant. This builds loyalty for the channel and the end-user.

As this examples shows data are the foundation upon which to build a loyalty system. Data can be derived from three principle sources; **registration details, profiles** (lifestyle data overlaid on the registration data to provide preferences by geographic area) and **activity data** which is ongoing and constantly updated with each transaction. The activity data is particularly useful for producing information on response to promotions, profiling of shopping habits and identifying niches for new products and services. The plastic cards, points and promotions are there only to attract customers to join and continue to use the scheme. The information derived can be used to build relationships by making targeted offers and personalising communications.

Kotler (1996) suggests that **frequency marketing programmes** and club marketing programmes are the most promising techniques to use when considering introducing a loyalty initiative. Frequency marketing programmes provide rewards to customers who buy frequently and/or in substantial amounts - British Airways Executive Club segments customers into three categories and provides a number of benefits such as quicker check-in procedures, executive lounges, improved in-flight services and rewards tied into the Air Miles scheme for its heavier usage customers. Many health clubs try to encourage more frequent visits by providing rewards such as free sun beds for reaching so many visits a month. Most of these initiatives provide financial benefits for loyalty. Club marketing programmes offer club membership either automatically upon purchase or by paying a fee. In addition to financial rewards, social benefits are also offered as illustrated in the successful Harley-Davidson Harley Owners Group.

When introducing a loyalty programme, a company should make decisions in seven areas.

(a) What are the programme's objectives? To increase average order size, build goodwill, prevent brand switching, attract new customers and target mailings

(b) Who is the target group? All customers or just heavy users?

(c) What will be the benefit bundle? Soft services and/or hard awards.

(d) What will be the communications strategy to promote the programme? Mass communication or targeted mailings?

(e) How much funding is required? Is a membership fee required, should co-sponsors be involved?

(f) What implementation strategy is necessary? Who needs to be trained and ready to deliver the programme?

(g) How will the programme's performance be measured and improved? On going control information will be required.

With the advent of computerised information systems and the growing realisation that customer retention is the smart way to improve profitability loyalty marketing is certainly a big issue for proactive marketing directors.

50 PRODUCT DEVELOPMENT (12/99)

> **Examiner's comments: summary/extracts.** This was a popular question and was generally handled well by candidates. Good answers outlined the new product development process and discussed ways in which it could be improved given the scenario presented in the question. Weaker answers talked about the new product development process but failed to discuss how it could be improved in the specific context of the manufacture of electrical cooking equipment.

Introduction

In the intensely competitive world of business, companies that fail to develop new products to meet the changing needs and wants of consumers expose themselves to the risk of having obsolete or unpopular products. This is particularly relevant in the electrical cooking market where technology and style is constantly changing.

However, new product development is very risky with figures of 60-90% failure rates per annum depending on the type of product.

It is therefore essential to have an effective new product development process to help minimise the risks arising from new products and ensure that innovative and profitable products are successfully launched. It is vital to have an understanding of the stages a new product goes through before it is launched. Booz, Allen and Hamilton suggest the following model:

New Product Development Process

Idea generation
↓
Screening
↓
Concept development and testing
↓
Marketing strategy
↓
Product development
↓
Market testing
↓
Commercialisation

To ensure the success of the process, an effective organisational structure must be established. There are a variety of alternatives available to create this structure, which are outlined below.

Product managers

The advantages of giving responsibility for new product development (NPD) to product managers are:

- They have expertise in their product
- They understand the markets
- New product management is only part of their job, so less resources are used

The disadvantages are:

- A lack of time to devote fully to the new product development process
- A risk of managers being preoccupied with existing rather than new products
- The fact that managers may lack the necessary skills for NPD.

New product section

The advantages of setting up a new product section are:

- It enables streamlining of ideas to be in keeping with market forces.

- Direct reporting to the chief executive can speed up decisions.

- Members are drawn from a cross-section of the organisation and so offer a different perspective on the products based on their experience.

  This is vital for rapid changes in technology and style, as in electric cooking.

- A centralised approach allows staff and channel ideas and information easily to the section.

The disadvantages are:

- It is costly to set up a new department.

- Recruiting staff internally that cannot be replaced easily may damage other departments.

- The department can be perceived by the rest of the organisation to be too remote.

- It is a permanent commitment, which may not be appropriate in future years.

Venture teams

Unlike a section, a venture team is brought together on a part-time basis to work on a specific product from conception to marketing. The advantages are:

- There is no permanent commitment to have the team.
- The team can be multi-disciplinary in nature.
- The team is solely focused on the specific product.
- A team is more cost effective than a section.
- The team may have an entrepreneurial spirit.
- A team is quick to set up.

The disadvantages are:

- It can be expensive, particularly to recruit specialists from other departments.

- Results can be of questionable quality, particularly if all the members of the team can return to their former role after the project.
- The team may operate out of anyone's direct control.
- The team will often be reactive to market needs.

New product managers

New product managers can be appointed across the full range of mainstream products. The advantages are:

- This can provide specialist knowledge in each cooking area.
- The managers will be exclusively focused on developing new products.
- Resources can be allocated specifically for each task.
- There will be natural competition between NPD managers to produce results.

The disadvantages are:

- Managers can promote product line extensions and modifications rather than new products.
- The lack of a centralised approach could result in the development of too many products across the range.

New product committees

Similarly to departments or sections, new product development committees are selected from key functional areas and are usually senior managers. They can co-exist with new product departments or sections to oversee crucial stages of development. This implies that there role is to give approval to and review existing programmes rather than be involved in the whole process of NPD.

The advantage of a committee is:

- The members will have substantial authority in the organisation.

The disadvantages are:

- The committee may be conscious of their other responsibilities in the organisation which may make decision making slow.
- This may also lead them to make compromises more easily than departments or sections would.

These factors may inhibit the development of new products which have good potential.

Customer involvement

From the beginning of the process of new product development, market research should be used to identify the gaps in the market for electrical cooking equipment in both the consumer and the commercial market. This can be fed back into the development process easily.

Further extension of this idea would be to involve the customers throughout the developmental stages of the product. Techniques such as panel testing can be developed. This can monitor the progress of the product both pre and post launch, giving valuable feedback and assisting in targeting prime segments in both the industrial and commercial markets.

Answer bank

Recommendation

Out of all the above options, I feel that the most viable option is to set up a new product development department. This is particularly true if the competitive strategy of the organisation is to produce new products.

The benefits of this method are:

- Co-ordinated approach to new products
- Focus for the departments to liase with in respect of new product ideas and information
- Resources dedicated to generating new ideas and products

This is probably the most costly venture. However, in the longer term, speed is essential in bringing new products onto all markets, but particularly the electrical cooking market. If a new product department can reduce the time span from conception to launch, the company will grow faster and maintain an advantage over its competitors.

51 FEASIBILITY STUDIES AND RISK EVALUATION

In order to get a marketing plan implemented in real life, marketing managers need to persuade their superiors and peers of its financial viability as well as its marketing feasibility. It is unrealistic to expect a **carte blanche** to spend large sums of money without any regard to a return on these investments. The production of a feasibility study, especially in the situation of a new venture, should help in generating support for the plan, assuming of course that the results of the study are positive.

The assessment of the feasibility of any strategy is concerned with whether it can be implemented. The scale of the proposed new venture needs to be achievable in resource terms.

Within the planning and control process the assessment of feasibility should start during the identification of strategic alternatives, has a large role to play in strategic evaluation stage and continues through into the process of assessing the details of implementation.

Johnson and Scholes discuss the concept of feasibility in particular in relation to the evaluation of strategic options. They suggest a number of fundamental questions which need to be asked when assessing feasibility.

(a) Can the strategy be funded?

(b) Is the organisation capable of performing to the required level, for example (quality and service)?

(c) Can the necessary market position be achieved and will the necessary marketing skills be available?

(d) Can competitive reactions be coped with?

(e) How will the organisation ensure that the required skills at both managerial and operative level are available?

(f) Will the technology, both product and process, to compete effectively be available?

(g) Can the necessary materials and services be obtained?

This is not a definitive list but it does illustrate the broad range of questions which need answering within the feasibility study. It is also important to consider all of these issues with respect to the timing of the required changes for the new venture.

Pearson states that very little appears to have been written specifically on feasibility studies in the marketing literature. However he provides guidelines for the form and content of a feasibility report.

(a) **Corporate audit**

- Objectives, five year plan
- Key criteria for project evaluation

(b) The **scenario or project**

(c) **Assumptions**

(d) **Feasibility research**

(i) Experimental/technical research
Design studies, performance specification, timings, costs

(ii) Market research
Demand analysis, competition, buying motives, pricing etc.

(iii) Commercial potential
Outline income and expenditure analysis

- DCF projections over five years, prices, breakeven analysis
- Venture capital required
- Cost of capital at current interest rate
- Working capital
- Short term loans/overdraft requirements
- Cash flow projections - funding periods
- Contingencies
- Payback periods and net gains.

In terms of the new venture for the **leisure centre**, the purpose of the feasibility assessment would be to reduce or avert risk under conditions of incomplete knowledge and thereby assist in confident forward planning.

(a) The **corporate audit** would outline the corporate mission statement and objectives in order to see if the leisure centre proposal harmonised with the organisation's intended business purpose. Also included here would be senior management's key financial and non financial criteria for any proposed investment evaluation such as ROI and market share targets. It would include an ongoing analysis of corporate strengths and resources.

(b) The marketing manager should gives details of the content and context of the proposal. The leisure centre is likely to have strategic synergy with current products and markets and these should be emphasised. Highlighting the **strategic logic** of the proposal is important.

(c) Next, should come the operational details such as the size of the centre, the **target markets** and **positioning**, the sports and leisure services to be offered and the prices to be charged. For example, the new venture could be a private members club with an emphasis on exclusivity, health care and premium services such as aromatherapy and weight loss or it could be an opportunity to run a contracted out public leisure centre offering a wide range of sports such as swimming, squash, badminton and aerobic classes to residents within a three mile radius of the centre.

(d) Any necessary assumptions should follow, such as the successful completion of negotiations with the local authority or the generation of funds from the sale of other interests.

Answer bank

(e) The feasibility research should cover three areas: supporting department contributions; marketing research; and financial analysis.

  (i) **Experimental/technical research** would cover design studies of the technical alternatives and the feasibility of any construction work required. An estimate would be needed for development time and costs.

  (ii) The **marketing research** would centre around forecasting market potential. Research would be commissioned to examine the characteristics, size and trends in the leisure centre market place. The nature of competition would need analysis together with customer research to ascertain buyers' motivations to initiate and complete a membership transaction. **Focus group research** would highlight the attractiveness of the proposed positioning and provide information on the best target market and marketing mix requirements.

  (iii) **Financial analysis** would be required in terms of cost and profit forecasting for a venture requiring substantial investment. Costs and revenues will need to be projected using discounted cash flow techniques over a five year period. Leisure activities tend to be seasonal in nature so price analysis should be undertaken to exploit seasonal peaks and troughs, breakeven analysis completed with cost-volume-profit projections forecasted. Estimates will be required for expenditure including: venture capital needed to design, build and equip the centre, cost of capital for the duration and working capital and short term loan/overdraft. A cash flow statement should be produced and it would be prudent to utilise some form of sensitivity analysis indicated optimistic and pessimistic revenue, cash and profit projections. Payback periods and the opportunity cost of capital should also be evaluated against the desirability of the leisure centre new venture.

The marketing implications arising from any feasibility study are the go/no go decision. Should the study prove favourable against the corporate criteria established, time dependent marketing objectives with an outline marketing strategy statement would flow naturally from such a study.

52 CRITERIA FOR A NEW PROPOSAL

> **Examiner's comments: summary/extracts.** Not a popular question, but it generated some good answers. The better candidates did well by relating their answer to **services** and showing how the criteria could be applied.

Introduction

Whether a good or service, any new product proposal should be professionally evaluated against a number of marketing, financial and internal criteria. It is only by making explicit use of such criteria that more objective and consistent decision-making can be achieved. Ennew (1990) outlines the five stage new service development process; new service development strategy, idea generation, screening, development and testing and service launch. Criteria are used at the third stage before large investments are made in product development. There a definitive list as it will depend on the individual service being evaluated. However the following criteria are likely to be included.

Financial criteria

- Sales volume
- Expected return on investment
- Cost of service operation

Answer bank

- Profit opportunities
- Profit-volume variations and breakeven point
- Pricing issues
- Costs of the marketing support necessary
- Cross subsidy from other operations

Marketing criteria

- Compatibility with current marketing strategy
- Consumer behaviour patterns
- Trends in the industry
- The size of the potential market
- Growth prospects
- Competitive profiles/strategies
- Attractiveness of the market
- Position in the overall product/service offering
- Pricing issues
- Promotional needs/opportunities
- Organisational abilities
- Perceptions of current brand offerings

According to Donelly, screening requires thorough **evaluation** and the application of **weights** to the different criteria according to the key factors for success in the particular service market.

These criteria can then be used in several ways to screen the new service proposal. Specifically they can be used to make the following comparisons.

- This proposed development against other alternative opportunities that the organisation could address.
- The profitability of alternative potential pricing/positioning proposals.
- Our offering against competitors' services.
- Our potential positioning strategies in the market against our competitors.

Conclusions

Should the service proposal score highly enough against the weighted criteria, detailed profit sales and cash flow projections should be developed. More detailed consumer research should follow in the development and test marketing stage of the new service development process.

53 PAN-EUROPEAN BRANDING

Introduction

The first issue to clarify is what is brand strategy? Different authors (Arnold, de Chernatony, Macrae, Hankinson and Cowking) suggest different components. Taking Arnold's definition, brand strategy comprises target market, brand positioning, brand name and extension decisions. Many authors, including Doole, Lowe and Phillips who take an international perspective, focus on the brand name decision as a key element of strategy. As we are dealing with a pan-European issue we should also include a consideration of the globalisation/adaptation strategic options as well.

Brand name options

Brand name decisions are an important aspect of branding strategy. Mihailovic and de Chernatony suggest five brand name options for managers along their Brand Bonding Spectrum:

(i) **Zone one: Total reliance on house brand.** ICI is the only brand name that is emphasised. Products are identified by a descriptor, ICI polyurethanes. Close to this in the U.K. confectionery market is Thorntons. This can be the best route where there are not enough resources to establish a new name or where a new name will not provide the right set of associations as a platform for future growth.

(ii) **Zone two: House brand umbrella, sub brand names.** The Escort sub brand name is subordinate to the Ford house brand umbrella. Nestlé adopt this strategy in many European markets. This can be the best route for companies seeking global recognition via their house brand, but require continuation of domestic recognition for their product brand. Also in situations where the house brand can add value to a newly launched product brand.

(iii) **Zone three: Balanced reciprocity between house and product brand.** L'Oreal's Studio Line where the branding of the product always communicates the company as the source. Cadbury's Caramel is another example. This approach is more costly as it requires each brand to be supported. However it reinforces the brand values of the house brand which in turn strengthens the product portfolio.

(iv) **Zone four: House brand endorsement.** Kit Kat is promoted as an independent brand endorsed by the Nestlé name in the U.K. Here the product may be more easily transferred to other house brands in an acquisition. A strategy used to gradually introduce a house brand.

(v) **Zone five: Independent product brand.** Marlboro cigarettes stand by the product brand alone. With the exception of the Mars Bar, Mars confectionery products use this approach. This requires greater investment to establish new products than the four other approaches. P&G and Unilever have used this strategy for years but you may have noticed the gradual introduction of 'Lever' on certain advertisements. Unilever is 'overbranded', that is they have too many separately identified strong brands, making it difficult to bring the brand values together under one umbrella. They are urgently re-engineering their brands and rationalising their portfolio under a smaller number of labels, in an attempt to rival the strength of the multiple retailers.

National, regional or global brand names?

A key decision will be whether to have National, European or Global brand names. This will of course be affected by the history of the brand name decisions already taken. Within the confectionery market a number of brand names have been changed to move from a national to regional/global strategy such as Marathon bar to Snickers and Opal Fruits to Star Burst. The brand strategy adopted here has been global product brand names.

Quelch, in a recent article on global branding in Long Range Planning, suggests that global consumers are younger, richer, more urban and exist with non-culture bound product categories. Global brands such as Coca-Cola, Sony, IBM and Nestlé have the following characteristics:

- Strong in home market
- Geographical balance in sales
- Address similar consumer needs
- Consistent positioning

- Consumers value country of origin
- Product category focus
- Corporate name

So whilst many confectionery companies are simply nationally based, exploiting the particular culture-bound aspects of this particular food product category, at least one brand, Nestlé, is adopting a global brand strategy. Quelch provides a useful summary of which aspects of brand strategy can be most easily standardised and which usually require adaptation.

Building Global Brands

	Standardization		Adaptation
	Full	Partial	Full
Brand name			
Brand positioning			
Brand slogan			
Brand logo			
Brand icons			
Copy platform			
Copy execution			
Product design			
Pricing			
Sales promotion			
Distribution			
Customer service			

Even with Nestlé however, certain local adaptations are required such as the house brand endorsement with the acquisition of Rowntrees and KitKat.

Conclusion

Clearly there exist a number of strategic options for pan-European branding. An evaluation of our past strategy, current position, competitor strategies and consumer preferences should help inform our final decision.

54 PIMS

Every strategic marketing text advises managers to use tools such as Product Life Cycle (PLC), Portfolio Models and the Profit Impact of Marketing Strategy (PIMS) database in the analysis and strategy generation stage of the marketing planning process.

PIMS is an international business consultancy based on the most extensive strategic information database in the world. PIMS began in the early 1970's with a number of researchers from the Marketing Science Institute, a non-profit research organisation associated with the Harvard Business School. The aim of this empirically based research was

'..to provide... insights and information on expected profit performance of different kinds of businesses under different competitive conditions'

(Schoeffler, Buzzell and Heany - HBR, 1974)

Currently PIMS is only available to subscribing clients who answer questions on a data form on such factors as market environment, competitive position, production structure and cost and performance ratios.

A key finding from analysis of the database is that there is much more variation in profit performance within industries than there is between them. This indicates that being a 'winner' in your particular industry is much more important in determining margins than being in the right industry. So what determines performance?

Thirty-seven factors explain more than 80% of variability of profit performance among the businesses on the database. A number of these are outlined below.

Marketing & corporate performance: PIMS

	Bad	Good
Relative Share	Weak	Strong
Relative Quality	Inferior	Superior
Investment Intensity	High	Low
Investment Mix	Fixed	Liquid
Capacity Utilisation	Low	High
Productivity	Below Par	Above Par
Real Market Growth	Decline	Growth
New Products	Many / None	Some
Marketing Spend	High	Low
Customer Power	Strong	Weak
Logistics	Complex	Simple

The profile of the business on the chart determines profitability. According to Pimsletter No. 47, businesses with weak profiles in every industry sector make 10% ROCE over a four-year period. In contrast a strong profile business makes 30% ROCE.

Key drivers are:

(a) **Market share.** The higher the share, the higher the profits and cash flow. On average, businesses with market shares above 36% had more than 3 times the ROI by comparison with businesses that had less than a 7% share of their respective markets. The main reason for this relationship is experience effects and E/O/S. However other factors influence the affects of market share on ROI -

- High marketing expenditures are negatively correlated to ROI but, when spend is high, market share matters more.

- Market share matters more when R&D intensity is high (R&D/Sales). Only high share players benefit from higher expenditure on R&D.

Buzzell & Gale in 'The PIMS Principles' state that:

'There are some trade-offs between current profitability and long term value enhancement... the most visible trade-offs have to do with levels of spending on marketing and R&D and with capacity expansion. In each of these areas, the SBUs that performed best over the long term were more aggressive.'

PIMS Associates do highlight that some high share businesses fail to achieve ROI's greater than 15% and that some low share businesses do achieve ROI's greater than 25%, but these are the exceptions to the rule.

(b) **Product quality.** Superior product quality has a positive influence on ROI for any given market share, thus the best position is high market share and high quality products. Inferior quality products and increasing marketing expenditure have a negative affect on ROI.

Given a certain product quality/market share position what strategy should be adopted?

Suppliers of higher quality products could contemplate the use of higher marketing expenditures as a means of inflicting damage on weaker competitors, whereas lower quality suppliers should avoid such a strategy.

(c) **Investment intensity.** The analysis shows that there is a negative relationship between this and ROI.

These and other PIMS findings can provide useful insights for the process of strategy development.

Using the evidence built up in the database, clients receive diagnostic and prescriptive information contained in four detailed reports:

- Par report: this specifies what ROI is normal for a particular type of business.

- Strategy analysis reports: the likely outcome of several broad strategic moves, based on evidence of similar moves by similar businesses.

- Optimum strategy report: shows the combination of moves most likely to give the client optimum results for their business.

- Report on 'look alikes' (ROLA): indicates successful tactics used by strategically similar businesses.

Clearly such reports would be useful in the formulation of marketing strategy.

That stated, PIMS is not without its criticisms. As early as 1982, Wensley in 'PIMS and BCG: new horizons or false dawns' argues that successful firms are those that have a sustainable competitive advantage attained via private information and not generally known strategic recommendations. In addition PIMS can not assess the effects of competitive response. Abell & Hammond in 'Strategic Marketing Planning' also add:

- Demanding and time-consuming nature of data input.
- Related to a single business rather than a portfolio.
- Fails to present insights to future market evolution.
- Specification problems, has the regression model included all variables?
- Measurement error by eliminating outliers.

Woo & Cooper point out the surprising case for low market share. Thus PIMS can mislead marketers into thinking increasing market share is the only option. They studied 126 low share companies that demonstrated superior performance. The key characteristics were industries with slow growth and few product changes that produced frequently bought items and a strategy of differentiation focus.

Given an awareness of these potential problems, PIMS is still the most sophisticated marketing planning tool available which can provide company specific confidential data and strategy suggestions, dependant upon company performance and market characteristics.

Despite PIMS' limitations, which all practitioners should be aware of, it does prove useful in the analysis and ideas generation stage of strategy formulation. PIMS was not designed to replace management judgement simply to inform it. It is best used in combination with other tools such as PLC and portfolio models to ensure consistency.

55 RELATIONSHIP MARKETING STRATEGY

Relationship marketing has been variously defined, one often quoted definition from Gronroos (1994) being that relationship marketing, '..is to establish, maintain and enhance relationships with customers and other parties at a profit so that the objectives of the parties involved are met. This is done by a mutual exchange and fulfilment of promises.'

Relationship marketing is also variously applied in different sectors including consumer, service and business-to-business. For example, Sim Kay Wee at Singapore Airlines states that 'we think it's important to have the loyalty of a passenger so that he appreciates what you do for him. So, we have a scheme called Priority Passenger Service whereby we ensure that the passenger's needs are met, we gather data about him... and we look after him really well.'

Russ Shaw at American Express discusses the Relationship Bill. 'Something that we launched here in the UK, and are now rolling out throughout the world, is something called 'relationship billing', which uses our database as a fundamental resource behind the way we bill our customers. We capture a lot of information about the way our customers use the American Express Card and, through the relationship bill, we can reflect back to them'. American Express also use relationship marketing with their channel members to link consumers with outlets via promotional programmes.

To provide an industrial business-to-business example, David Welch at 3M graphics works with their distributors. 'The main requirement is to be competitive and to grow their own businesses, so that the relationship we build with them is one of constantly enhancing their own business process and to make them more competitive against their competitors.'

The first step for the IT company to build a relationship marketing programme should be to establish a planning framework. Clark -and Payne (1994) have developed a customer retention improvement framework which can be applied:

Customer Retention Improvement Framework

Step 1	Step 2	Step 3
Customer Retention Measurement ■ by time ■ by market segment ■ by product / service offered Profitability analysis by segment	Identification of cause of defection and key service issues ■ Root cause analysis ■ Trade-off ■ Competitive benchmarking ■ Complaints analysis	Corrective action to improve retention ■ Top management endorsement ■ Employee satisfaction ■ Best demonstrated practice ■ Implementation plan

Clark, M. and Payne, A. (1994)

A decision should be taken to segment their market according to relationship potential based on a cost/benefit analysis. Kotler (1997) suggests marketing managers use number of customers and margin potential to identify which customers should be targeted for a relationship marketing programme.

Research & Segmentation

	Margin High	Margin Medium	Margin Low
Many Customers	Accountable	Reactive	Basic
Medium	Proactive	Accountable	Reactive
Few Customers	Partnership	Proactive	Accountable

Basic: sale without further contact
Reactive: customer encouraged to contact co.
Accountable: co. contacts customer to check they are satisfied, get ideas
Proactive: co. contacts customer with NPD suggestions
Partnership: co. works continuously with customer

Once identified, the second step should be to identify why customers in this segment are defecting and then to put together a relationship marketing plan to increase retention levels.

The IT company should move from a focus on customer recruitment to customer retention and management. This will involve the building of trust, commitment and loyalty. This will focus the company's attention on the importance of process, quality, personal relationships, databases and information, communication and keeping promises with key accounts. A customer retention plan should be written and contain the following aspects.

- Research and segmentation
- How to build financial/social/structural bonds
- Customer retaining mix
    - Product service system
    - Reinforcing promotions
    - Key account management
    - Specialised distribution
    - Post-purchase communication
- Reorganisation and internal marketing

Key account managers will be vital to this process and should manage the implementation of the plan in consultation with the IT company's board.

56 TUTORIAL QUESTION: BUDGETS

(a) **Behavioural arguments for including managers in budget preparation**

    (i) Managers will be more likely to adopt targets as realistic goals if they have been involved in setting them.

(ii) Motivation may improve as the result of a 'team spirit' developing through the involvement of more managers.

(iii) Managers are encouraged to think more innovatively and use their own initiative if they are involved in the planning process, as opposed to having budgets imposed on them.

(iv) Managers aggrieved by imposed budgets may under-perform intentionally, in order to discredit the budget.

(v) Goal congruence - where an individual's personal goals are congruent with those of the organisation - is more likely to exist in a participatory system. Involving managers in setting their budgets enables individual aspiration levels to be taken into account.

(b) **Behavioural arguments against involving managers in budget preparation**

(i) Managers may try to build unnecessary expenditure - budgetary slack - into their budgets, in order to reduce the risk of overspending.

(ii) Communication problems can arise if too many managers are involved.

(iii) It is difficult to develop co-ordination if several managers are involved in the process, each having a different personal perspective of the business and its environment.

(iv) There is a danger that participation will be cosmetic only, because managers are 'consulted' about something that in reality has already been decided. Such pseudo-participation can only generate cynicism.

(v) Individual managers may not be able to take the wider view of the whole business which is required in the budget setting process. There is a danger that 'empire building' will develop, with managers attempting to secure resources for their own budgets without considering the effect on other parts of the business.

Many of the behavioural factors which limit the effectiveness and efficiency of budgets can be overcome with the use of zero base budgeting. Traditional budgetary planning processes often use the current year's budget as a starting point for the budget for the following year. This leads to many problems including the following.

(i) **Overspending** to prevent subsequent year's budgets from being reduced.

(ii) The inclusion of unnecessary expenditure in the budget as a cushion against overspending.

(iii) Continuation of expenditures and practices from one year to another, without questioning their validity.

(iv) Lack of incentive for managers to be forward thinking and innovative.

Zero base budgeting practices can overcome these problems because each budget is started from scratch without being based on the previous year. Managers are required to quantify the benefits to be received from expenditure in their budgets and resources are allocated according to a cost-benefit ranking.

57 IMPLEMENTATION PROBLEMS

Implementation is not separate from but an integral part of the marketing planning process as illustrated by Wilson, Gilligan and Pearson's cycle of planning.

McDonald conducted a four year research project interviewing 200 industrial goods companies regarding their marketing planning process. In reality, it is a far easier job to establish objectives and strategies following the types of prescriptive approaches offered by several authors, than to manage the complex behavioural issues of putting these decisions into action - the implementation dimension of the marketing planner's role.

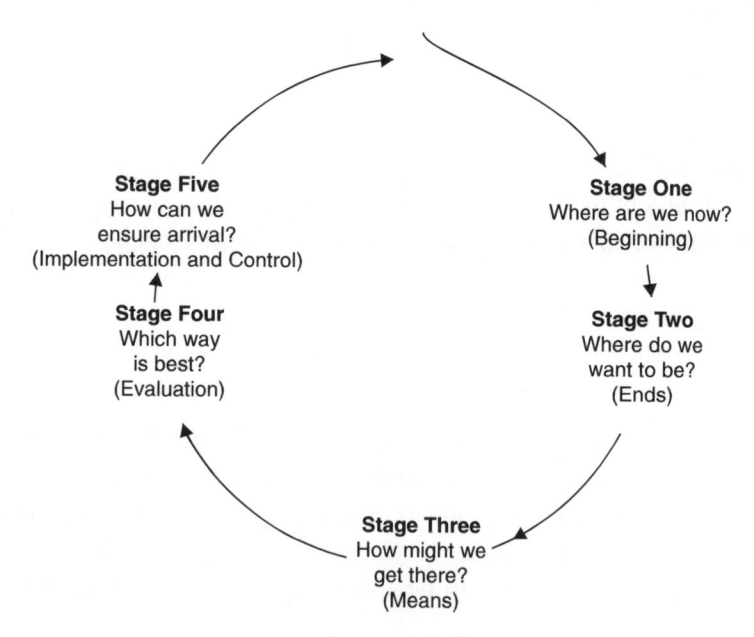

Stage One — Where are we now? (Beginning)
Stage Two — Where do we want to be? (Ends)
Stage Three — How might we get there? (Means)
Stage Four — Which way is best? (Evaluation)
Stage Five — How can we ensure arrival? (Implementation and Control)

Frequently encountered implementation problems

(a) **Weak support from the chief executive and top management.** Without the support, understanding and involvement of the chief executive it is unlikely that other functional managers will take the marketing manager's initiatives very seriously. Marketing planning has to be seen to be important to those in power if 'political' difficulties are to be minimised.

(b) **Lack of a plan for planning.** It is naive to assume that once a marketing planning system has been designed that it will operate smoothly from day one. The evidence indicates that a period of around three years is required in a large company to overcome resistance to the change that planning inevitably brings. Internal marketing is required which will be discussed later.

(c) **Lack of line management support.** Operational managers are often unwilling to participate fully because of hostility, lack of skills, lack of information, lack of resources and an inadequate organisational structure without a fully integrated marketing function.

(d) **Confusion over planning terms.** The initiators of the system are often graduates who have a tendency to use academic planning terminology which line managers see as meaningless jargon. It is unrealistic to expect a process to work if it is not explained clearly and simply and sold in the language of those whose support is required.

(e) **Numbers in lieu of written objectives and strategies.** Prior to a planning system often all that is used is sales forecasts and financial projections. Making explicit the route to achieving these objectives is a new and difficult skill. It requires managers to express the logic of their objectives and in this sense is a creative process requiring qualitative rather than quantitative information.

(f) **Too much detail, too far ahead.** Over planning is often associated with too much information and ends with piles of paperwork which confuses and demotivates rather than promoting positive participation. Marketing auditing can result in far too many issues demanding management attention. Key issues need to be identified - the wood needs to be drawn from the trees. However without practice, training and experience it is difficult to extract truly key strategic issues which are buried in piles of detail.

(g) **Once a year ritual.** This is a common barrier to effective implementation, when the task is seen as just another job to do which gets in the way of the really pressing day-to-day activities. Plans which are written and then filed away until next year do not work. Planning needs to be an integral part of the manager's job with progress towards objectives being reviewed and discussed on a regular basis.

(h) **Separation of operational planning from strategic planning.** This represented a major problem in McDonald's research. It is the lack of integration between the shorter term plans of operational managers and the longer term plans of senior management. If the activities of the former are not consistent and contributory to the latter then strategic plans are bound to fail. Strategic plans need to be built up from sound analysis at grass-roots level, and all managers need to consider not just continuing in the same direction but what longer term changes may be required.

(i) **Failure to integrate marketing planning into a total corporate planning system.** This is really a facet of the last point. Unless marketing plans are considered in relation to the plans of finance, production and personnel it becomes impossible to resource accurately the plan's product/market requirements. Many companies require cross-functional planning teams to be able to exploit internal strengths through synergistic efforts.

(j) **Delegation of planning to a planner.** When planning is divorced from the reality of operations, and the people who are expected to put the ideas into action are not involved, it is not surprising that resistance and lack of commitment can exist. In addition, for a planner to be effective it will require him or her to initiate changes in management behaviour and for this to happen top management need to be involved and not simply delegate the task to the 'planner'.

Explicit recognition of these potential barriers is necessary before an internal plan can be developed to try to reduce them, and thereby allow the organisation to reap the benefits of a strategic approach to its business.

The 'flipside' of external marketing is internal marketing which involves 'selling' your marketing plan to your internal customers, ie employees. The following quote from Foreman and Woodruff helps to illustrate the internal culture strived for:

'Two stone cutters in the middle ages were asked what they were doing: "I am cutting this damned stone into a square", one of them answered. "I'm working on a cathedral", the other one responded'.

The transformation of emphasis from the stone cutter to the employee building the cathedral is the essence of internal marketing.

58 INTERNAL MARKETING

> **Examiner's comments: summary/extracts.** This question on internal marketing produced some very good answers.

Bonoma and Clark have developed a model of marketing implementation in which four skills are outlined as being necessary for the effective implementation of a marketing plan; allocating, monitoring, organising and interacting skills. Interacting skills focus on how managers deal with employees in order to win their co-operation and support for the changes needed as a result of a new marketing plan. The flipside of external marketing is

Answer bank

internal marketing which involves selling your marketing plan to your internal customers, ie employees.

(a) **The principles of internal marketing**

- **Implementation** needs planning.
- Staff needs must be identified.
- Key influencers and decision-makers must be identified and targeted.
- Plans need packaging and promoting.
- Managers must make use of both formal and informal networks of communication.

Piercy and Morgan in 1990 created a model for internal marketing and we see that it can be described in the form of the internal marketing mix.

```
                    Missions
                       ↓
                   Objectives
                       ↓
             Strategic marketing audit
                       ↓
             Strategic marketing plan
               ↙              ↘
   Internal marketing      External marketing
      programme               programme
    • Product               • Product
    • Price                 • Price
    • Communications        • Communications
    • Distribution          • Distribution
         ↓                       ↓
    Key target groups        Key target
     in the company        customer groups
```

Product is the marketing plan which management wish to implement.

Price highlights that the costs and benefits to staff need to be assessed and with any situation there may need to be negotiation.

Place in external marketing represents when and where the product is available. Internally the timing and build-up to the announcement of the new plan can be vital, for example the positive impact at a company wide conference where all senior management are present.

Promotion in terms of poor communication is probably the biggest area for failure when evaluating internal company problems. Involvement of staff is key therefore meetings and discussion to take account and exploit the skills of the workforce is essential.

The key point to be taken from this model is that in addition to developing marketing programmes aimed at the external marketplace, to achieve the organisational change that is required to make those strategies work, there is a need to carry out substantially the same process for the internal marketplace within organisations.

Answer bank

A good strategy **incorrectly implemented** leads to no real advantages in the market place. Recently this fact has led to growing concern from academics, consultants and marketing executives alike to the issue of implementation. Reinforcing this, is the superficial implementation of marketing strategies by British firms who achieve the trappings of change but not the substance.

The original ideas of internal marketing were developed in the 1980s (by the **Nordic School of Services Marketing** by researchers such as Gummerson and Gronroos). Marketing success is frequently largely dependent on employees who are far removed from the excitement of the marketing office - service engineers, production and finance personnel, the delivery driver and so on. These are the employees called 'part-time' marketers by Gummerson. Interest in internal marketing has grown from here because empirical work has highlighted the fact that few firms put the standard text book model of marketing planning into practice. Consequently, much of the recent research on marketing planning, by such people as Greenley and McDonald, is now focusing on managerial perceptions and problems of implementation.

(b) **Factors to be considered when developing internal marketing programmes**

   (i) Internal training: to build awareness of marketing and customer-consciousness.

   (ii) Internal interactive communication: between managers and employees.

   (iii) Internal mass communication: using various communication tools to inform and create interest.

   (iv) Personnel administrative tools: bonus systems, recruitment procedures etc., to attract and retain key staff.

   (v) External mass communications and advertising: present advertising and promotional campaigns to staff before external launch to increase interest/involvement.

   (vi) Market research: collect information from employees and consumers to assess performance in non-sales areas.

   (vii) Market segmentation: to lead to more effective recruiting efforts.

Piercy in 'Market Led Strategic Change' highlights the hidden factors which should also be taken into account when developing an internal marketing programme. He suggests marketers should distinguish between a level of rational analysis, which is about techniques and systems as indicated above, and the level of power and political analysis. These factors are concerned with who runs the organisation and who has influence in the organisation. Cultural and political implications of a new plan should also be considered when developing an internal marketing programme.

It is likely that both academic and practitioner interest in internal marketing will continue to grow as conceptual frameworks and analytical tools for the strategy of marketing implementation develop. The benefit for marketing managers of an effective internal marketing plan is significant. It will ensure that the investment of time and resources in the external marketing plan is fully exploited.

59 INTERNAL MARKETING IN A HOTEL

> **Examiner's comment: summary/extracts.** This popular question produced some of the best answers, which expanded on communications and resource issues, although only the best candidates highlighted industry problems, such as low pay and high staff turnover.

Answer bank

Briefing Paper: Internal Marketing
To: The Managing Director
From: The Marketing Manager

Please find outlined below an overview of an **internal marketing** programme as requested.

Key elements of an internal marketing programme

What is internal marketing?

'Treating with equal importance the needs of the internal market - the employees - and the external market through proactive programmes and planning to bring about desired organisational objectives by delivering both employee and customer satisfaction'

Originally the scope of internal marketing was considered to be the motivation, training and development of employees involved at the customer interface, with the aim of delivering a better service to the end customer. This is obviously important in a service industry like Hotels. However internal marketing is now seen to include non-contact employees as well. In fact internal marketing covers any planned effort to overcome any resistance in an organisation to change and to ensure through proper communication, motivation and training that employees effectively implement corporate and functional strategies/plans (Woodruffe, 1995).

This concept is obviously important in the Hotel Industry where customer's expectations of the service encounter are rising. The interchange staff and back office systems are critical in terms of delivering customer satisfaction.

Development and implementation

People inside the organisation, to whom the plan must be marketed, are considered internal customers. The first stage is to group these internal customers. The first stage is to group these internal customers into three segments.

- Supporters: Those likely to gain from any changes.
- Neutrals: Those whose gains and losses are in balance.
- Opposers: Those who are likely to lose from the change or are long term opponents.

An internal marketing mix has to be developed for each of these target groups.

- **Product:** This is the plan/strategy itself together with the attitudes, values and actions that are needed to successfully carry it out.

- **Price:** The price is what internal customers have to pay as a result of accepting the plan/strategy. This could be lost status or resources, change in work pattern etc.

- **Promotion:** This is a critical area in the mix, and involves any communication medium that can be used to effect the attitudes of key groups. The promotional mix includes: presentations, discussion groups, written reports etc. It is important to note this communication has to be a two way process. At times it may be necessary to adapt the plan in order to gain support.

- **Distribution:** this categorises the places where the product and communications are delivered to internal customers, such as: meetings, seminars, informal conversations and away days.

Although an internal marketing programme gives a framework within which to work, successful implementation is reliant on three key skills:

(a) Persuasion

- Present a shared vision
- Communicate and train
- Eliminate misconceptions
- Sell the benefits
- Gain acceptance by association
- Support words with action

Answer bank

    (b) Negotiation

- Make the opening proposition high: leave room for negotiation
- Trade concessions

    (c) Politics

- Build coalitions
- Display support
- Invite opposition in
- Warn opposition
- Control the agenda
- Take incremental steps

Potential problems

Time is also important and potential problems can arise by not taking enough *time* to allow people to adjust to the changes implied by the plan. Persistence is required in the face of opposition, modifications to the strategy may be necessary on the way. Key detractors and recalcitrant players may exist, and if negotiation and persuasion are not successful, these people can be removed. A final potential problem is lack of resources, both human and financial. Internal marketing programmes require a budget for training, communications and staff time. If this is not available the likely chances of success are greatly reduced.

60 EFFECTIVE CONTROLS

> **Examiner's comments: summary/extracts.** The least popular question on the paper, but well answered. A lack of clear cause and effect relationship has led to a lack of accountability. A marketing control system would include objectives, targets, feedback and accountability.

Planning and control can be seen as a five stage process involving the regular analysis of the current situation, the establishment of objectives and strategies, tactics and controls for their achievement (Dibb, Simpkin & Bradley, 1996). The first four stages are the planning processes. Control is often less practised and this answer will consider a number of reasons for this together with the weaknesses of such a situation and suggestions for how an effective control system can be established.

Marketing control is the process of objective setting, performance measurement against these objectives, performance diagnosis and taking corrective action where necessary.

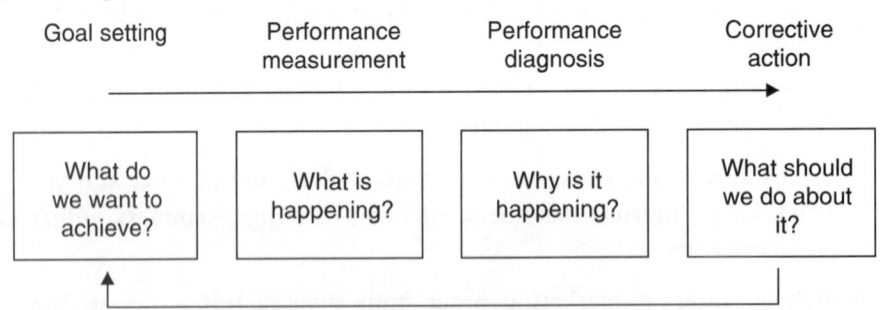

Goal setting	Performance measurement	Performance diagnosis	Corrective action
What do we want to achieve?	What is happening?	Why is it happening?	What should we do about it?

Evaluation and control is a natural part of the marketing planning process, ensuring that planned strategy really happens and that results of such actions are properly monitored. Successful companies rely on the effective implementation and monitoring of strategy.

Kotler (1995) reports on a study of 75 companies and their control processes and the findings give some explanation for poor practice in this area.

    (a) **Resources and experience:** small companies had poorer controls than large companies in terms of setting clear objectives and establishing systems to measure performance.

(b) **Lack of adequate information systems:** less than half of the companies knew the profitability of individual products, could compare their prices with competition, could analyse their warehousing and distribution costs or evaluate their advertising effectiveness.

(c) **Lack of systematic review procedures:** less than a third of the companies had regular review procedures for spotting and deleting weak products.

(d) **Out of date information:** many companies took four to eight weeks to develop control reports which were occasionally inaccurate.

Taken together these factors indicate a lack of focus on control which is likely to stem from control not being seen as important from a senior management perspective. Often marketers are employed for their creativity which is vital in strategy development but not the skill needed for controlling the implementation of the strategy.

The consequences of relying on inadequate control information are typically manifested in terms of **partially developed understanding** of the market, an **inadequately focused** marketing strategy and programme development, a heightened probability of the company being forced into a **reactive mode** as environmental shifts take the organisation by surprise and the possibility of **overspend** as costs escalate beyond revenues achieved. Given these consequences the arguments for a formal and well-structured control system are strong.

Establishing a control system not only involves deciding what approaches to adopt but also in deciding what information systems will be used, who should be involved and how the system will be sold via internal marketing techniques.

Kotler (1995) details a number of different types of control; **strategic plan control** which includes the marketing and effectiveness rating audit; **annual plan** control which includes sales, market share, financial and satisfaction analysis; **profitability and efficiency control** rather than reporting on every result, it is sensible to simply report on those areas which go above or below acceptable variance levels.

A sound marketing information system will need to be in place which gathers and processes internal records, marketing intelligence data and specific continuous and ad hoc research studies such as the customer satisfaction information.

The marketing manager together with marketing budget holders should be involved. This is likely to include the sales manager and the various product/brand managers. Employees from manufacturing, finance and personnel should also be included together with the specialist agencies who will be employed to do specific evaluation tasks such as the market research agency. Distributor performance is likely to be evaluated so representatives from our various channels would help with the decision-making and communication process. Wilson and Gilligan (1995) highlight the importance of clearly defining the extent and limits of functional control and ensuring that those responsible for performance should be fully involved in the planning process.

Good communication, both within the marketing department and between departments, will be vital. This should include regular review meetings, performance reports and publication of good results to recognise achievements in this area. Means should also be established to enable plans to be revised in line with actual performance in such a way that the responsible individuals are involved.

Effective implementation will greatly depend on internal marketing to employees, motivation of personnel and effective co-ordination of planning and control activities.

61 CONTROL SYSTEMS

> **Examiner's comments: summary/extracts.** Strongest answers included reference to a variety of inputs to the control system and how this information could be used for decisions on product range and development and so on.

Marketing control system

Control can be defined as the continuous comparison of actual results with those planned and taking management action to correct adverse variances or to exploit favourable variances. To be able to do this targets and standards need to be set and measurement and evaluation of performance needs to be undertaken as illustrated below:

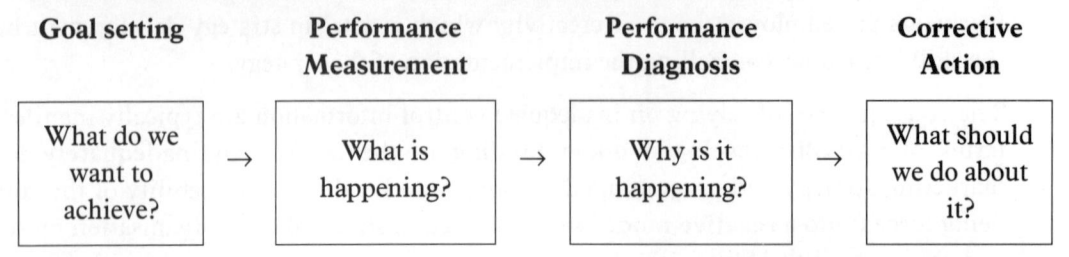

Goal setting	Performance Measurement	Performance Diagnosis	Corrective Action
What do we want to achieve?	→ What is happening?	→ Why is it happening?	→ What should we do about it?

Control information can be financial or marketing in nature. Sales and profit information is financial whereas customer satisfaction ratings and market share analysis are examples of non-financial control information.

Considering the fact the personal computers are sold through multiple distribution channels a system is required which:

- Gives a picture of absolute and relative performance of the channels
- Allows for regular monitoring
- Allows us to feedback information and modify behaviour

The types of information required include:

(a) **Financial information**

This will be mainly concerned with cost efficiency and profitability, although information about incremental costs and benefits of providing more or fewer channels of distribution should also be made available.

(i) For each category of distribution channel, the direct costs of operations, for example costs of: warehousing, transportation, discounts to resellers, insurance, handling costs and charges. Direct costs should be analysed into fixed and variable costs.

(ii) For each category of distribution channel, the volume of each type of product sold per period and the contribution from those sales.

(iii) The gross profit from each distribution channel, being the difference between the contribution in (ii) and direct cost in (i).

(iv) The distribution cost of products sold.

(v) For each category of distribution channel, budgeted direct costs, sales volumes, contribution and gross profit.

(vi) Share of central promotion costs (if relevant). For example marketing and advertising may be centrally organised, but its activities may relate to specific channels of distribution and as a consequence this should be brought into the information.

(vii) Ratio analysis, indicating the returns on capital employed per product before and after the deduction of the already-analysed distribution costs; also ROCE per distribution channel.

(viii) The value of stocks owned by the company and held unsold in each distribution channel.

This information should be available through the internal records system of the company.

(b) **Marketing information**

(i) Details of market shares in the various channels.

(ii) Estimated future growth or decline of the channel.

(iii) Details of the strength of the competition and competitive activity in terms of product launches, price reductions and communications activity.

(iv) Customer satisfaction ratings for resellers.

(v) The volume and nature of customer complaints.

(vi) Willingness to support marketing activity ie uptake of trade marketing merchandisers, support literature, joint warranty initiatives etc.

(vii) Dealer design, display and merchandising standards.

(viii) Customer profile and accessibility by channel (Geographic profile).

Some of this information may be available from secondary sources, such as competitive shares and activity, but a lot will require investment in primary research such as customer satisfaction ratings and complaint data. The use of a specialised marketing research agency to conduct on-going research together with ad-hoc dealer mystery shopper and store audits would be advisable.

This information would be used to assess the success of the overall marketing plan for the range of personal computers the brand manager markets. The monitoring of the successful implementation of the plan in such a dynamic market is likely to be on a weekly basis with more thorough reviews quarterly. Where sales, costs and customer satisfaction ratings are above or below pre-set variance levels corrective action will be required. This may be in the form of additional trade marketing support, possible rationalisation of channel strategy or additional customer care training initiatives.

62 MARKET-LED STRATEGIC CHANGES

To: Managing Director

From: Marketing Manager

Briefing paper: What does Market-Led Strategic Change Mean for Us?

It is likely that you have been to a conference at which Professor Nigel Piercy was presenting his best selling strategic marketing text. So what does Market-Led Strategic Change entail?

According to Piercy (1997) the three things a manager needs to get a handle on in the process of going to market are:

- **Customers.** Understanding customers and focusing on the market offering made to them, what it produces in customer value, satisfaction and loyalty.

Answer bank

- **Market strategy.** Choosing market targets and a strong market position, based on differentiating capabilities to create a robust and sustainable value proposition to customers and networks of critical relationships.

- **Implementation.** Driving the things that matter through the corporate environment to the marketplace.

Thus 'market-led' is all about focussing the whole businesses' attention on customer needs and wants. 'Strategy' is about segmentation, targeting and positioning and deciding who to partner with to achieve and maintain a competitive advantage. 'Change' is about the organisational and behavioural dimensions, rather than the analytical ones, within the marketing planning process. The rest of this briefing paper will consider these three dimensions in more detail.

(a) **Market-Led**

Piercy provides a useful diagnostic to assess the current level of customer-orientation.

How Serious are We About Measuring Customer Satisfaction?

How good are we at each of these?	Score out of 10
1. Measuring customer satisfaction	
2. Using customer satisfaction measures to change our marketing policies	
3. Using customer satisfaction measures to evaluate and reward our staff	
4. Ensuring all staff understand out strategy on customer service and quality	
5. Setting staff measurable goals for customer service and quality, and evaluating performance	
6. Consulting staff about customer needs, expectations and complaints, and taking notice of what they say	
7. Managers setting a good example in providing service and quality to customers	
8. Working together to remove obstacles and barriers to quality and service delivery	
9. Regularly evaluating our competitors' service and quality provision	
10. Having a clear and actionable service and quality strategy compared to out competitors	

In addition to measuring the current levels of customer satisfaction we should display some, if not all, of the following internal/cultural characteristics:

Strategy
- Integrated plan for development of marketing orientation
- Formalised definitions of markets and mission
- Detailed specification of marketing objectives
- Commitment to implementation

Shared values
- "We will become a fully customer-driven organisation"
- "Customers come first"
- "Marketing expenditures are an investment"
- "Service is paramount"

Style
- Top management support for marketing through symbolic actions and commitment of time to marketing and customer-related activities
- Open communications between all functional groups and marketing staff
- Recognition and reward of customer/market-orientated behavior

Systems
- Customer intelligence reports
- Competitor intelligence reports
- Marketing planning and control systems
- Remuneration and performance appraisal systems geared to support marketingorientation

Skills/staffing
- Recruitment of an adequate number of people with requisite marketing skills
- Marketing training programs and facilities
- Knowledge of Market
- Analytical skills in segmenting markets and identifying decision making units (DMU's)

Structure
- Simple structure based on markets/geography
- Key account sales structure to service most important customers
- Decentralised marketing staff to provide close and fast support to customers
- Staff rotation of non-marketing staff through customer contact positions

(b) **Strategic**

According to Piercy, market strategy involves choosing market targets and developing a strong market position based on differentiating capabilities to create a robust and sustainable value proposition to customers and networks of critical relationships.

Brooksbank (1991) suggests it includes similar dimensions:

(i) **Setting Strategic Focus.** Profitability can be improved by either raising volume or improving productivity. This focus mirrors the basic difference between Porter's (1980) generic strategies of differentiation and cost.

(ii) **Defining Competitive Advantage.** This is a company's chosen route to distinguishing its offering from the competition and should be based on something of value to the target market. It can be derived from any of the firm's strengths relative to competition. It is embodied in the company's positioning strategy which, according to Brooksbank, is the amalgam of the following two components.

(iii) **Selecting Customer Targets.** Emphasises the role of marketing segmentation and target marketing in the development of marketing strategy.

(iv) **Selecting Competitor Targets.** Emphasises the role of competitor intelligence and analysis in the development of marketing strategy.

(v) **Assembling the Marketing Mix.** Translates the segmentation and positioning plan into action in the marketplace and is, in fact, the tangible elements of strategy as far as customers are concerned. Each target market will require a separate mix of product, price, promotion and distribution offering which should be superior to that offered by the competition.

Dibb, Simkin and Bradley (1996) offer a similar list of components for marketing strategy, but also include business mission and marketing objectives.

(c) **Change**

Piercy offers a model for the process of going to market which, he suggests, is driven by placing the customer centre stage.

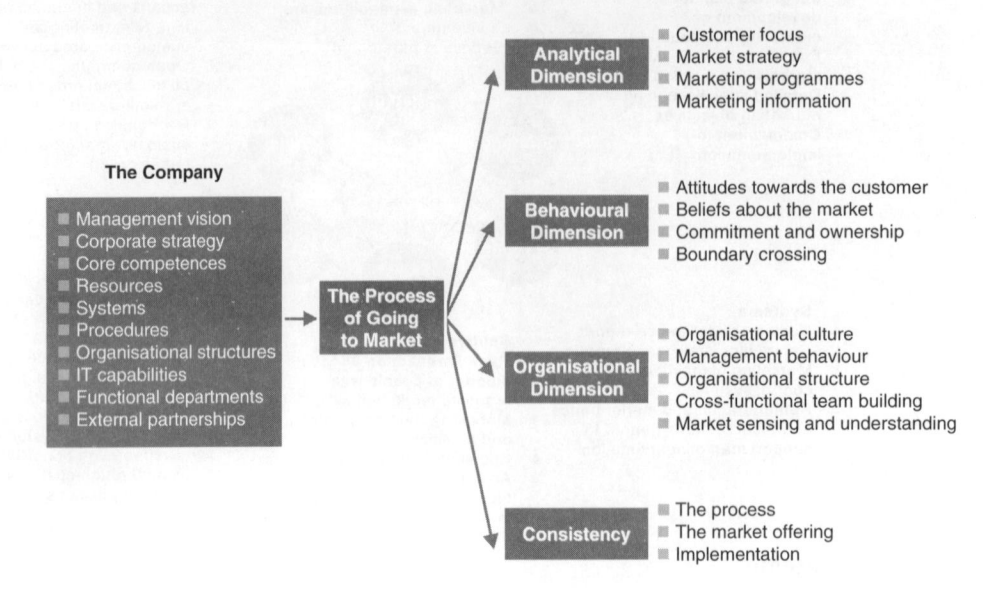

The Process of Going to Market

The Company
- Management vision
- Corporate strategy
- Core competences
- Resources
- Systems
- Procedures
- Organisational structures
- IT capabilities
- Functional departments
- External partnerships

→ **The Process of Going to Market** →

Analytical Dimension
- Customer focus
- Market strategy
- Marketing programmes
- Marketing information

Behavioural Dimension
- Attitudes towards the customer
- Beliefs about the market
- Commitment and ownership
- Boundary crossing

Organisational Dimension
- Organisational culture
- Management behaviour
- Organisational structure
- Cross-functional team building
- Market sensing and understanding

Consistency
- The process
- The market offering
- Implementation

Implementation involves driving the things that matter through the corporate environment to the marketplace. Barriers (McDonald 1997) can include:

- Weak support from the chief executive and top management.
- Lack of a plan for planning.
- Lack of line management support.
- Confusion over planning terms.
- Numbers in lieu of written objectives and strategies.
- Too much detail, too far ahead.
- Once a year ritual.
- Separation of operational planning from strategic planning.
- No ownership or commitment.
- Delegation of planning to a planner.

Piercy suggests managing the process of strategic planning can reduce these barriers. This involves recognising the analytical, behavioural and organisational dimensions of the process and managing these in a consistent way. Chunking by champions, managing participation, building effective planning teams, facilitating the process, making implementation strategic and ownership the top priority are all important ingredients for success.

Clearly, this brief overview explaining what market-led strategic change entails can not do full justice to what is essentially a strategic approach to marketing. This, by definition, encompasses many aspects of the total marketing management process.

63 THE LEGAL BUSINESS

> **Examiner's comments: summary/extracts.** Part (a) answers concentrated on the purpose and structure of the audit, but little detailed attention was paid to how it might be used, and its importance in underpinning the strategic marketing process. Answers to part (b) for some reason concentrated on SWOT and marketing plans, rather than the particular problems such as culture, or introducing a strategic marketing orientation to the Legal Business.

Answer bank

(a) To: Managing Partner
From: Marketing Manager
Date: December 1996
Subject: Conducting a Marketing Audit

(i) **Purpose of the marketing audit**

'A marketing audit is a comprehensive, systematic, periodic and independent examination of a company's marketing environment, objectives, strategies, organisation and performance.' (Kotler, Gregor & Rodgers, 1977)

Organisations usually carry out marketing audits with the view to determining problem areas and opportunities so that the company's marketing performance can be improved. As such it represents the most appropriate basis for generating the necessary information to take forward the marketing activities of The Legal Business.

More specifically, the purpose of the audit is to do the following.

(1) Summarise current activities and results in terms of sales, costs, prices and profits.

(2) Identify any opportunities/threats in the environment that should be taken into account when developing the marketing plan.

(3) Gather information about customers, competition and environmental developments that may affect marketing strategy. This will enable The Legal Business to stay very close to its marketplace and customers.

(4) Ensure that objectives set are realistic and provide an opportunity to revise them in light of any environmental changes.

(5) Reveal any aspect of the marketing mix which is not operating effectively.

(6) Ensure that all marketing activities are operating productively and achieving maximum cost-effectiveness.

(7) Provide an overall database of marketing information which can be fed into the management information system and used as an invaluable aid to strategic decision-making.

(ii) **Focus and components of the audit**

To realise the above benefits a detailed examination of the following areas is required. Kotler, Gregor and Rodger suggest six elements for a marketing audit which can be categorised under three headings.

(1) **Macro environment** which includes: political/legal, economic, social and technological trends likely to affect the organisation in the short, medium and long term. A particularly important trend is the rise in consumerism in the public and professional sector and the resultant increase in customer expectations of the legal service we provide.

(2) **Micro environment** which includes: customers, competitors, suppliers and distributors. This is an in-depth investigation of our immediate marketplace. It is clear that a number of competitors have become more aggressive, hence a detailed analysis of our competitors strengths and weaknesses is vital to support our plans to arrest our decline in market share.

The external environmental analysis outlined should highlight key opportunities and threats together with an understanding of the key factors for success in the market.

(3) **Internal company analysis:** This should highlight our marketing strengths and weaknesses.

- **The marketing strategy audit.** Marketing objectives and strategy review - how well suited is this to the realities of the external environment?

- **The marketing organisation audit.** Evaluation of structural capability and suitability for implementing the strategy outlined in the marketing plan.

- **The marketing systems audit.** Evaluation of the quality of systems for analysis, planning and control. This will particularly focus on the marketing information system and marketing planning system.

- **The marketing productivity audit:** examines the profitability of the marketing programme and cost effectiveness of marketing expenditure.

- **The marketing functions audit:** evaluates each of the elements of the marketing mix to include the service portfolio, pricing programme, distribution channels, promotional mix, our service processes, physical evidence and customer focus of all our employees.

From the consultant's report we already have some indication of a number of opportunities to improve in this area.

(iii) **How we might conduct the audit**

Best practice suggests that we employ an independent auditor to carry out the audit. Since I have only recently been employed I feel confident that, as Marketing Manager, I should conduct the audit. However, to ensure the necessary degree of objectivity, all primary research such as the customer service quality ratings and the internal employee attitude survey, should be conducted by an external marketing research agency.

It is necessary for us to work out an agreement on the objectives, coverage, depth, data sources, report format and the time period for the audit. From this I will develop a detailed plan as to who will be interviewed, the questions, time and location and agree a date for the presentation of the findings. In order to generate support for marketing, we should include a session which asks the senior partners to discuss, debate and develop recommendations for needed marketing actions in light of the findings.

(iv) **How the results might be used**

Having conducted the audit it is important that the time, effort and expense is used to take the necessary actions to improve the performance of The Legal Business. To ensure that the results are incorporated effectively within the strategic planning process, the major findings need to be incorporated into an appropriate framework. The most often employed framework is that of SWOT: strengths, weaknesses, opportunities and threats. Strengths should be matched with opportunities and a summary of the reasons for good and bad performance included. It will be against this background that I will move on to writing the marketing plan to include the establishments of objectives, marketing strategies, tactics and an implementation plan including the necessary internal marketing activities needed to develop a far greater strategic marketing orientation within the organisation.

Answer bank

(b) To: Managing Partner
From: Marketing Manager
Date: December 1996
Report: Developing a far greater Strategic Marketing Orientation

What is a strategic marketing orientation (SMO)?

According to Brooksbank (1990), '...marketing is a company-wide commitment to providing customer satisfaction. It is also a managerial process involving the regular analysis of the firm's competitive situation, leading to the development of marketing objectives, and the formulation and implementation of strategies, tactics, organisations and controls for their achievement'. This definition of strategic marketing orientation is illustrated below:

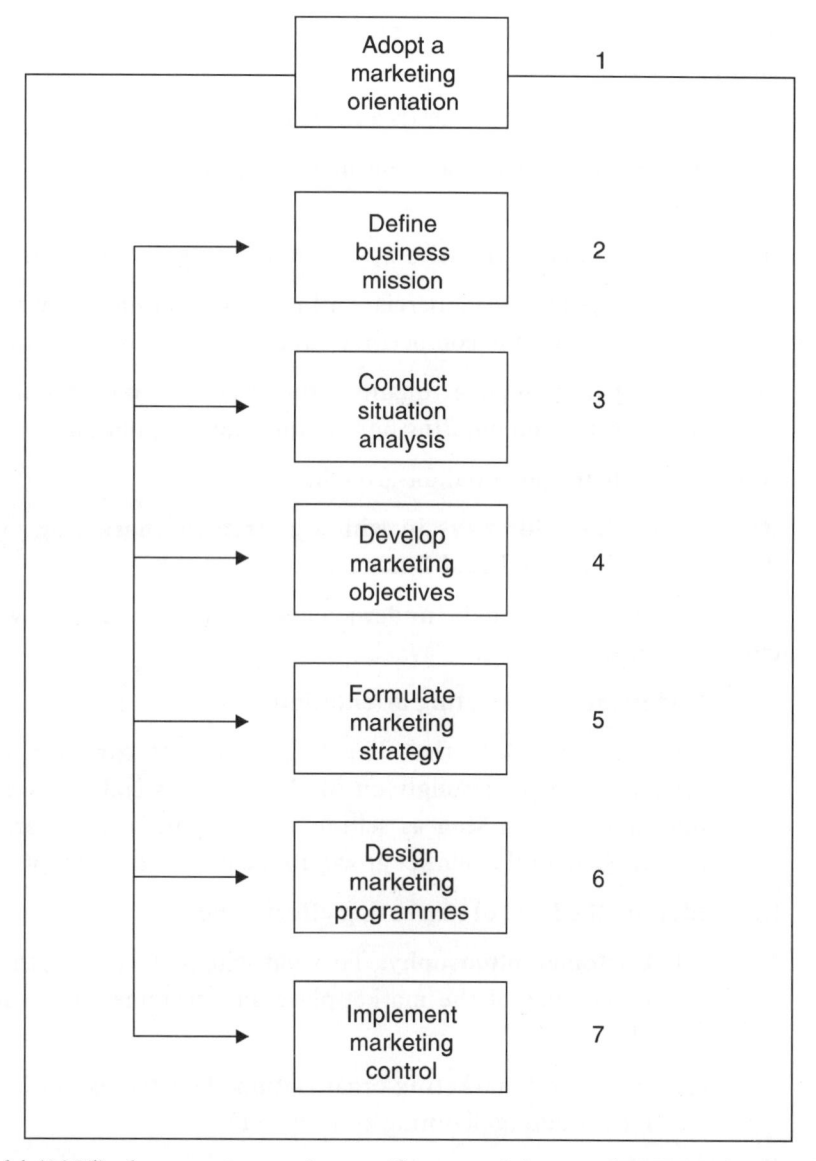

1. Adopt a marketing orientation
2. Define business mission
3. Conduct situation analysis
4. Develop marketing objectives
5. Formulate marketing strategy
6. Design marketing programmes
7. Implement marketing control

McDonald (1995) also comments that, ... 'few practising marketers understand the real significance of a **strategic** marketing plan as opposed to a **tactical**, or operational marketing plan'. The difference can be explained as follows:

Tactical. A detailed, one year plan based on last year's products and customers, focus on marketing mix eg advertising.

Strategic. A three to five year plan based on defining scope of product/market activities and matching activities of the firm to its environment and distinctive competencies.

Thus for The Legal Business to become more strategic in relation to its marketing activities a more customer focused, longer term planning approach needs to be undertaken. A SMO is a combination of marketing and organisational factors which contribute to improving effectiveness (Kotler 1995) and form the basis of sound organisational performance. It is made up of the following elements.

- Customer philosophy
- Integrated marketing organisation
- Adequate marketing information
- Strategic orientation
- Operational efficiency

Why should a professional service organisation adopt a SMO?

There are several reasons why a professional service organisation like ourselves should adopt a SMO.

(i) To understand client needs and wants.

(ii) To develop and operate the most appropriate service offerings to meet those needs.

(iii) To communicate the offerings to our clients and attract interest and business.

(iv) To become more commercial and marketing orientated which is vital to success in the dynamic and competitive environment we operate in.

(v) To enhance service quality, thereby ensuring client satisfaction whilst safeguarding and building our organisation's reputation.

(vi) To create the potential for growth.

Recommendations for ways in which a strategic marketing orientation might be developed within The Legal Business

A number of steps need to be undertaken when trying to change what is essentially the culture of the organisation. (Payne's (1988).

(i) **Understand the existing orientation**

It seems very likely that The Legal Business currently holds a 'professional orientation' based strongly on the law society's code of conduct. Marketing has traditionally been seen as selling and only in recent years has the number of practitioners in the market grown to the point where supply exceeds demand.

(ii) **Identify the level of marketing effectiveness**

(1) **Customer philosophy.** To what extent do the partners acknowledge the importance of the market-place and customer needs in shaping company plans?

(2) **Integrated marketing organisation.** To what extent is the company staffed for marketing planning and control?

(3) **Adequate marketing information.** Does management receive the quality of information necessary to conduct an effective planning process?

(4) **Strategic orientation.** Does the company's management generate innovative strategies for long term growth and profitability, and to what extent have these plans proved successful?

(5) **Operational efficiency.** Is marketing implemented in a cost-efficient manner and are results monitored to ensure necessary corrective action is taken?

The primary purpose of this audit is to find and communicate to the senior partners the current level of perceived marketing effectiveness and provide evidence of the need for a programme to improve the firm's marketing orientation.

(iii) **Identify a marketing champion**

Ideally the **senior partner** should champion the adoption of a marketing orientation because the attitude of this person can be the determining factor in the success or failure of the plan. Without top management support, the programme can degenerate into a token management-training exercise. Leading by example is vital so, for example, the senior partner should allocate regular time to marketing planning meetings, new service development meetings and marketing research associated with client satisfaction ratings.

(iv) **Conduct a needs analysis**

The next step is to conduct a management-development needs analysis based on interviews with appropriate partners, fee earners and support staff within the firm. The sorts of knowledge, skills and attitudes that can be developed through training include competitive strengths and weaknesses, clients' motivations, planning, motivating and communication skills and customer focused attitudes.

(v) **The management development programme**

Based on step 4, appropriate courses can be developed to include different types and levels of staff to explain the knowledge, skills and attitudes necessary for the development of a strategic marketing orientation. A workshop approach, where a series of sessions are designed to focus on current problems and apply new knowledge to solve them, works well.

(vi) **Key support activities**

(1) Establish a **marketing task force** to oversee the development of marketing activities

(2) **Organise for marketing.** The Legal Business is currently structured around services such as debt recovery and commercial litigation, and not around customers and markets. This has resulted in lost opportunities for cross-selling.

(3) **Acquire and develop marketing talent.** My appointment is one step in this direction, we should also develop marketing skills in internal staff.

(4) **Use external consultants.** Marketing research, customer care training and communication agencies seem appropriate areas.

(5) **Promote marketing-orientated lawyers.** This will aid in developing an appropriate culture which clearly sees customer service, planning and innovation as important.

(6) **Develop a marketing-information system.** In particular regular studies of clients and competition. A greater awareness of sales potential and profitability of different markets and the measurement of the cost effectiveness of different types of marketing expenditure.

(7) **Install an effective marketing planning system.** The planning process, including feedback mechanisms should be formalised. The time spent and people involved in developing the marketing strategy needs to be improved. Thought should be given to contingency planning and a more strategic use made of the elements of the marketing mix.

(8) **Recognise the long term nature of the task.** Developing a strategic marketing orientation represents a major change in attitudes and a fundamental shift in core values. Change can take from three to six years and will be gradual in nature.

Problems likely to be encountered in a professional service organisation and suggestions to overcome these problems

The particular characteristics of services (variability, intangibility and inseparability) are likely to bring particular problems. Other problems include the fact the service is delivered by '**professionals**' with the regulations and traditions of the professional body, the short time marketing has been practised, the lack of appropriate structures, processes and systems, and the management of highly skilled individuals.

(i) The **individual** nature of the legal service, typically performed on a one-to-one, client-professional basis can lead to the problem of **variability** in delivered service quality from partner to partner and from exchange to exchange making quality difficult to assure. Solutions include the selection of customer focused employees, establishing clear service standards, training current employees and monitoring standards through customer satisfaction research.

(ii) The legal service is highly **intangible** and therefore difficult for the client to understand and assess in terms of quality and value. This characteristic will make it more difficult to clearly define performance criteria and monitor standards. It also places a strain on marketing communications and makes trial before purchase difficult. The service marketing mix, particularly physical evidence, can help to reduce uncertainty. Building our reputation and brand name will help to enhance consumer confidence.

(iii) The '**people**' element in service is a critical factor as our service is dependent on the skills and competence of individual lawyers. Customer retention will be highly dependent on the trust and empathy developed between lawyer and client in what is an **inseparable** exchange process. Heightening our lawyers' sensitivity to this fact may be a problem. Internal marketing, staff development and customer care training will help solve this problem. Developing a relationship marketing plan will also be crucial.

(iv) Advertising of legal services has only recently become common therefore we may have a problem of low consumer awareness of our practise. We will need to inform the market about our service to communicate our availability and service standards.

(v) The service is delivered by 'professionals' who are affiliated to the regulations and traditions of the Law Society. They are influenced by strict codes of conduct. Until recently marketing was equated with advertising and promotions and this was banned. It is only necessary to review the comments made in discussion with the partners to see that this is a pervasive view in The Legal Business. Consequently we are very passive in waiting for clients to come to us and viewing marketing activities as unnecessary or even contrary to professional standards. This view of marketing will need to be changed over time through all the initiatives previously outlined.

(vi) The short time marketing has been explicitly practised is likely to mean that there is a lack of appropriate structures, processes and systems to support the marketing task. Law firms have traditional been structured around the professional partnership and individual's specialisms and not around market needs. Information and planning systems will all need developing.

(vii) **Managing highly trained individuals** can be problematic and requires sensitivity. They should be involved and their views canvassed and acted upon whilst recognising the time constraints imposed on busy professionals who actually carry out the activities associated with the provision of the service (Woodruffe, 1995).

Conclusions

The effective implementation of a strategic marketing orientation will require the commitment and co-ordination of efforts of all employees. Their co-operation is essential in realising the marketing plan which will be designed to increase service efficiency and effectiveness thereby enhancing our overall share of the market.

64 MJS CATERING SUPPLIES

> **Examiner's comments: summary/extracts.**
>
> (a) Generally well answered with coverage of both short term tactical and longer term strategic steps that might be taken to combat the competitive threat. Problems arose where candidates produced a SWOT analysis and/or general marketing plan and failed to pay attention to the organisational implications of developing a proactive stance.
>
> (b) Rather disappointing answers with many candidates discussing internal marketing rather than how strategic relationships with customers might be developed. Amongst the other common mistakes was the failure to relate the discussion to the issues raised in the case study.

(a) **Briefing Paper**

To: The Main Board
From: Marketing Manager
Date: June 1997

This report will outline the offensive marketing strategies which we can use against the emerging market challengers and market nichers in our industry.

We are currently being squeezed by the entry of several new competitors and increasingly more aggressive marketing by existing competitors. In order to react to this market structural change we can use the philosophy of offensive marketing strategies.

Offensive marketing strategies are based upon military theory and tactics. These strategies are based upon the concept of establishing a defendable advantage over the competition (Porter 1980, 1985). There are two generic approaches.

(i) Offensive strategies: usually associated with market challenger and the aim is to grow market share.

(ii) Defensive strategies: usually employed by market leaders and the aim is to defend market share against market challengers.

It is **offensive** marketing strategies that we will be focusing on within this report. Offensive strategies can be split into five main strategies (Kotler et al 1981) which are:

- Frontal Attack
- Flank Attack
- Encirclement Attack
- Bypass Attack
- Guerrilla

Frontal attack

The most risky option. The attacker meets the competition head on, product for product, cost for cost. History has indicated that in order for this approach to succeed the attacker needs to have three times the resources of the defender.

You can have a variation on the frontal attack which is called modified frontal attack or limited frontal attack, this is where you lure away selected customers by shifting resources to a single marketing element for example advertising or price. This tends to work best where there is no or slow competitor reaction.

Flank attack

Gain advantage in areas where the competition is geographically weak or market segments that have not been fully developed.

(i) Geographical flanking: focus attention on those geographical areas that are weak.

(ii) Segmental flanking: focus on segments where customer needs are not being fulfilled (similar to a focus/niche strategy).

Encirclement attack

The aim here is to dilute the defender ability to retaliate which strength in any one area. Attacking the defender on as many fronts as possible, for example: price/quality/distribution/ service. This is very expensive in the first instance because all resources are mobilised in a lot of areas, however this can be extremely successful in the long term for example, Seiko watches.

Bypass attack

The most indirect approach is to develop new markets through:

(i) Unrelated products
(ii) New geographical markets for existing products
(iii) Technological leapfrogging

This approach avoids confrontation.

Guerrilla Attack

This is best suited to smaller companies with a limited resource base. This approach basically involved small attacks on different areas - hit and run. The aim is to demoralise the defender and to keep him off balance. Examples of guerrilla tactics are damaging PR, sudden & intense advertising, poaching key members of staff. A good example is Virgin's dispute with British Airways.

Who to attack?

MJS cannot possibly attack all of our competitors so we have to decide on one of these options:

(i) **Attack the market leader**

We are not prepared to do this at the moment. Risk of retaliation is high and the market leader is not perceived to be our major threat.

(ii) **Attack firms of similar size to us who are under-financed or re-active**

The nature of our competitors is that they are highly financed and are pro-active in the marketplace. These companies are a threat to our position; we know that they are pursuing aggressive strategies and the risk of retaliation is high.

Answer bank

(iii) **Attacking smaller regional firms**

There have been a number of small firms following a niching strategy which have entered the marketplace and it is to these companies that we have lost business.

It would be best for us **to launch our efforts against weaker companies.** This is likely to cost us less in the first instance, threat of retaliation is smaller and we have more likelihood of being successful. Competition is strong and we can not afford to tie all of our resources into offensive strategies, as we also need to hold our market share.

We need to **identify** new or smaller companies who are weaker then us in terms of finance and resources.

What strategy to pursue?

If we target smaller, weaker companies then a **frontal attack** would be likely to succeed. Although this strategy is generally perceived to be the most risky option we have a number of advantages.

- Our resource base is more than three times the size of any of these competitors.
- We have superior economies of scale.
- We have a premium reputation.
- We have the experience and capacity to produce more innovative recipes.
- High level of customer service.
- Degree of retaliation is small.

Bypass attack and Guerrilla attack are not appropriate because of the size difference between our target competitors and us. Encirclement attack is appropriate; however this is likely to take quite a while and ties up our resources. Flanking attack again is a possibility, however if we look at the relative strengths of RJS in comparison to the competition I believe that a more direct assault would work more effectively.

By focusing on the new and small companies we would effectively raise barriers to entry so high as to deter new competitors entering the market. However we still have information gaps. We do not know what factor or combination of factors has enabled them to be successful in their markets. We have been able to make certain assumptions, however we need to establish these more detailed factors before deciding on the elements for our strategy.

Through this flanking activity we will pick up more market share in niche areas. Essentially we are performing a segmental flanking manoeuvre attack on firms similar to ourselves.

Longer-term strategy. The initial frontal attack could develop into an encirclement strategy on other targeted competitors. Rather that focus of one element of strategy, we need to pull together several elements for our strategy to succeed in the long term and for us to be able to survive in this increasingly competitive environment. Initial thoughts are these.

- Product innovation
- Improved service
- Distribution
- Prestige image
- Cost reduction

In order to be able to make an informed decision on these elements of strategy, we need to implement a competitor information system immediately.

Answer bank

Implications

The implications for MJS on adopting a more pro-active and offensive marketing strategy are going to be widespread.

To develop and implement an offensive marketing strategy we are looking at changes in the organisation. We are looking at a culture change from that of a sales orientation to a marketing orientation. This means that we must focus on the 4 C's.

Competitors

Who are they, what are their objectives, what strategies they are pursuing, their strengths and weaknesses and how they will react to an offensive move?

Customer needs

In order to sustain competitive advantage we need to understand our customers better, build relationships with them and make sure that we are servicing their needs better than the competition.

Company capabilities

The fit between what we want/need to do and the capabilities of the company.

Changing environment

Environmental monitoring and analysis systems need to be put in place.

These values need to be adopted throughout the organisation and to have top level support. We will need systems (MKIS), structures, management style, staff and skills. This is a major task and one that we will need to consider in detail and will be the subject of my next presentation to the board.

(b) To: Managing Director
    From: Marketing Manager
    Date: June 1997
    Subject: Relationship Marketing Programme

1 **Introduction**

A relationship marketing programme concerns the development of long-term relationships between a firm and its different stakeholders. The programme will therefore focus on developing loyalty between the firm and its customers and immediate business partners such as suppliers and distributors. Further, when developing a programme for customers, the focus is on retaining existing customers rather than concentrating on attracting new customers.

This report will firstly define relationship marketing. Then, utilising the market research findings of the 'customer perception survey' the report will outline the principal dimensions of a relationship marketing programme before examining the programmes effective implementation within MJS.

2 **Defining relationship marketing**

Berry (1983) first introduced the concept of relationship marketing in the service context with the definition of 'attracting, maintaining and - in multi-service organisations - enhancing customer relationships'. In this practical paper, he offered five strategies for enhancing relationships: core service strategy, customisation, service augmentation, relationship pricing and internal marketing. Similar ideas were also emerging at this time from The Nordic School of Services with Gummerson's (1981) paper on the marketing cost of services. Gronroos later wrote extensively on relationship marketing, his 1990 paper introducing the 'marketing strategy continuum' was a key contribution.

The essence of relationship marketing is the developing of long-term relationships with stakeholders. It is particularly applicable to companies which seek a long-term continuous series of transactions with their customers. As MJS relies on repeat purchase from its customer base, this type of marketing orientation is appropriate. Relationship marketing is situated on the opposite end of the marketing strategy continuum to transaction marketing, where parties are concentrating on a one-off negotiation in order to maximise their profitability.

3   **MJS Relationship marketing initiatives**

The MJS customer perceptions survey results show a rapid decline in perceptions in all areas over the last three years. Starting from an acceptable base in 1994 we have fallen quickly in our customers estimation. This situation could be due to either an actual decline in our service levels, or a perceived decline when compared with offerings from our competitors. Whatever the reason, MJS must react to these results in order to increase the current perception levels. A relationship marketing programme will assist us to achieve this goal by concentrating our efforts on our customers and their developing needs.

A relationship marketing programme will allow MJS to bring together the elements of customer service, quality and marketing (Christopher, Payne & Ballantyne 1991).

The dimensions of relationship marketing are as follows.

- Focus on customer retention
- Orientation on customer benefits
- Long time scales
- Higher customer commitment
- High customer contact
- Quality as the concern for all

By implementing a programme of this type MJS will move much closer to their existing customers and develop a much greater understanding of their needs. This will assist the company to make more informed decisions on issues such as product range and quality, customer support and pricing. Working with the customers, MJS can then address these issues in order to increase customer perceptions in all the research areas.

In order to implement a programme of this type Kotler (1993) identified 5 steps of implementation.

- Identify key customers
- Assign a skilled relationship manager to each
- Develop clear job descriptions
- Appoint manager to supervise the relationship managers
- Long-range and annual relationship plans

Implementation raises a number of resources and skills issues. After key customers have been identified, MJS will appoint Customer Relationship Managers (or Key Account Managers) to look after them. These staff will deal with communication and co-ordination issues in order to ensure customer satisfaction. Training will be required for the Customer Relationship Managers, unless we recruit suitably experienced personnel from outside the organisation.

Through the relationship marketing activities, we may identify organisations with whom we could develop strategic links. This would be beneficial with regard to new

Answer bank

product development and sharing of information and resources between the organisations.

The MJS customer perception survey has shown that we have decreasing scores in may vital areas. A Customer Relationship Programme of this type will help us to address these problems and to reverse the trend.

65 WILD OUTDOORS

> **Examiner's comments: summary/extracts.** This question was generally answered poorly with few candidates demonstrating any real understanding of how an organisation determined to go on the offensive might behave. Choices included attacking the market leader, attacking firms of a similar size in trouble or attacking smaller companies. To do this a detailed understanding of competition, the market, key factors for success and core competence is required. Also candidates were asked to refer to the resource, cultural and implementation implications of their recommendations which many failed to do.
>
> The answers proved to be generally disappointing but where they were good, candidates focussed on the need for brand vision, detailed understanding of the market, resource implications and so on related to WOBC.

(a) **Briefing Paper**

To: Marketing Director
From: Marketing Analyst
Subject: Challenger Strategy
Date: December 1997

(i) **Background**

This briefing paper will outline the possible dimensions of a market challenger strategy which we can use against the weaker competitors in our market place. Reference will be made to the resources, cultural and implementation issues associated with such as strategic approach.

We are currently experiencing a **polarisation** of the mountain bike market towards price at one end and product innovation at the other and increasingly more aggressive marketing by existing competitors. In order to react to these structural changes we can consider applying offensive marketing strategies.

Offensive marketing strategies are based upon military theory and tactics. These strategies are based upon the concept of establishing a defendable advantage over the competition (Kotler and Singh 1981, O'Shaunessy 1996). There are two generic approaches.

(1) **Offensive strategies:** usually associated with market challenger and the aim is to grow market share by taking this from competitors.

(2) **Defensive strategies:** usually employed by market leaders and the aim is to defend market share against market challengers.

It is dimensions of a market challenger strategy that will be the focus of this report.

(ii) **Defining the strategic objective and opponent(s)**

Our strategic objective is to increase market share. We can decide to take share from the market leader, firms of our own size who are vulnerable to attack or smaller local and regional firms who are vulnerable to attack.

(iii) **Choosing a challenger strategy**

(1) **Generic strategy**

At the broadest level we should decide what basis of competitive advantage to pursue. Porter (1980, 1985) suggests four possible generic strategies:

	Broad	Cost	Differentiation
Competitive Scope			
	Narrow	Cost Focus	Differentiation Focus
		Cost	**Differentiation**

Basis of Advantage

(2) **Offensive strategies**

Offensive strategies can be split into five main strategies (Kotler 1996).

- Frontal attack
- Flank attack
- Encirclement attack
- Bypass attack
- Guerilla attack

Frontal attack

The most risky option. The attacker meets the competition head on, product for product, cost for cost. History has indicated that in order for this approach to succeed the attacker needs to have three times the resources of the defender.

You can have a variation on the frontal attack which is called modified frontal attack or limited frontal attack, this is where you lure away selected customers by shifting resources to a single marketing element for example advertising or price. This tends to work best where there is no or slow competitor reaction.

Flank attack

Gain advantage in areas where the competition is geographically weak or market segments that have not been fully developed.

- Geographical flanking: focus attention on those geographical areas that are weak
- Segmental flanking: focus on segments where customer needs are not being fulfilled (similar to a focus/niche strategy)

Encirclement attack

The aim here is to dilute the defender's ability to retaliate with strength in any one area. Attacking the defender on as many fronts as possible (for example, price/quality/distribution/service) is very expensive in the first instance because all resources are mobilised in many areas. However this can be extremely successful in the long term (for example, Seiko watches).

Bypass attack

The most indirect approach is to develop new markets through:

- Unrelated products
- New geographical markets for existing products
- Technological leapfrogging

This approach avoids confrontation.

Guerrilla attack

This is best suited to smaller companies with a limited resource base. This approach basically involved small attacks on different areas - hit and run. The aim is to demoralise the defender and to keep him off balance. Examples of guerrilla tactics are damaging PR, sudden and intense advertising, poaching key members of staff.

(3) **Challenger tactics**

Challengers rarely succeed by relying on just one element of strategy (Gilligan 1995). Instead success depends on designing and implementing a strategy made up of several tactical elements. This can include the following.

- Trade price discounting
- Cheaper products to the consumer
- Product innovation
- Product proliferation
- A differentiated brand image
- Improved service
- Distribution innovation
- Intense advertising

(iv) **What strategy to pursue?**

WOBC is **not a niche player** so that leaves us with either pursuing a cost and therefore a **price positioning strategy** or a strategy based on **competitive differentiation** which can come from any element of the marketing mix (for example new product development, brand management, promotional or channel innovation). According to PIMS research, high relative quality and market share bring the best ROI results. When this is linked to our above average sales and profits, it seems strategically logical to adopt a differentiation approach.

Flanking and bypass attack would seem attractive as they are indirect strategies which would help avoid competitive retaliation. Perhaps we could base are 'Wild Outdoor' theme to better satisfy the needs of the more 'extreme' seeking segments of the market. In addition, a bypass strategy based on product/feature innovation would help us to leapfrog to the front of the market. For example the innovators in hybrid cycling technology and sophisticated suspension features have all taken share.

Rather that focus of one element of strategy, we need to pull together several elements for our strategy to succeed in the long term and for us to be able to survive in this increasingly competitive environment. Initial thoughts are these.

- Product innovation to bypass the market leaders
- Improved service to build positive channel relationships
- Clear, credible and competitive brand values
- Cost reduction to remain price competitive

(v) **Resource, cultural and implementation implications**

The implications for WOBC of adopting a more pro-active and offensive marketing strategy are going to be widespread.

To develop and implement a challenger strategy we are looking at changes in the organisation. We are looking at a culture change from that of a sales orientation to a marketing orientation. This means that we must focus on the 4 C's.

Competitors

Who are they, what are their objectives, what strategies are they pursuing, what are their strengths and weaknesses, and how they will react to an offensive move?

Customer needs

In order to sustain competitive advantage we need to understand our customers better, build relationships with them and make sure that we are servicing their needs better than competitors.

Company capabilities

We must assess the fit between what we want/need to do and the capabilities of the company.

Changing environment

Environmental monitoring and analysis systems need to be put in place.

The McKinsey 7S framework can be used to consider the implementation implications of a challenger strategy.

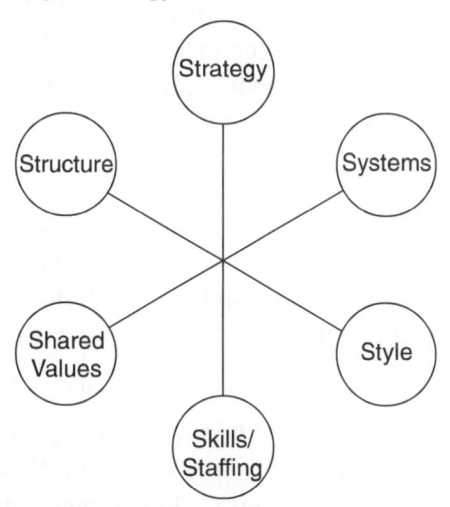

In order to be able to make an informed decision on these elements of strategy, we need to implement a marketing information system immediately. We will also need the right planning system, structure, management style, staff and skills in order to adopt a more competitive focused culture or set of shared values.

Needless to say, an effective challenger strategy will need resourcing and so a cross-functional project team together with an aggressive budget should be provided. The resultant competitive plan should be monitored for results in terms of market share and profit gains.

(b) **Briefing Paper**

To: Marketing Director
From: Marketing Analyst
Subject: Brand Strategy
Date: December 1997

Answer bank

(i) **Introduction**

Let's begin with a definition:

'A brand is a simple thing, it is in effect a trade mark which through careful management, skilful promotion and wide use, comes in the minds of consumers to embrace a particular set of values and attributes both tangible and intangible.'

John Murphy, Group Chairman, Interbrand

Brands in the 1990s are coming under increasing pressure from low economic growth, peer-group competition and thrusting own-label rivals. However as the PIMS database shows, return on investment is far greater for brand leaders:

Rank	ROI
Market leaders	
Dominator	34
Marginal leader	26
Competitors	
No.2	21
No.3	16
Followers	12

Doyle in 'Marketing Management and Strategy' (1994) suggests that brands are at the heart of marketing because marketing is about decommoditising products. If an organisation's products are deemed to be the same as competitors then customers will be indifferent and choose the cheapest and most available. Companies that compete on price rarely make satisfactory profits. Brand management is about creating a preference for the company's products thereby reducing price sensitivity.

(ii) **Key elements of brand strategy**

Arnold (1992) suggests that brand strategy comprises a detailed profile of the target market, our brand positioning approach to include clear, credible and competitive brand values - both functional and image based and brand scope ie product line depth and breadth.

In more detail a brand can be thought of being built up of 4 layers.

A good quality product. Having a quality product is the anchor upon which all other brand associations are built. New products need to offer demonstrably superior performance. Functional advantages are usually short-lived as competitors imitate them as can be seen by the plethora of mountain bike products on the market today.

However, the most common barrier is to build a brand that has values beyond those of functionality.

The basic brand comprises the core elements of the marketing mix eg brand name, design, packaging, price, advertising and distribution. These elements should seek to differentiate and develop a brand's personality. Our company name is distinctive and conveys certain brand values we may be able to exploit.

The augmented brand adds additional services (or added values) to the brand to create a competitive edge. The company seeks ways to meet expectations beyond that required by the buyer. Examples include service, delivery, credit terms and guarantees.

The potential brand. A brand reaches its potential when its added values are so great that customers will not willingly accept substitutes even when the alternatives are substantially cheaper or more widely available. Here the psychological benefits (or image truths) make possible brand dominance.

Doyle suggests that the major characteristics of brands that achieve their potential are as follows.

(1) **A quality product.** If this is allowed to deteriorate then its position will be undermined.

(2) **Being first.** It is easier to stake a position in the consumer's mind when the brand has no competitors to rival its claims.

(3) **Unique positioning concept.** This is a benefit proposition or augmented brand that will distinguish it from the competition.

(4) **Strong communications programme.** The brand should communicate functional and psychological values - also referred to as product truths and image truths.

(5) **Time and consistency.** Brands require investment to build adoption, and then consistent but evolving brand values to remain relevant in a changing environment.

(iii) **How brand strategy can be developed and implemented**

Arnold (1992) in The Handbook of Brand Management uses the following framework to guide the process of brand development and implementation.

(1) **Market analysis:** includes market definition, market segmentation, competitor positions and environmental trends.

(2) **Brand situation analysis:** includes brand personality research to identify the brands current individual attributes. Internal analysis involves asking questions such as; is advertising projecting the right image? Is the packaging too aggressive? Does the product need updating? Fundamental evaluation of the brand's character can be assessed through using focus group research with key buyers at present and non-purchasing members of the target market. Both consumer and trade research would be necessary.

(3) **Targeting future positions.** This involves developing the brand strategy. Any brand strategy should incorporate what has been learnt in steps 1 and 2 into a view of how the market will evolve and what strategic response is most appropriate. Target markets, brand positions and brand scope as discussed should be the outcome of this stage in the process.

(4) **Testing new offers:** tactically, the individual elements of the marketing mix come next. Test marketing the overall offer is recommended at this stage.

(5) **Planning and evaluating performance.** Finally if test marketing proves positive we will need to establish a brand budget, activity planner and measure results against objectives set. Objectives such as awareness, availability and attitudes are required. Information on tracking of performance feeds into step 1 on analysis.

The process of brand planning mirrors the marketing planning process and is usually built into an annual planning cycle which in turns feeds into the medium term 3-5 year planning process.

Answer bank

66 TMM INDUSTRIES

> **Examiner's comments: summary extracts.** Good answers used the formats requested. In part (a) poorer answers merely listed the criteria (as opposed to explaining why they had been chosen). Poorer answers to (b) covered MkIS generally not EMS.

(a) **Briefing Paper: Criteria that should be used to evaluate our response to price-based attack.**

　　To:　　　　　　　The Marketing Director
　　Prepared by:　　 The Marketing Analyst
　　Date:　　　　　　June 1998

Introduction

A variety of external and internal criteria should be used in deciding whether to use an aggressive price-based attack on the south-east Asia market challenger (Kotler & Singh, 1981). The management team at TMM should also give full recognition to the dangers of responding in this way. The focus of this paper is on the option of maintaining and improving market position through an aggressive cut price-based strategy and the criteria to use in deciding whether this is a logical option.

External factors

(i) **The profile of the competitor**

　　(1) How large is the competitor? This can be measured in several ways, market share, financial strength, number of employees, and such like. Does it have the backing of a larger group?

　　(2) What volumes is it currently producing? This information would give some indication as to any economies of scale that the competitor may be achieving.

　　(3) Any indication of the resources available to this competitor would allow us to calculate whether their action is a short-term strategy.

(ii) How will other companies in the industry respond? If a majority of our competitors actively respond then it will make it more difficult for us to restrict reacting. You may be able to anticipate your competitors' actions, if you undertake an analysis of their current brand positioning.

(iii) The nature of the market: What stage is this industry at in its life cycle? If the industry has reached maturity, then with the tightening market, weaker competitors may be squeezed out of the market.

(iv) **The profile of the target market**

　　(1) How important is price to the consumer?

　　(2) What weighting is put on technical excellence and on high levels of after sales service?

　　(3) Are we still seen as offering technical excellence and high level after sales service compared to our competitors?

　　(4) Do we have strong customer loyalty?

　　(5) Can we cut prices enough to attract consumer attention?

　　(6) Are there a number of market segments with different product requirements and price sensitivities?

(v) **Brand positioning.** How is our brand perceived? Is it deemed to be worth a premium price? How are competitor's brands perceived?

(vi) Reaction of members of the distribution channel. Although some distributors have been lost, what would the reaction of our other distributors be if we cheapen the image of the brand?

Internal factors

(i) Are we experiencing excess supply leading to spare capacity?

(ii) Will the price cut take our price below our costs?

(iii) Will the resultant increase in demand bring significant economies of scale?

(iv) Ability to respond: Are the management skills available to handle a price-based response?

(v) Resources: What are the resources at our disposal? Entering a price war is likely to be an expensive and damaging process.

(vi) Funding: In particular what is the financial position of the organisation?

(vii) Culture: How aggressive is the organisation's managerial approach?

Conclusions

The company has lost market share in its two biggest SBUs. To sustain a price advantage we have to deliver superior value to our customers. It is vital that we conduct marketing research to aid in our pricing decision in relation to the questions posed above. Published research data from PIMS (Buzzel, 1987) indicates that the most profitable position to be in is that of market leader with the highest quality levels which justifies higher than average prices. The reality may be that short term profits will need to fall in order to invest in the necessary equipment to reduce our cost of sales, R&D to maintain technological leadership and marketing to establish a defendable and valuable brand.

(b) To: The Marketing Director
Prepared by: The Marketing Analyst
Date: June 1998

Report on the development of an environmental monitoring system.

Introduction

TMM face an increasingly competitive and changing market. In such dynamic circumstances, the need for an effective environmental monitoring system (EMS) is intensified. This report includes recommendations for the structure of such a system, the outputs, organisational and resource implications we can expect together with a discussion of the value of the information generated in relation to the development of the company's future marketing strategy.

Structure of an EMS: Inputs/Processing/Outputs

An EMS has a three-part structure; input data on the various aspects of the external environment, processing of this data into useful management information and output or dissemination of the various types of information produced. Simply, the system:

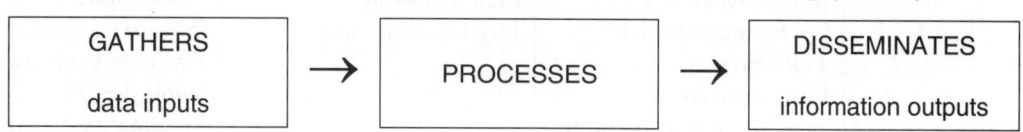

GATHERS data inputs → PROCESSES → DISSEMINATES information outputs

Answer bank

(i) **Data inputs:** data is required on both the micro and macro environment. A number of key factors make up these environments as illustrated below:

(1) **Macro environment.** A popular aide memoir used for grouping the various factors under this main heading is PESTLE standing for - Political, Economic, Sociological, Technological, Legal and Environmental ('Green' issues). Clearly advances in packaging machinery and materials will be affected by technological advancements.

(2) **Micro environment.** This part of the audit embraces customers, competitors, suppliers and distributors. Clearly, we need to know how we are doing against our competitors and what our customers and distributors think about products services and us.

Considering the situation that TMM finds itself in, information on key aspects, trends and implications of factors in the micro environment will be most useful at present. However in setting up the system I would recommend all the factors above are monitored on a regular basis.

A detailed breakdown of the types of data, regularity of collection and the sources of data for all of the above factors are required to ensure the systematic identification and collection of data. Competition is exerting a significant influence on TMM at present so this will be used as the example for this report.

(3) **Competition and competitive advantage**

Data is required on:

- Who are we competing against?
- What are their objectives?
- What strategies are they pursuing, with what success?
- What strengths and weaknesses do they possess?
- How are they likely to behave, especially to offensive moves?

In addition, the difference between 'winners' and 'losers' should be examined to pinpoint the central heating industry's '**key success factors**'.

We should also widen the analysis to the **competitive structure** of the industry.

- Threat of new entrants
- Threat of substitute products
- Power of buyers
- Power of suppliers
- Extent of competitive rivalry (Porter, 1985)

Three sources of this data can be identified:

RECORDED DATA	OBSERVABLE DATA	OPPORTUNISTIC DATA
Market research reports Credit reports Annual reports Government reports Trade press Business press Sales/advertising literature	Sales force feedback Advertising Merchandising Buying competitors'	Exhibitions Conferences Distributors internal newsletters Poaching competitors' employees Private investigators

(ii) Processing data into usable information: once data has been collected on all the aspects above it needs to be converted into information which can be used to guide subsequent marketing action. I would suggest the 6-stage process as advocated by Jain (1985) be employed within the EMS:

(1) Maintain an awareness of broad trends in each of the key environmental factors.

(2) Delineate those trends, which are most significant for further, more detailed investigation.

(3) Undertake an in-depth analysis on the possible impact of these selected trends on WGP's current products or sectors. In particular this analysis should indicate whether the trend is an opportunity or a threat and the potential magnitude of its impact.

(4) Forecast future direction of the isolated trends

(5) Further analyse the possible effects of the forecasted trend on future performance (a) on the assumption of no action (b) on the assumption the trend is responded to.

(6) Assess and predict the implications of the preceding analysis for overall strategic decision making.

(iii) **Information outputs:** three types of information will be available as a result of this EEMS.

(1) **Firstly,** raw data in the form of research reports, competitors' annual reports, sales force market place reports etc. I would recommend that an Information Resource Room be established for executives to access and scan when required.

(2) A number of reports will be produced and circulated to an agreed mailing list:

- Cuttings service - regular circulation of abstracts from key publications (trade journals, research reports etc.)
- Macro-environmental Trends Report - regular report highlighting key occurrences and trends in the PEST factors.
- Micro-environmental Trends Report - regular report highlighting key occurrences and trends in the immediate market place.

(3) More detailed and specific reports on significant trends - opportunities or threats - with the analysis, interpretation and implications of this trend for future marketing strategy included, for example, competitive changes reports and changing buyer behaviour reports.

With each level, confidentiality increases, circulation decreases and regularity of publication decreases. The regularity of production of the above outputs will be dependent on the resources invested in the EEMS.

Organisational implications

For the successful implementation of the EMS a number of requirements exist.

(i) **Top management commitment** - there needs to be support in terms of investment in personnel and equipment. Visible and verbal support is necessary to ensure the co-operation of middle management. The importance of a planning culture needs to be endorsed and promoted by senior management.

Answer bank

(ii) Incorporation within the decision making process - the EMSS has to be seen as a major input into the company's planning and control process and in turn the market analyst has to be aware of and take information from the current marketing plan.

(iii) Co-operation of senior and middle management in systematically determining **their needs** for market information; co-operation by certain managers in the **collection of the data**, that is the sales manager promoting the gathering of data by the sales force.

(iv) Training concerned with how best to use the information.

(v) Awareness and management of the potential political influences on the EEMS. Information should be as valid and reliable as possible; potential bias and subjective interpretation to further individual motives is likely.

(vi) Likely need to incorporate the EEMS into a larger MkIS in the future with not just marketing intelligence but also an internal records system, decision-support system and marketing research system.

Resource implications

Resources will be required in terms of personnel, time and a budget. The exact amounts can only be determined after an information needs audit and consideration of TMM's objectives and strategy. It is likely that a significant percentage of the marketing budget will be required for the ongoing research plus initial personnel and equipment set up costs.

How output may be used in developing marketing strategy

A marketing strategy outlines the future direction of an organisation in relation to which markets it plans to serve with what products and services. Formulating marketing strategy involves matching the capabilities of the organisation with the demands of the marketplace. To be able to do this, the starting point is information, which highlights environmental opportunities and threats. The EMS provides this type of information. The market analyst should also analyse this information to forecast future trends and changes and interpret the significance of these environment trends and changes for future marketing strategy.

Benefits of an EMS

- Increased management sensitivity to environmental changes
- Better informed organisational planning and control process
- Identification and exploitation of opportunities before competition
- Better image for the firm by illustrating that it is sensitive to its environment
- Skill development opportunities for executives and strategists
- Ultimately, improved market place results and financial performance
- Improved strategic decision making

67 THE WET SHAVE MARKET

(a) From: Marketing Manager
To: Marketing Director
Date: June 1999
Briefing Paper: Gillette's Spend on NPD and Promotion

Introduction

In looking at the new product development literature, there is a focus on the new product development (NPD) process and the factors which differentiate between new

Answer bank

product successes and failures (for example Cooper and Kleinschmidt, 1986; Johne and Snelson, 1990).

New Product Development Process

1. Idea Generation
2. Screening
3. Concept Development & Testing
4. Marketing Strategy
5. Business Analysis
6. Product Development
7. Market Testing
8. Commercialisation

Storey and Easingwood (1996) suggest that there has been little consideration of the product beyond the core benefits offered. An area that has been neglected is the potential contribution that the marketing of the product and the support given to the product can make to new product performance. Yet most new products are not radically different from existing products (Booz, Allen & Hamilton, 1982):

Types of New Products

Newness to the Company (High → Low) vs. Newness to the Market (Low → High):

- New product line: 20%
- New to the world products: 10%
- Revisions/improvements to existing products: 26%
- Additions to existing product line: 26%
- Cost reductions: 11%
- Repositionings: 7%

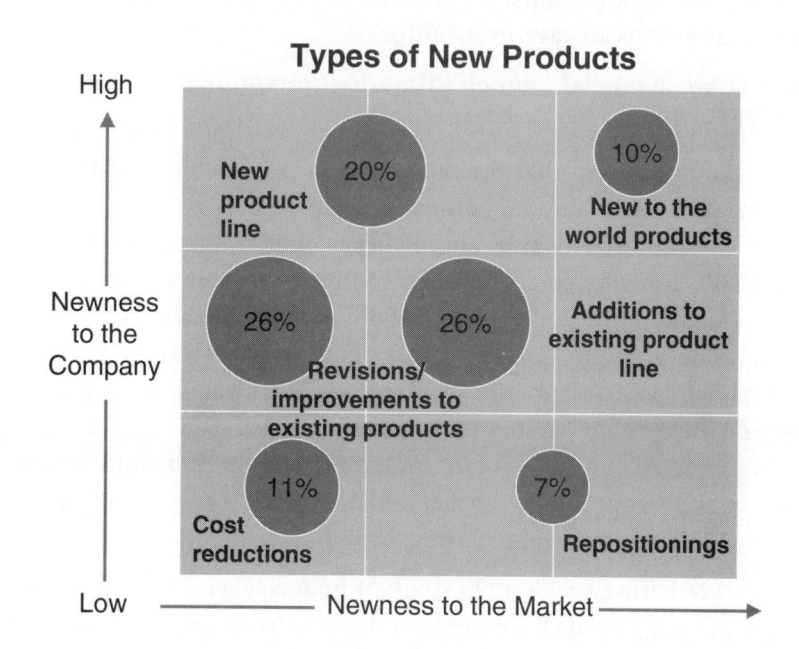

Source: New Product Management for the 1980's (New York: Booz, Allen & Hamilton, 1982)

and thus the marketing support in the form of promotion, may be one area where competitive advantage can be gained.

This briefing paper therefore focuses on the strategic role which NPD can play and the reasons why our major competitor, Gillette, continue to spend large amounts of money on the NPD process (£460m on the Mach 3) and promotional support (£215m on product launch).

The Strategic Role of New Products

Based on the work by Wong (1993) the following table indicates the strategic roles which NPD can play.

Strategic Role (Rationale) of NPD	New Product Type
Maintain technological leadership	New to the world
	New product line
Enter future/new markets	New to the world
Pre-empt competition or	New to the world
Segment of the market	New Product Line
	Repositioning
Maintain market share	New Product line
	Repositioning
	Additions to existing lines
Defend market share position/	Repositioning
Prevent decline	Cost reductions
	Revisions/improvements to existing lines
Exploit technology in a new way	New to the world
	New product line
Capitalise on distribution strength	Additions to existing line

Analysing Gillette's approach to NPD, we can surmise that the Mach 3 is likely to maintain technological leadership for Gillette which pre-empts us and other competitors and thereby maintains their market share. In light of their aggressive approach to the market, it is vital that we respond by maintaining product parity with Gillette and, through our own innovation process, continue to seek new innovations which may give us an edge in the future.

Why £215m on Global Launch (Majority Promotional Spend)

Referring back to the research conducted by Storey and Easingwood (1996), the potential contribution that the marketing of the product and the support given to the product can make to new product performance is great. In general, marketing efficiency and effectiveness have been cited as contributing to success. More specifically, a misdirected sales/distribution effort can affect success adversely and an effective communication strategy ideally should educate users about the value of the product (for example Cooper, 1980). The launch strategy is the link between the development process and the marketplace. A strong launch effort, with appropriate targeting and pricing strategies, is linked to success (Storey & Easingwood, 1996). In addition, advertising and promotion have been found to work best when geared to the creation of a strong brand image, which Gillette has certainly cultivated (Berry and Hensal, 1973; Easingwood & Storey, 1991).

In Storey & Easingwood's 1996 study of financial service product launches they found that promotion played an important role in NPD success and that it should:

Answer bank

- Be effective in raising awareness
- Be effective in explaining/convincing
- Result in more effective advertising/promotion
- Be responsible for creating the 'brand' image
- Be consistent with marketing strategy

Gillette spends £215m on launch promotion because it is important to any product's success to raise awareness of that product with the target customers. Both these goals can be aided by the creation of a strong brand image for the product and by attractively positioning the product in the market. Consistency with the rest of the marketing strategy helps ensure that a uniform image is presented to the consumer. A strong corporate advertising campaign, as run by Gillette prior to the Mach 3 launch, in general will also help in the selling of specific products.

Conclusions

It is clear that our main competitor, Gillette, will gain significant advantage through the launch of their innovative new product, the Mach 3. The second part of this briefing paper addresses the question of the options we have for response to this significant global product launch.

(b) **Strategic Options available to Wilkinson Sword in the Wet Shave Market**

The first key strategic option for us is to decide whether we are a market follower or market challenger (Kotler and Singh, 1981) in this sector. This part of the paper will therefore be divided into the options under each positioning decision.

(i) **Market Follower Strategic Options**

Market followers accept the status quo and avoid risks of confrontation following a 'me-too' strategy - product imitation, not product innovation. Our options include:

- Cloner: copies, in extreme a counterfeiter.
- Imitator: copies some things but maintains some differentiation.
- Adapter: takes leader's products and improves them growing into future challenger.

We should be aware that PIMS research shows low ROIs for followers (Hooley, Saunders & Piercy, 1998).

(ii) **Market Challenger Strategic Options**

Kotler (1997) provides a number of possible market challenger, or attack, strategies for challengers trying to take share from market leaders such as Gillette, as illustrated below.

(1) **Frontal Attack**

This is the direct, head-on attack meeting competitors with the same product line, price, promotion, and so on. In principle, to succeed the attacker needs three times the resources as the defender and, because you are attacking your enemy's strengths rather than weaknesses, it is generally considered the riskiest and least advised of strategies. A modified frontal attack tempts away select customers by shifting resources to a single marketing element (for example, via price or advertising) but this depends on no or slow competitor reaction. Direct attacks are risky but there are numerous indirect alternatives.

(2) **Flanking Attack**

The aim is to engage competitors in those product markets where they are weak or have no presence at all. Its overriding goal is to build a position to launch an attack on the major battlefield later, without waking 'sleeping giants'. Porter refers to this as a niche or focus strategy. Segmental flanking is based on satisfying market needs not being met by competitors' different products or approaches to the market. Geographic flanking serves areas in a country or the world with similar products and approaches, but where opponents are weak or non-existent.

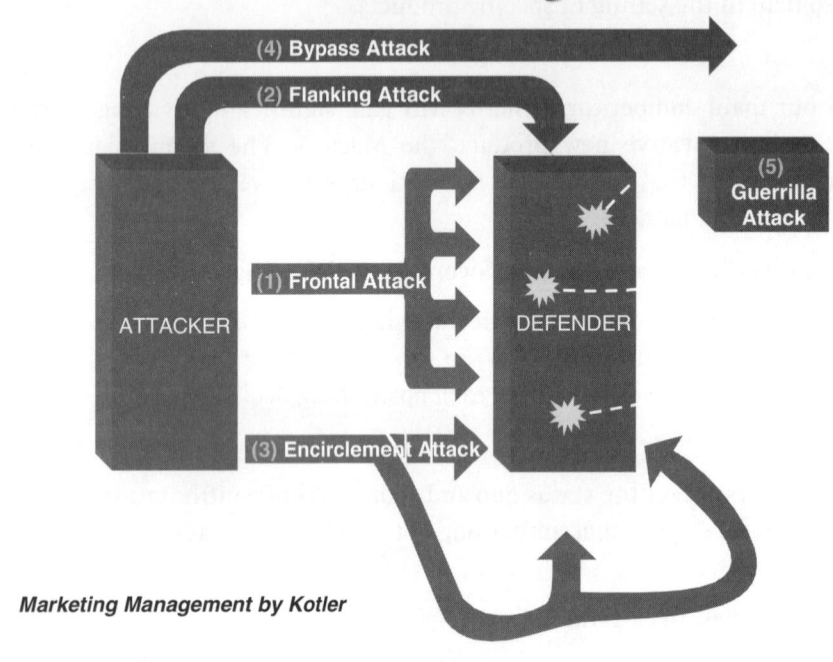

Attack Strategies

Marketing Management by Kotler

(3) **Encirclement Attack**

Encirclement involves a multi-pronged attack aimed at diluting the defender's ability to retaliate in strength. The attacker stands ready to block the competitor no matter which way he turns in the product market. In business there are two conceptually distinct forms of encirclement: product and market. An attacker can encircle by product proliferation, or by expanding the products into all segments and distribution channels. Encirclement is feasible when the attacker has superior resources, is willing to commit these resources for a long time to achieve market dominance, has access to distribution channels and product development capacity.

(4) **Bypass Attack**

This is the most indirect form of competitive strategy as it avoids confrontation by moving into new and uncontested fields. Three types of bypass are possible: develop new products, diversify into unrelated products or diversify into new geographical markets. Developing new products is referred to as 'leap frogging' where a business takes advantage of a technological development emphasising the next generation of products and becoming the pioneer of the new demand/technology life cycle.

Answer bank

(5) **Guerilla Warfare**

Guerilla attack is less ambitious in scope and involves making small attacks in different locations whilst remaining mobile. They take several forms: law suits, poaching personnel, interfering with supply networks and so on. The overriding aim is to destabilize by pricks rather than blows. The risks are strong competitive retaliation if the threshold of tolerance is passed.

(6) **Strategic Alliances**

Both a defender and attacker can benefit from alliances, which is where independent partners pool resources in order to achieve a limited objective and promote reliable superiority where none existed.

Suggested Approach for Wilkinson Sword

We need to consider all the options listed and conduct cost/benefit analysis of each. Based on suitability, feasibility and acceptability criteria we will be able to make an informed strategic decision of our best response.

Due to our smaller size and resources, at this stage my gut reaction would be to favour a market follower approach in the shaving system sector:

- Adapter: takes leader's products and improves them growing into future challenger

and

- Frontal attack against Bic in the disposable sector as they are much weaker

I look forward to your comments in due course.

68 THE LENS SHOP

> **Examiner's comment: summary/extracts.** 'Good answers referred to Porter or Davidson and used one of these models as a framework and applied it to TLS directly. They then went on to discuss the factors that might influence the sustainability of TLS's position. Poorer papers merely listed factors, that may be giving TLS competitive advantage, without any discussion of theory.'

(a) Subject: Sources of competitive advantage
    To: The Managing Director
    Prepared by: The Marketing Manager
    Date: December 1998

Introduction

(i) **Competitive advantage** is anything which gives an organisation an edge over its competitors - the reason why a customer would select TLS's products or services over other competitive offerings. Once an advantage has been gained, competitors will try to copy or supersede it, so continuous improvements in offerings are needed unless the advantage can be protected.

(ii) **Competitive strategy** is the search for a favourable competitive position in an industry. The aim is to establish a profitable and sustainable position. Porter suggests three generic routes to achieving competitive advantage.

(1) Overall cost leadership
(2) Overall differentiation
(3) Focus (segmentation based on costs or differentiation)

Answer bank

Sources of competitive advantage for TLS

(iii) **Cost leadership**

This strategy seeks to achieve the position of **lowest cost producer** in the industry. This enables the company to compete on price and earn the highest unit profits. Porter (1985) has identified several major factors that affect costs which he terms 'cost drivers'. Not all of these apply.

(1) **Economies of scale** are not possible. TLS is a **specialist** retail store, as opposed to Dixons with many more locations.

(2) **Experience and learning effects** can bring efficiencies through repetition of tasks. Experience can be gained through hiring experienced staff and through training. The concept was derived from the manufacturing sector so its application to retail services may be questionable.

(3) **Capacity utilisation** is important to profits, especially for smaller firms. Our smaller, secondary sites with small stock holdings will be a source of cost advantages.

(4) **Linkages** between quality control and stock return, for example, can drive costs up or down. External linkages with suppliers can also reduce costs. Our access to discounted products of 'old' product lines will provide a cost advantage.

(5) **Interrelationships** with other SBUs in a corporate portfolio can help to share costs but this is not possible for our smaller, single business unit organisation.

(6) **Integration** such as contracting out delivery and/or service can affect costs. As we are not vertically or horizontally integrated this is not an option for competitive advantage.

(7) **Timing.** Being first to the market can provide access to low cost products, ensure prime locations and gain us technological leadership. As we operate in an established market with a number of general and specialist camera retailers, this is not a route to competitive advantage for us.

(8) **Policy choices** such as product line, service, warranties and so on all affect costs. They also affect the perceived uniqueness of the offer to customers and hence if the competitive strategy is not clear this can create a dilemma. If cost advantage is the strategy then the general rule is to reduce costs on factors which will not significantly affect valued uniqueness.

(9) **Location and institutional factors** can also reduce costs, such as sites near raw material and government regulations. This is not viable for TLS.

From this analysis, discounted 'old' products, small stores in secondary locations and low stock holding all create a cost advantage for TLS. This enables the company to offer lower prices with a price guarantee of being £10 below other local retailers for a similar brand of camera.

(ii) **Differentiation**

This is a competitive strategy based on raising the quality of the product and thus its costs and sale price. Loyalty is built up and, because customers are not so price sensitive, profits can be increased through higher prices. Organisations following this strategy must continually innovate in order to stay ahead of competitors in quality, thus necessitating larger R&D and promotional budgets.

Competitive advantage can be achieved through what Porter calls 'uniqueness drivers'.

(1) **Product differentiation** seeks to increase the value of the good or service on offer to the customer. Products are made up of four components. The **generic product** which is photography, the **expected product** which is a retail site with a range of products and prices with reasonable customer service, the **augmented product** which constitutes all the extra features and services that go beyond what the normal camera consumer expects and the **potential product** which is anything that could be offered. TLS offer an augmented product in the form of the buy-back service for upgrades, selection of recent reviews from Camera magazines and sales staff are also knowledgeable and helpful.

(2) **Brand differentiation** is related to the product offer and moves companies from thinking about **tangible product** benefits to **emotional image** benefits. TLS may be able to establish this in the future, through owning the value and service position in the camera market.

(3) **Distribution differentiation** comes from using different outlets, networks or coverage of the market. The less formal, friendly atmosphere of the shops may be a potential source of differentiation from the large, formal multiples.

(4) **Promotional differentiation** involves using different types of promotions at different intensity or content. The TLS colour catalogue is a 'fun' brochure distributed in an innovative way, especially through direct mail to existing customers. This should be a loyalty builder.

(5) **Pricing differentiation** can be successful if TLS enjoys a cost advantage. This is TLS's major point of differentiation with its £10 lower price guarantee, discounted price 'old' stock products, cheap three year extended warranty and buy-back service.

(iii) **Sustainability of current situation**

(1) TLS operate on a **differentiation strategy based on price differentiation** with elements of **product differentiation** based on information and customer service. This is financed through their low cost sources of 'old' product lines from distributors and their location and store size policy. (This is similar to Richer Sounds approach in the hi-fi sector.)

(2) The **risks** of this strategy are the **threat of competition** from lower cost specialist retailers and the vulnerability of a price-based attack by larger competitors such as John Lewis and Dixons, should they go for an aggressive strategy in this product category. Perhaps the greatest risk which needs to be protected is the relationship they have with distributors to clear their shelves of 'old' product lines. If this supply ceased, TLS would lose a significant advantage.

The most useful ways of creating a defensible position lie in exploiting the following.

(1) Unique and valued products
(2) Clear, tight definition of target markets
(3) Enhanced customer linkages
(4) Established brand and company credibility

In the future, creating closer bonds with customers through interactive communications and enhanced service through internal marketing initiatives

Answer bank

(see question 1(b)) should strength TLS's position. The buy-back service should help build in switching costs and should be retained together with building the awareness of the brand from specialist camera consumers to the general public. Public relations should help, following the lead of **Richer Sounds** with innovative employee relations policies and incentives together with shouting about their buy-back service.

(b)

> **Examiner's comment: summary/extracts.** 'This was a relatively straightforward question. Good answers were in report format and discussed fully the benefits of internal marketing, implementation and the potential problems. Poorer answers failed to tackle the issue of implementation effectively. There was very little mention of internal target markets and the internal marketing mix.'

To: The Managing Director
Prepared by: The Marketing Manager
Date: December 1998

Report on the development of an **Internal Marketing Programme**

Please find outlined below an overview of an internal marketing programme as requested.

(i) **What is internal marketing?**

'Treating with equal importance the needs of the internal market - the employees - and the external market through proactive programmes and planning to bring about desired organisational objectives by delivering both employee and customer satisfaction'.

Originally, the scope of **internal marketing** was considered to be the motivation, training and development of employees involved at the customer interface, with the aim of delivering a better service to the end customer. This is obviously important in a service industry like camera retailing. However, internal marketing also includes non-contact employees as well. In fact, internal marketing covers any planned effort to overcome any resistance to change in an organisation and to ensure through proper communication, motivation and training that employees effectively implement corporate and functional strategies/plans.

This concept is obviously important in the retail sector where customers' expectations of the service encounter are rising. The head office staff who support the shops are also critical in terms of delivering customer satisfaction.

(ii) **Development and implementation**

People inside the organisation, to whom the plan must be marketed, are considered internal customers. The first stage is to group these internal customers into three segments.

(1) **Supporters:** those likely to gain from improving service levels.

(2) **Neutrals:** those whose gains and losses are in balance.

(3) **Opposers:** those who are likely to lose from the change or are long term opponents.

An internal marketing mix has to be developed for each of these target groups.

(1) **Product.** This is the plan/strategy itself together with the attitudes, values and actions that are needed to successfully carry it out.

(2) **Price.** The price is what internal customers have to pay as a result of accepting the plan/strategy. This could be changes in work patterns and greater effort to achieve high levels of customer satisfaction.

(3) **Promotion.** This is a critical area in the mix, and involves any communication medium that can be used to effect the attitudes of key groups. The promotional mix includes: presentations, training workshops, discussion groups, written reports etc. This communication has to be a two way process. At times, it may be necessary to adapt the plan in order to gain support.

(4) **Distribution.** This categorises the places where the product and communications are delivered to internal customers, such as in-store, meetings, seminars, informal conversations, away days and so on.

Although an internal marketing programme gives a framework within which to work, successful implementation is reliant on three key skills.

(1) **Persuasion**

- Present a shared vision for the group through a customer service charter.
- Communicate and train.
- Eliminate misconceptions through two-way dialogue.
- Sell the benefits through success stories in the company newsletter, employee of the month awards, incentives for the best store etc.
- Gain acceptance by association, perhaps with Richer Sounds retail success and employee benefits.
- Support words with action, for example the MD rewarding best practice and reviewing the customer feedback comments.

(2) **Negotiation**

- Make the opening proposition high – leave room for negotiation.
- Trade concessions.

(3) **Politics**

- Build coalitions.
- Display support.
- Invite the opposition to contribute.
- Warn opposition.
- Control the agenda.
- Take incremental steps.

Benefits of internal marketing

For TLS, improved **employee satisfaction** and **customer responsiveness** will lead to improved **customer satisfaction**. The higher the relative service quality of any business the higher the return on investment (PIMS research). A clear customer service charter should lead to greater clarity in the purpose and objectives for each store. Customer complaints should reduce thereby saving time dealing with them. Employee turnover should reduce as well. As indicated in the first part of this report, excellence in customer service combined with a competitive pricing strategy should help achieve a sustainable competitive advantage for the business in the highly competitive market in which we operate.

Answer bank

Potential problems to overcome

To achieve the stated benefits, a number of implementation barriers need to be considered. Time is important and potential problems can arise by not taking enough time to allow people to adjust to the changes implied by the plan. Persistence is required in the face of opposition; modifications to the strategy may be necessary on the way. Key detractors and recalcitrant players may exist and if negotiation and persuasion are not successful these people can be removed or if this is not possible, you have to wait till that person leaves or changes job. A final potential problem is lack of resources, both human and financial. Internal marketing programmes require a budget for training, communications and staff time. If this is not available the likely chances of success are greatly reduced.

69 EASYJET

> **Examiner's comments: summary/extracts.** Goods answers used a theoretical framework upon which they could build an answer. Weaker candidates failed to use the value chain in their analysis of the company. Models are a key area of the syllabus and students need to understand a wide range of models and be able to apply and criticise them.
>
> Good answers discussed branding strategies in part b and identified the factors that need to be considered when evaluating these choices. These answers were also applied specifically to EasyJet's situation. Weaker papers failed to demonstrate an understanding of branding strategy options…(some) failed to identify that the question was about branding.

(a)

Report

Subject: EasyJet, core capabilities for use in family of companies
From: Tess Jessop, consultant.
Date: December 1999

Introduction

Identification of an organisation's current and potential capabilities requires assessment of the resources it possesses. In this particular case, a distinction is required between assets and competencies. Competencies are the abilities and skills available to the company to marshal the effective exploitation of the company's assets. The company's assets are:

- **Financial.** Working capital
- **Physical.** Ownership and control of the facilities
- **Operational.** Production and plant machinery
- **People.** Quality and quantity of human resources
- **Legal.** Ownership of copyrights and patents
- **Systems.** Management information systems and databases.
- **Marketing.** Marketing strategy

In contrast, the companies core **competencies** are:

- **Marketing.** Such as brand extension, business analysis and new product development
- **Selling.** Supply chain management, pricing and promotion
- **Operations.** Such as speed of response, total quality management, payment systems, cost management and health and safety

Answer bank

Value chain analysis

The value chain developed by Porter can be used to categorise the organisation of EasyJet into a series of processes. This will help identify EasyJet's key capabilities that generate value for their customers and stakeholders.

The Value Chain

Firm Infrastructure

- Headquarters based in Luton
- Easy access to major transport routes
- Low airport costs
- High emphasis on Internet bookings
- Low administrative paperwork, for example, free allocation of seating
- Sole ownership of EasyJet by Haji-Ioannou

Human Resource Management

- 'Hands on' approach from entrepreneurial owner
- Active search for opportunities to stretch the brand
- Pro-active marketing team breaking traditional airline establishment practices

Technology development

- Heavy investment in technology has led to simplification of processes, for example, Internet bookings
- Reduction of staff costs
- Improved profit margins

Procurement

- Customer friendly, simplified booking system
- Low airport costs
- Informal approach adopted by airline staff

The **support activities** will now be analysed in relation to EasyJet's **primary activities** in order to identify the activities that will be used to benefit future growth.

Inbound logisitics

Customer friendly, simplified airline service (achieved by investment in technology) has led to less bureaucracy and has reduced labour and airline costs leading to easy payment, easy booking and easy seat allocation.

Operation and outbound logistics

- The use of secondary airports and fast turn around times together with simplified and efficient processes has resulted in lower fares.
- Space and increased seat allocation has been created by not offering business class and reducing catering facilities. This has also led to lower fares.
- The airline has a less formal appearance and approach to customers than some competitors.

Sales and marketing strategy

- The airline has a clearly defined target market and segmentation. It combines this with an aggressive marketing strategy.
- Is has a 'Branson style' PR strategy and attracts high media attention at very little cost.
- It uses joint promotional ventures in national newspapers. It has also been the subject of television documentaries.
- EasyJet adopts a friendly, informal approach.

Service

- The company adopts a 'budget approach', offering only essentials, such as safety, single destination flights and fast turnarounds.
- It is also growing, providing increasing airport locations but maintaining reliability, flight frequency and low cost.

Conclusion

In conclusion, by using the value chain as a tool for analysis, it can be seen that EasyJet may be good at some of its primary activities (core capabilities). However, not all of these are transferable into other brands. This is because there is a unique interrelationship between EasyJet's assets and competencies. Those that can be transferred are:

- Low overheads
- Economies of scale
- An aggressive marketing approach
- Legal patents and copyrights
- A perceived high value of the brand.

(b) To: Haji-Ioannou

From: Keith Reed

Subject: Branding Strategy

Introduction: the importance of branding

It is useful to consider the importance of branding before the individual branding options as this will impact on the choice of branding strategy.

Brands are designed to enable customers to identify products or services which promise specific benefits. In the case of EasyJet, these are no nonsense, easy to book, cheap flights.

EasyJet have been able to differentiate their service from that of competitors based on these benefits.

EasyJet has a distinctive orange logo and has the booking telephone number painted clearly on the side of its aircraft. These have become good promotional tools which have motivated customers to choose EasyJet's service.

It is now necessary to evaluate the branding options open to EasyJet in terms of expansion into other business areas, primarily 'Easycafes'.

Options available

Family branding

This can be divided into two components. Firstly, a blanket family brand name such as Heinz. This has the advantage of enabling a global organisation to introduce new products quickly and successfully as well as consolidating expensive promotional activity behind one message.

Secondly, separate family names, such as Volkswagen use. They now own Skoda and Seat and are able to adopt a family approach, particularly in style and parts. This is more costly in terms of promoting each brand. However, savings are made by the economies of scale in production by using up to 80% of existing Volkswagen parts in some models of Skoda and Seat.

Corporate umbrella branding

This is where the company name covers a wide variety of products which the name suggests. A good example is Virgin. They operate an airline, Virgin Airways, but also have Virgin cola, Virgin direct, Virgin mobile phones, Virgin trains and Virgin clothes under their corporate umbrella.

The important issue when using corporate umbrella branding is that all of the businesses must be seen to be successful so that they can add value to each other. Until recently it has been a successful strategy for Virgin, but the closure of the Virgin clothing operation in the UK and the failure to deliver good service on Virgin trains may have damaged consumer perception of the brand.

Multi-brand approach

This approach has been taken successfully by competitors Unilever and Proctor and Gamble for a number of years. They each have a range of products under different brand names within the same product line. Examples are: Bold, Persil and Dreft (washing powder). There are many other examples. Each brand satisfies the needs of particular segments within that line. Also, if any brand fails, it doesn't adversely affect the parent company or other brands in that line.

Individual brands need separate marketing mixes which is costly. However, an additional benefit to those mentioned above is that a multi-brand approach stifles competition because other companies may have to launch several brands to successfully compete in that line.

Company and individual branding

This is when a company produces a range of similar products, targeted at a particular segment in the market. An example of this is Kellogg's, who target cereal eaters in the food market. Kellogg's have a range of products to cater for differing tastes within that segment. They range from Special K, for the health conscious, to Crunchy Nut Cornflakes.

The existence of the related products in the same market segment does not benefit the other products in the range. However, in the case of Kellogg's, the image of quality is transferable. It is costly to operate such a branding system, but the benefit lies in the fact that consumers are targeted precisely.

Answer bank

Key issues

In making a choice of branding strategy for the future, several key questions need to be answered. These questions are listed below.

- Can the existing brand values be extended to other products and services easily?
- Will the brand extension damage the core business or strengthen it?
- Are there sufficient resources available to carry out a systematic and planned expansion?
- How will the branding strategy be managed?
- Can similar marketing communications be used for all new products and services?
- Would EasyJet's current client base have similar needs for Easycafe services?
- What are the needs, wants and values of 'Joe Public' for Easycafe services?
- It will also be necessary to undertake an audit of any competitor's branding strategy.

Conclusions

Once the questions above have been successfully discussed a value judgement can be made. This will be aided by market research information on current and potential customer groups on their perception of the EasyJet brand and its extensions. The results of the competitor branding audit can also be used to make this judgement.

My preference would be an umbrella branding strategy such as Virgin uses. Easycafe could build on EasyJet's existing reputation and image which could be transferred to other services and products. The distinctive orange logo could be utilised. There would be no need to redesign separate names for each product and service, similar communications messages could be used and the website and other printed material would need little adaptation.

Another advantage is seeing Virgin's recent experience. EasyJet could learn from Virgin's setbacks in brand stretching by trying to make more judicious choices in the future, based on market analysis.

Test your knowledge

Test your knowledge

1. The primary objective of the marketing concept is which one of the following?

    A   Product quality
    B   A fair price
    C   Customer satisfaction
    D   Maximising profits

2. What are the four major factors which marketers should monitor in the macro-environment?

3. What are the six competitive marketing strategies which can be used to attack market leaders?

4. Which one of the following statements is true? **Inelastic demand** means that

    A   Customers will not make a modified rebuy purchase.
    B   Demand depends on how many items are purchased.
    C   When supply is reduced the price will increase.
    D   A price increase or decrease will not significantly change demand for the item.

5. Distinguish between marketing efficiency and marketing effectiveness.

6. What personal and psychological factors affect consumer buying behaviour?

7. Which one of the following statements is true? **Test marketing** is

    A   Conducted after the product development stage.
    B   Conducted after the commercialisation stage.
    C   Used predominantly by small companies.
    D   An extension of the screening process.

8. What are the five stages of Wilson, Gilligan and Pearson's cycle of control?

9. Distinguish between price skimming and penetration pricing.

10. What are the additional 3 'Ps' of the service marketing mix?

11. List five responsibilities of a sales manager

12. Which one of the following statements is true? Relative to marketers of consumer products, you would expect **industrial marketers** to

    A   Rely more on publicity.
    B   Rely more on personal selling.
    C   Rely more on advertising.
    D   Rely more on sales promotion.

13. Define strategic marketing as fully as possible.

14. Which one of the following statements is true? According to *product life cycle theory*, profits:

    A   And sales peak during the growth stage.
    B   And sales peak during the maturity stage.
    C   Reach a peak during the growth stage, but sales peak during the maturity stage.
    D   Never actually peak.

15. Distinguish between market research and marketing research.

16. Distinguish between aims and objectives.

17. The statement 'We will advertise only in controlled circulation media' is which one of the following?

    A   A promotional policy
    B   A sales tactic
    C   A marketing objective
    D   A promotional objective

Test your knowledge

18 Describe the contents of the four reports which can be produced from the PIMS database.

19 What is the formula for the ROCE ratio?

20 List at least five benefits of the process of marketing planning.

21 What is the third stage in the consumer buying decision process?

22 What are the major bases for segmenting industrial markets?

23 List the **four** major characteristics of services that greatly affect the design of marketing programmes.

24 Which stage of the new product development process is missing?

- Idea generation
- Screening
- Concept development testing
- Marketing strategy
- Product development
- Market testing
- Commercialisation

25 Fill in the missing phrases. The General Electric multifactor portfolio model is a two dimensional **matrix** with _____ on the vertical axis and _____ on the horizontal axis.

A   Market growth rate, relative market share
B   Market attractiveness, competitive position
C   Competitive position, market attractiveness
D   Industry attractiveness, business strength.

26 Which type of models are most widely used when assessing risk and uncertainty?

27 Define **budget**.

28 List Ansoff's four suggested marketing strategies for growing sales.

29 List four financial and four non-financial criteria which can be used in making the **strategy selection** decision.

30 Distinguish between intensive, selective and exclusive distribution channel **strategies**.

Test your knowledge: answers

1. The primary objective of the marketing concept is customer satisfaction (c).

2. 'PEST': Political/legal, Economic, Social/cultural, Technological factors.

3. Frontal Attack, Flank Attack, Encircle Attack, Bypass Attack and Guerrilla Warfare.

4. Inelastic demand means that a price increase or decrease will not significantly change demand for the item (d).

5. Marketing efficiency relates to 'doing things right' whereas marketing effectiveness means 'doing the right things'.

6.
   Personal factors:
   Age and life cycle stage
   Occupation
   Economic circumstances
   Lifestyle and personality

   Psychological factors:
   Motivation
   Learning
   Perception
   Beliefs and attitudes

7. Test marketing is conducted after the product development stage (a).

8. Stage One
   Where are we now? (Beginning)

   Stage Two
   Where do we want to be? (Ends)

   Stage Three
   How might we get there? (Means)

   Stage Four
   Which way is best? (Evaluation)

   Stage Five
   How can we ensure arrival? (Implementation & Control)

9. Price skimming is where price is set high in order to generate large profits. Penetration pricing is where prices are set low in order to generate large sales.

10. The three additional 'Ps' are: People, Process and Physical evidence.

11. Sales managers have a number of responsibilities which include: sales planning; organising the sales force; recruiting sales people; training sales people; monitoring sales force performance; motivating sales people and selling (especially to key accounts).

12. Relative to marketers of consumer products, you would expect industrial marketers to rely more on personal selling (b).

13. Your definition should include as many of the following key elements as possible,

    'Strategic marketing is a process of: strategically analysing environmental, competitive, and business factors affecting business units and forecasting future trends in business areas of interest to the enterprise; participating in setting objectives and formulating corporate and business unit strategy; selecting target market strategies for the product markets in each business unit, establishing marketing objectives, and developing, implementing, and managing program positioning strategies for meeting target market needs.'

14. According to product life cycle theory, profits reach a peak during the growth stage, but sales peak during the maturity stage (c).

15. Market research provides information on the marketplace that is market size and growth, competition, customer segments and such like. Marketing research provides information on all aspects of marketing i.e. the marketing environment, The market, product, price, promotion and distribution research. Market research is one aspect of marketing research.

Test your knowledge: answers

16 Aims are general statements of intention which focus attention and lead to the need for certain, definitive action, for example 'Our aims is to be the best employer in town', 'Our aim is to produce the highest quality products'. These are not objectives, because they are not performance specific or time related.

Objectives are clear statements of what the business or function intends to achieve. Objectives should be hierarchical, measurable, realistic and consistent. A marketing objective could be, to achieve total sales revenue of £18 million in 1993 (a 9% increase from 1992)'with the related promotional objective being, to increase consumer awareness of the brand from 15% to 30% in 1993'.

17 'We will advertise only in controlled circulation media' is a promotional policy (a).

18 **Par report:** this specifies what ROI is normal for a particular type of business.

Strategy analysis report: this indicates the likely outcome of several broad strategic moves, based on evidence of similar moves by similar businesses.

Optimum strategy report: shows the combination of moves most likely to give the client optimum results for their business

Report on 'look alikes' *(ROLA):* this indicates successful tactics used by strategically similar businesses.

19 $$\text{ROCE} = \frac{\text{Profit on ordinary activities before interest and tax (PBIT)}}{\text{Capital employed}}$$

20 The process of marketing planning has a number of benefits which include the following.

   (a) It motivates staff and improves commitment
   (b) It secures participation and involvement
   (c) It leads to better decision-making
   (d) It requires management staff to state assumptions
   (e) It prevents 'short-termism'
   (f) It ensures a systematic approach to the future has been taken
   (g) It creates a climate in which change can be made
   (h) Standards of performance are established
   (i) Control systems can be designed and performance assessed more objectively

21 The third stage in the consumer buying decision process is the evaluation of alternatives.

22 Major segmentation bases for industrial markets are: demographic, operating variables, purchasing approaches, situational factors and personal characteristics.

23 The four major characteristics of services that greatly affect the design of marketing programmes are; intangibility, inseparability, variability and perishability.

24 Stage 5, Business Analysis, is missing.

25 The General Electric multifactor portfolio model is a two dimensional matrix with industry attractiveness on the vertical axis and business strength on the horizontal axis (d).

26 Decision trees are the models most widely used when assessing risk and uncertainty.

27 Your definition should be similar to the following:

'A budget is a quantitative plan of action that aids in the co-ordination and control of the acquisition, allocation and utilisation of resources over a given period of time.'

28 Ansoff's four growth strategies are: market penetration, market development, new product development and diversification.

29 Financial and non-financial choice criteria include the following.

Financial	**Non-financial**
Liquidity	Sales volume
Value-added	Market share
Earnings per share	Growth rate
Shareholders value	Competitive position
Share price	Consumer franchise
Profit	Risk exposure
Cost leadership	Customer satisfaction
Cash generation	Reliance on new products
Profitability	Sustainable competitive advantage

30 Intensive distribution is where products are placed in as many outlets as possible. Here the image of the outlets is not the key criteria, coverage is, whereas with selective distribution, products are placed in a more limited number of outlets. This strategy seeks to show products in the most promising or most profitable outlets only. Exclusive distribution is where only one distributor is used in a relatively large geographic area.

Diploma in Marketing

Test Paper: June 2000

9.53 Strategic Marketing Management: Planning and Control

3 Hours Duration

This examination is in two sections.

Part A is compulsory and worth 40% of total marks.

Part B has six questions, select three. Each answer will be worth 20% of the total marks.

DO NOT repeat the question in your answer but show clearly the number of the question attempted.

Rough workings should be included in the answer book and ruled through after use.

DO NOT OPEN THIS PAPER UNTIL YOU ARE READY TO START UNDER EXAMINATION CONDITIONS

PART A

Weetabix

The breakfast cereal market in the UK is estimated to be worth around £1 billion a year and has been growing at around 2%-3% a year in terms of value. Consumers in the UK eat 17lbs of breakfast cereal a year, more than in any other country in the world. The nearest rivals are consumers in the United States of America who eat 10lbs a year. This sector of the UK market is highly competitive with both Kellogg's and Nestle - two of the world's biggest food companies - being actively involved ('Cereal Partners' being Nestle's joint venture with General Mills). The market share breakdown is shown in Table 1.

Table 1: Share of the UK breakfast cereal market by company

Company	Market Share %
Kellogg's	43.5
Weetabix	15.2
Cereal Partners	12.0
Others	29.3

Source: Marketing

As well as having major global players active in market, retailer own label brands have been growing in strength. In the last three years alone retailers' own label brands have increased their share of the market from 22% to 33%.

Weetabix is a medium-sized company employing 2,000 people in the UK. Yet, against this market background in the year ending February 1999 Weetabix's turnover had risen 12% from £274 million to £308 million. Pre-tax profits had grown 23% to £52 million from £42 million. In fact Weetabix has shown steady growth for a number of years. Back in 1982 Weetabix has a turnover of just £55 million with profits of just over £1 million.

Weetabix (the product) was developed in Australia around 1900. It is a sugarless flaked wheat biscuit with a consistency that turns into a soft pulp once milk is poured over it. When eaten this biscuit delivers nourishment in the form of a strong mix of complex carbohydrates. Due to its consistency it can be eaten by any age group. In particular, it is ideal for weaning babies. It is currently the number two brand in the UK breakfast cereal market (see Table 2). Unlike the other leading brands, no other retailer or manufacturer has managed to launch successfully a 'me-too' product. The majority of own label flaked wheat biscuits are actually manufactured by Weetabix.

Weetabix (the company) has six major products which are: Weetabix (plus a variation, Frutibix), Alpen, Crunchy Bran, Weetos, Ready Brek and Advantage. This gives the company some advantages in concentrating investment and management effort over a small range of products. Some observers see this situation arising because Weetabix is poor at innovation and see the company as having a conservative new product development policy. This is especially noticeable given that the other major players in this market have launched a number of minor variations on their breakfast cereal products in recent years.

Table 2: The UK breakfast cereal market

Position	Brand	1998 Listing (£m)	% Change on Previous Year	Company
1	Kellogg's Corn Flakes	Over 90	-7.8	Kellogg's
2	Weetabix	75-80	0.7	Weetabix
3	Kellogg's Frosties	60-65	-5.9	Kellogg's
4	Nestle Shredded Wheat	45-50	14.2	Cereal Partners
5	Kellogg's Rice Krispies	35-40	-6.2	Kellogg's
6	Kellogg's Crunchy Nut Corn Flakes	35-40	-3.7	Kellogg's
7	Kellogg's Healthwise Bran Flakes	30-35	-5.2	Kellogg's
8	Kellogg's Special k	25-30	0.9	Kellogg's
9	Quaker Sugar Puffs	25-30	8.8	Quaker
10	Kellogg's Optima Fruit 'n' Fibre	25-30	-2.5	Kellogg's

Source: AC Nielsen MEAL

Weetabix does not compete in every segment of the market and does not have multiple products in each category. However, it does not tend to dominate the categories where it chooses to compete. For instance, Alpen is the brand leader in muesli, Ready Brek created and still dominates the hot cereal sector and Weetabix leads the wholewheat biscuit category.

Table 3: Advertising spend, cereals

Company	Advertising spend in £m (April 1998-March 1999)
Kellogg's	55
Cereal Partners	19
Weetabix	15
Quaker Oats	1.7
Others	2.2
Total	**92.9**

Source: Media Monitoring Services

One of Weetabix's key strengths is its high level of service. The Federation of Wholesale Distributors awarded the company a gold medal for service levels in 1995. Weetabix has a reputation of having products in stock, delivering when they say they will deliver and of offering merchandising and marketing support. This is in an industry where wholesalers are using to being let down on as many as one in ten orders.

At the end of 1998 Kellogg's decided to increase its advertising expenditure by 40%. At the same time it cut its prices on six of its leading brands by 12%. This price war was started in retaliation to the growth of the own label brands - however, it has obvious implications for Weetabix. The chairman of Weetabix said in February 1999 that he was 'concerned that the tactics of our major competitors may harm the whole breakfast cereal sector'.

Trends are also changing in the breakfast cereal market. Fewer consumers are having a sit down breakfast and are instead eating food such as croissants that can be eaten while travelling. A number of manufacturers have developed products to address this market (see Table 4). Kellogg's in particular has been active in this area of product development. Kellogg's Nutri-Grain is a bar high in fibre that the company is branding as a 'morning bar'. This product is now being extended with the addition of Nutri-Grain Twists, containing separate sections of yoghurt and fruit puree that are twisted into the Nutri-Grain bar. Kellogg's is also extending three of its breakfast bar brands into cereal bars. The Kellogg's brands of Frosties, Coco Pops and Smacks are all being launched in a cereal and milk bar format. Cereal and milk bars are bound together with dried milk and are claimed to contain the equivalent amount of milk as in a traditional bowl of breakfast cereal.

Table 4: Estimated manufacturers' shares in the UK cereal bar market in 1997

	£m	%
Kellogg's	14.1	25
Jordan	13.9	25
Mars	11.4	20
Quaker	6.3	11
Other brands	0.8	1.5
Own label	9.8	17.5
Total	**56.2**	**100**

Source: Mintel

This mini case study has been prepared from secondary sources.

PART 1

Question 1

(a) As a consultant, write a report to Weetabix outlining and evaluating the strategic options open to the company in responding to the developing price was initiated by Kellogg's.

(b) Weetabix has decided to review the company's innovation activities. Prepare a report advising the board of Weetabix on the auditing process necessary to undertake this analysis successfully.

(20 marks)

(40 marks in total)

PART B - Answer THREE Questions Only

Question 2

Write a report critically evaluating the usefulness of the value chain in analysing an organisation's capabilities and in the formulation of marketing strategies. **(20 marks)**

Question 3

Having undertaken a market analysis a company that designs female clothing in Hong Kong is considering launching a new range of garments. What criteria would you advise them to use in evaluating which potential target market or markets to enter? **(20 Marks)**

Question 4

Evaluate the usefulness to organisations of the balanced score card approach as advocated by Kaplan and Norton. **(20 marks)**

Question 5

A Western European soft drinks company is negotiating an agreement with a bottler and distributor in the Russian market. In its own domestic Western European market, the brand is seen as nonconformist and slightly maverick in nature. You have been asked to write a report to the Marketing Director advising the soft drinks company of the branding issues they need to consider before finalising any agreement. **(20 Marks)**

Question 6

A major bank is considering a strategic partnership with a mobile phone operator to provide customers with a package that offers home banking, bill paying and smart cards. Discuss the bank's motivation for such a move and assess the issues that are likely to be critical to a successful alliance. **(20 Marks)**

Question 7

The Marketing Director of an academic book publishing company has asked you to write a report evaluating the use of scenario planning in helping their organisation to develop an understanding of how this sector of the market may develop in the future. **(20 marks)**

Answers

**DO NOT TURN THIS PAGE UNTIL YOU
HAVE COMPLETED THE TEST PAPER**

1

(a) **Report**

To: Marketing Director
From: Consultant
Subject: Price Wars/Strategic Options open to Weetabix

Introduction

Professor Piercy (1997) states 'Price wars are dangerous and highly contagious'. This results in reduced margins, the product or service becomes a commodity, sold on price alone, and the weakest companies go to the wall.

It is important to consider and try to understand why Kellogg's is initiating a price war. It is probably initially to respond to the growth of own label brands, but the repercussions will affect all the brands within the sector. If Kellogg's maintain the strategy of price war, over a significant time frame they hope to increase market share.

This will be mainly at the expense of own label brands but it will also result in reduced margins for any competitors who wish to compete. It will also seriously weaken smaller producers.

Kellogg's assumptions are based on:

- The fact that they are a low cost producer
- The fact that they have dominance in the sector
- The fact that customers are responsive to price cuts

For Kellogg's, trying to re-establish lost market share in a mature market will be costly as historical evidence shows it is rarely cost effective. However, their aim is to recover lost sales.

Response of Weetabix

Before considering any strategic response a complete competitor analysis of Kellogg's needs to be carried out. This should be based on the following:

- Size of the company
- Costs (own and competitors)
- Perception of the company
- Financial state
- Resources
- Company objectives
- Historical behaviour in other markets
- Demand elasticities
- Interrelationships within the product lines

Once this has been evaluated, Weetabix can respond.

The response to entering the price war should be based on the following criteria:

- Reduction of price is compatible with brand
- Costs can be reduced or fall to help maintain reasonable margins
- Company's marketing objectives are to maintain and increase market share
- Excess supply in the sector.

Conversely, Weetabix should abstain from entering the price war if:

- Costs are rising

Test paper: suggested answers

- There is excess demand for the product
- Price fall is incompatible with brand image
- Objective is to harvest
- Customers are price insensitive

Options available to Weetabix

Below are some of the options open to Weetabix

(a) **Respond to Kellogg's by entering the price war.** This may cause other players to react by also entering the war. This will squeeze margins throughout the market. Only those with the most resources, particularly cash, will survive the war.

(b) **Focus on core strengths.** One way is to focus on Weetabix's core strengths, looking at other niches in the market, for example, the eat while you travel segment.

(c) **Form a strategic partnership.** This is an ever increasing undertaking by companies to maintain a competitive advantage. This could take the form of collaboration with Jordan's to develop new products, thus adding to the product portfolio, an obvious current weakness in the company. Alternatively, Weetabix could launch a promotional alliance with Jordan's crunch bars, for example, giving one free with every large packet of Weetabix. Whatever the collaboration, a small company like Jordan's could be squeezed out in the cereal war and might welcome an alliance.

(d) **Total withdrawal of the brand.** This must be the last resort, but in the baked beans price war when supermarkets sold own labelled beans as low as 6p, Crosse and Blackwell withdrew from the market with their own brand. Your company manufactures own label products and have a vested interest in the growth of this market as well as the survival of the Weetabix brand. The margins for Weetabix become too prohibitive and you are forced to withdraw, the shortfall in the UK may well be met by manufacturing more own label cereals. Promotional costs will drastically be reduced. However, returning to the market when it becomes more attractive could be prohibitive, as the re-launch costs could be enormous to recapture market share.

(e) **Increase promotional activity.** Conduct detailed research into your current and potential market segments, particularly attitudinal responses to price and preferences. From analysis of this research a schedule of promotional activities can be arranged to meet the outcomes of the analysis.

Conclusion

Generally, the only beneficiary of a price war in the short term is the consumer, not the business or the brand. Therefore, very careful consideration is needed before entering into any price war. The options highlighted may well be better alternatives than responding too quickly to Kellogg's stance.

(b) **Report**

To: Board of directors, Weetabix
From: Consultant
Date: June 2000
Subject: Audit process for innovation

Introduction

Innovation and new product development is essential for companies' survival in the market place today. With core technologies widely available and shortening product life cycles, getting new products to the market place quickly is essential. It is essential for companies to remember that the key driving force behind new product ideas and innovation is the human resource.

Resistance to change

New methods of management thinking can experience some resistance from established managers. This lack of management enthusiasm may be due to lack of knowledge or concern to maintain the status quo. Management can tend to focus too heavily on methods and products that have been successful in the past and see budgets for innovation and product development as taking resources away from core business. Similarly there can be a tendency, especially in the West, towards short-term profits rather than long term growth and stability

Old planning systems

Often old planning systems have been downgraded and inputs can take over from outputs. Large organisations that have been split into functional areas which operate at different sites tend to develop their own goals without knowledge about the customers needs through an integrated marketing communications strategy.

Old structures/functional specialists

Individuals often have limited responsibilities and this inhibits new thinking and creativity. Product development itself is often slow with poor planning and lack of market research or even an allocated budget for innovation in the first place.

An 'innovation audit'

Top management needs to create a priority for innovation by making it one of the organisation's goals. By assessing the company's innovation record all internal obstacles can be identified and steps started to incorporate 'innovation and learning' as part of the company culture. 3M expects each of its divisions to have a minimum of 25% of its profit from products introduced in the last five years. This goal demands that management and financial resources are devoted to innovation.

An audit to assess the company's position regarding innovation can take the following steps:

Step 1. **Benchmarking**

Compare the company's innovation record with other leading businesses. What is achievable can be discovered by examining what others have achieved. Managers within the organisation will also be able to see that proposed goals are not unrealistic. Research into competitor activity can also teach much about allotted research time, allocated product development budgets and employee involvement, for example, and this can be compared with profit margins and market share.

Step 2. **Assess creativity**

Management should undertake an attitude survey assessing the key areas of the organisation's climate of creativity. This should cover the following areas:

- Allocated resources for creativity and product development
- Supervisory support.
- The degree of teamwork/taskforces working within a creativity infrastructure.

Test paper: suggested answers

- The personnel involved (Teams should consist of experienced people from R & D, marketing, engineering, production and sales sharing multifunctional skills.)

- Recognition, unity and co-operation

- Political problems and leadership styles of senior management, attitudes that might be blocking innovation and creativity

Step 3. Measurement of current in innovation

This will involve analysis in the following areas:

(a) **Innovation/value portfolio analysis.** Are there regular review meetings focusing on opportunities in the market, analysis of innovation performance, and are objectives being met?

(b) **Customer satisfaction ratings.** What level of customer involvement and feedback exists in product development? To what extent is research identifying new target markets? Teams should be working together, talking to different customers, looking and listening

(c) **Rate of product development.** Many organisations fail to use profits on a continuous basis from current successes to develop more innovations. Processes should exist for idea generation, market testing and assessment of commercialisation. Effective planning and scheduled product development is essential as delay to the market place may result in loss of potential sales.

(d) **Staff turnover.** Are the staff motivated and rewarded for creativity? If a company is not investing in its people providing training and incentives a culture of creativity will be hard to achieve. A good communication structure is essential as is an understanding of the market environment and investment in technology help to develop the core capabilities for innovation.

Conclusion

As a company grows there is the danger that they lose the often close contact with customers that a small organisation can maintain. A vision and priority for innovation needs to be incorporated into the mission statement which should permeate throughout the culture of the organisation. Innovation and creativity should not be left to the research and development department.

With multi-skilled task forces from all functional departments from the organisation potential conflicts can be eliminated and time schedules co-ordinated thereby reducing some of the risks involved in encouraging innovation, and product development.

2

Report

Date: June 2000
Subject: Role of value chain in analysing capabilities and formulating marketing strategies

Introduction

Porter's value chain model is useful in identifying how an organisation's resources can be organised and activities performed in ways that add value to customers. This will provide a unique product or service and a sustainable market strategy.

Test paper: suggested answers

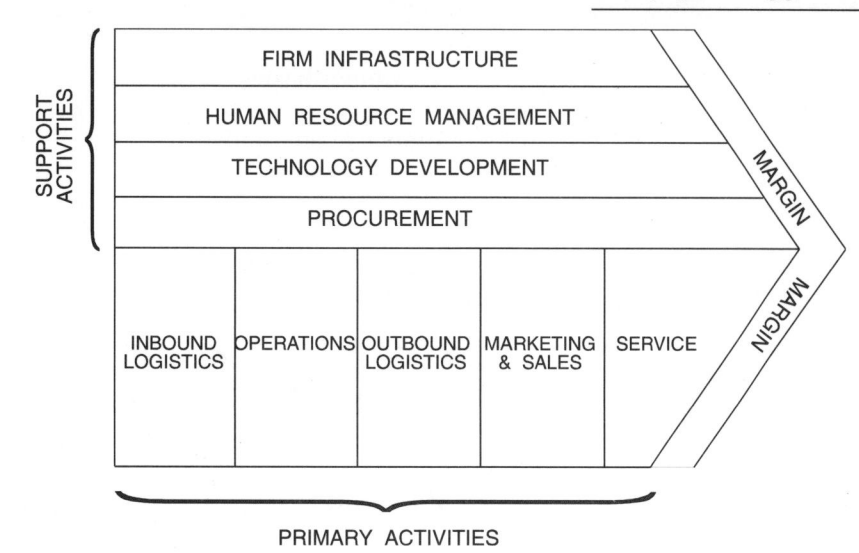

```
                    ┌─ FIRM INFRASTRUCTURE ─────────┐
         SUPPORT    │  HUMAN RESOURCE MANAGEMENT    │  MARGIN
         ACTIVITIES │  TECHNOLOGY DEVELOPMENT       │
                    │  PROCUREMENT                  │
                    ├────┬──────┬────────┬────────┬─┤
                    │IN- │OPERA-│OUTBOUND│MARKET- │SER-│ MARGIN
                    │BOUND│TIONS │LOGIS-  │ING &   │VICE│
                    │LOGIS│      │TICS    │SALES   │    │
                    │TICS │      │        │        │    │
                    └────┴──────┴────────┴────────┴────┘
                           PRIMARY ACTIVITIES
```

adapted from Michael Porter, 1996

The margin is the excess the customer is prepared to pay over the cost to the firm of obtaining resource input and providing value activities.

Primary Activities

These are directly related to production, sales, marketing, delivery and service

(a) **Inbound logistics.** Receiving, handling and storing inputs to the production system, for example, warehousing, transport and stock control.

(b) **Operations.** Convert resource inputs into a final product. Resource inputs are not only materials. People are a resource, especially in service industries.

(c) **Outbound logistics.** Storing the product and its distribution to customers, for example, packing, warehousing and testing.

(d) **Marketing and sales.** Informing customers about the product, persuading them to buy it and enabling them to do so through advertising and promotion.

(e) **After sales service.** Installing products, repairing them, upgrading them, providing spare parts and so forth.

Support activities

These provide purchased inputs, human resources, technology and infrastructure functions to support the primary activities.

(a) **Procurement.** Acquire the resource inputs to the primary activities, for example, purchase of materials, subcomponents and equipment

(b) **Technology development.** Product design, improving processes and/or resource utilisation.

(c) **Human resource management.** Recruiting, training, developing and rewarding people

(d) **Management planning.** Planning, finance, quality control: Porter believes they are crucially important to an organisation's strategic capability in all primary activities.

An organisation's **capabilities** are made up of its **assets** and **competencies**. Marketing assets refers to all those intangibles which can impact on the customer's perception of the organisation's products and services for example, reputation, expertise or brands. Hugh Davidson (1983) suggests that assets will come from such areas as:

Test paper: suggested answers

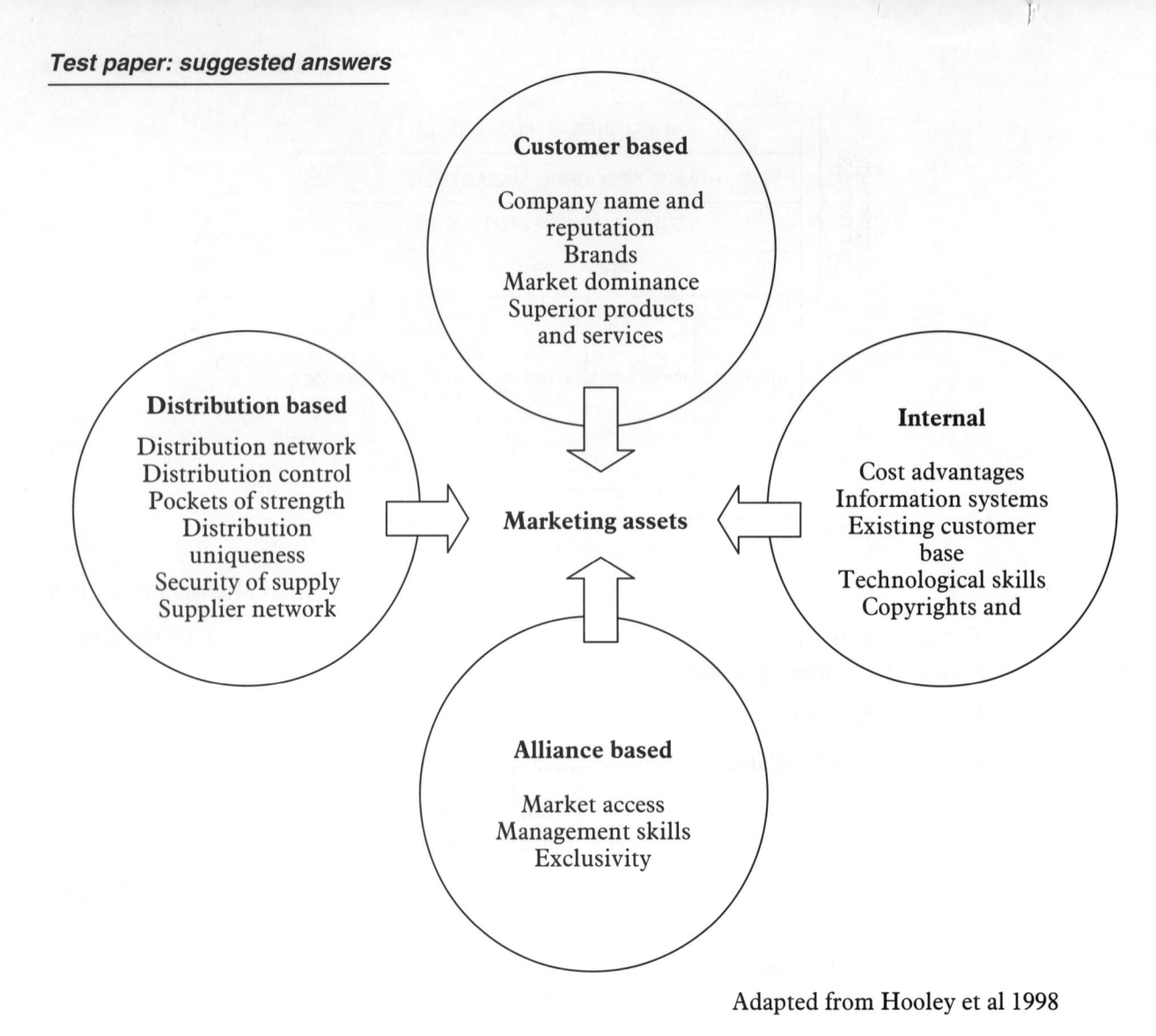

Customer based

Company name and reputation
Brands
Market dominance
Superior products and services

Distribution based

Distribution network
Distribution control
Pockets of strength
Distribution uniqueness
Security of supply
Supplier network

Marketing assets

Internal

Cost advantages
Information systems
Existing customer base
Technological skills
Copyrights and

Alliance based

Market access
Management skills
Exclusivity

Adapted from Hooley et al 1998

Competencies are the skills that are used to deploy the **assets** to best effect in the market. These will come from areas such as:

- **Marketing.** Brand extension, business analysis or new product development
- **Selling.** Supply chain management, pricing, and promotion
- **Operations.** Speed of response and payment systems

Many companies now focus on core competencies as a basis for strategy instead of managing a portfolio of brands and businesses in the belief that superior performance will come from focusing on these. For example, Canon's core competencies, skills and technologies in optics, has led to their survival in many markets, for example, laser printing, cameras and copiers. Similarly, Virgin's perceived high value brand has been used to develop other business units for Branson.

The identification of core competencies enables a company to penetrate wider markets especially if they are difficult for competitors to copy. The emergence of strategic alliances enables companies to compete effectively in globalisation and technology driven markets. Costs in developing internal skills and investment in technology that are needed to compete effectively can be reduced with strategic alliances where each partner can concentrate on applying its own core competencies.

The focus on shared objectives, in strategic alliance, enhances joint competitive positions in the industry and ultimately gives distinct customer benefits, for example, improved innovation and quality and customer service. Hewlett Packard and Matsushita combined their capabilities in the development of ink-jet faxes to provide a product that if produced separately would have taken much longer.

However, management has to be aware that whilst some risks may be avoided by the development of strategic alliances there are also significant risks in such ventures. The relative dependence and power within such relationships can make some companies very vulnerable. This was true of the relationship between Marks and Spencer and Coates Viyella.

Also, alliances require commitment from all parties which permeates throughout the organisations involved. In other words synergy is essential. It also demands appropriate management planning and communication at all levels in order to build trust and co-operation between the members of the alliance.

Conclusion

Whilst in Porter's value chain model it appears relatively simple to identify a company's core capabilities, in reality the identification of them may be not be so easy. In the long run success depends on possessing 'superior core competencies' in which the organisation operates. For example, Honda has core competencies in design and development skills. They produce motor cycles, cars, lawnmowers and outboard engines and as the market changes can adapt their core capabilities and maintain innovation and differentiation. However, a company buying certain goods and services from a supplier who at a later date decides to enter the market is not a successful strategy.

Focusing on core capabilities requires total organisational commitment and strategic investments. Such core capabilities are not static and need to be adapted within an organisation that is prepared to focus on change. The organisation needs to know what the customer wants and values and have the appropriate 'unique core capabilities' to offer by way of a product or service.

3

When evaluating which potential target market or markets to enter the company needs to consider the degree to which a market segment fits with their goals and capabilities. Segments which are most attractive will be those whose needs can be met by building on the company's strengths and where forecasts for demand, sales profitability and growth are favourable.

Hooley and others provide a comprehensive list of factors for evaluating **market attractiveness**, which is outlined here.

Factors	Characteristics to examine
Market factors	
	• Size of the segment
	• Segment growth rate
	• Stage of industry evaluation
	• Predictability
	• Pride elasticity and sensitivity
	• Bargaining power of customers
	• Seasonality of demand
Economic and technological factors	
	• Barriers to entry/exit

- Bargaining power of suppliers
- Level of technology
- Investment required
- Margins available

Competitive factors

- Competitive intensity
- Quality of competition
- Threat of substitution
- Degree of differentiation

Environmental factors

- Exposure to economic fluctuations
- Exposure to political and legal factors
- Degree of regulation
- Social acceptability

Internal factors

- The fit with 'internal' company needs
- Corporate strategies, size and profitability thresholds
- The availability of 'suitable' collaborative relationships

It is then necessary to assess the company's strengths and resources (assets and **competencies**) when evaluating attractiveness and targeting a market. This can help determine the appropriate **strategy** because once the attractiveness of each identified segment has been assessed it can be considered in relation to the strengths of the organisation to determine its potential advantages.

Company Assets

The assessment of company assets might show strengths or weaknesses in any of the following areas:

- **Physical assets**, for example, property, land and machinery
- **Financial assets**, for example, cash in hand, credit rating or worthiness, working capital
- **Operation assets**, for example, systems and production processes, advantages of scale
- **Human assets**, for example, intangible qualities and abilities, company culture
- **Marketing assets**, for example, sales/distribution network, relationship with customers (value perceived by the customer), brand name and reputation, relationship with other organisations
- **Legal assets**, for example, patents/copyrights and licences
- **Systems**, for example, information systems and market intelligence

How the strengths and weaknesses are assessed in these areas will impact on the choice of target market. Another key thing to consider, however, is the competencies of the company. Essentially **competency** is the ability to use the company assets through particular skills and processes in which the company excels. The following list gives examples of such competencies.

- **Strategic competencies**, for example, an organisation which is good at researching, assimilating and acting on information (strategy formation)

- **Functional competencies**, for example, marketing, (including brand management or market research techniques), financial management, production or research development

- **Operational competencies**, for example, motivation and control, inventory control or industrial relations

Success in choosing which market to enter depends on identifying one or two activities in which the company excels and applying them strategically. This area has been developed recently, with collaboration between companies. Companies create links to the 'value-added' competencies of other companies. For example, BP is jointly marketing petrol and groceries in partnership with Safeway and there is joint collaboration with Smart card with companies like Shell, Menzies, Victoria Wine and Dixons.

Overall, the Hong Kong company will have to match their assets and **competencies** to the target market/s they assess to be the most 'attractive.' The company needs to identify which 'competencies' are valuable in a particular market and ask themselves the following questions:

- Will their competencies provide continued value for the customer?
- Can their 'competencies' be copied?
- How long will it take for competitors to catch up with them?

Obviously, these are significant questions which have to be answered when deciding on the identification of a target market and strategic positioning in the market. Porter's Value Chain model of corporate activities could be used here to identify their 'value activities' and that of competitors' capability profiles, their strengths, weaknesses and likely future responses.

4

In developing a successful strategic direction today a company needs to recognise the importance of identifying broad objectives which have been negotiated and mutually agreed between all stakeholders within the organisation. The balanced scorecard technique is designed to ensure that the different functions of the business are integrated together in order that they work to achieve the corporate goals.

The balance score card is 'a set of measures that gives top managers a fast but comprehensive view of the business. The balance scorecard includes financial measures that tell the results of actions already taken. And it complements the financial measures with operational measures on customer satisfaction, internal processes, and the organisation's innovation and improvement activities - operational measures that are the drivers of future financial performance.' (Kaplan 1992).

For most businesses, the diverse objectives can be incorporated into four perspectives:

Financial perspective

Goals	Measures
Survive	Cash flow
Succeed	Monthly sales growth and operating income by division
Prosper	Increase market share and ROCE
Recognition	Share price

Customer Perspective

Goals	Measures
New products	Percentage of sales from new products
Responsive supply	On-time delivery (defined by customer)
Preferred supplier	Share of key accounts' purchases
	Ranking by key accounts
Customer partnership	Number of co operative engineering efforts

Internal Business Perspective

Goals	Measures
Technological capability	Manufacturing configuration versus competition
Manufacturing excellence	Cycle time
	Unit cost
	Yield
Design Productivity	Silicon efficiency
	Engineering efficiency
New Product introduction	Actual introduction schedule versus plan

Innovation and Learning Perspective

Goals	Measures
Time to market	New product introduction versus competitors
Manufacturing learning	Process time to maturity
Product focus	Percentage of products that equal 80% of sales
Technology leadership	Time to develop next generation of products

The Balanced Scorecard approach (BSA) helps an organisation focus on 'effectiveness', that is, the company's attainment of goals. It develops consistency between the goals. Often organisations that lack strategic direction focus on cost cutting in difficult periods, adopting a short time perspective. In contrast, the BSA helps managers to adopt a more holistic approach, developing their understanding of the complexity of relationships that exist between the traditional functional structures.

Clear, quantified corporate objectives and the co-ordinating influence of a corporate strategy allow unit managers to develop their own functional plans. However the BSA can be difficult to operate in practice as objectives are formed not only in a range of areas but at different levels and time scales.

Overall, this approach only measures strategy it does not indicate that the strategy is the right one. Its biggest contribution is that it serves to remind management that all areas of the company, for example, quality, response time, productivity or new products benefit the company as they are translated into financial results. Good finances are the result from successful handling of customer, internal processes and innovation and learning issues and the BSA enables all the vital perspectives (not just the financial ones) to be taken into account.

5

Report

To: Marketing Director, Quench soft drinks
From: Consultant
Subject: Branding Issues for the Russian market

Branding

Before discussing the key issues to be considered in your possible expansion into the Russian market, here is a brief outline of what advantages branding has to offer:

- Creates a unique identity for the product
- This uniqueness differentiates the product from the competition
- Helps customers to identify their preferred choice reducing purchase time
- Builds brand loyalty
- Reduces the importance of price differentials between products
- Aids market segmentation

A good example in the soft drinks industry is the blind/open testing of Pepsi and Coke. Pepsi significantly came out on top by 7% in the blind testing. However, in the open test, Coke's lead was an astounding 42%. This clearly indicates the power of the brand.

The success of Quench in Western Europe has been built on its image as a nonconformist and slightly maverick product, and targeted at those segments that display those types of characteristics. Quench need to ascertain if this can be transferred to the Russian market. To assist the decision making process, an audit of the current state of the Russian market and the company needs to be conducted.

Audit

The audit needs to cover the following:

- Market or (segment) attractiveness and position, that is, how will the opportunity fit into Quench's current capabilities and plans?

- Do management think Quench can succeed in this market?

- Legal requirement

- Market trends

- Profitability

- Competitor analysis: evaluate direct/indirect competitors

- Distribution systems

- Reputation of the Russian Company

- Current performance in the market place

- Culture of the company

- Profitability of the company

Test paper: suggested answers

Once the information has been assembled, key issues can be drawn that affect the branding decision.

Key Issues

Below are the key issues that need to be considered before any agreement is reached.

(a) **Does it fit the strategic plan?**

- Are the business objectives to globalise the product or manufacture for the Russian company as a "private" brand?
- If the aim is to develop the brand globally, has the company the resources?
- Can it be standardised, that is, can the name easily translate like Pepsi or Coke or must it be adapted?
- Does the taste need to change to suit a more eastern palate?
- If the aim is to manufacture as a private brand, is the company prepared to relinquishing control of marketing?

(b) **Cultural differences**

Culture is too complex to define in simple terms. One fundamental is it is learned behaviour, and is the distinctive way of life of a group of people. One of the important aspects of Russian society is its cultural diversity and must not be categorised as one whole. Therefore, research is vitally important to clearly categorise these differences in language, taste and so on across the whole of Russia. However, issues such as:

- Will the current brand position in the west, that is nonconformist/maverick, translate successfully into the Russian market or must it be re-positioned?
- Do the potential segments across Russian mirror the behaviour and attitude to the current European segments?

All these points and questions need to be addressed for the whole of Russia, along with a clear perspective that brands are about delivering lifelong customer value rather than a single transactional value.

I hope this report will assist in helping with your decision. In my opinion, the culture barrier and question of brand translation the key issues for the company to make a decision about.

6

Introduction

A strategic alliance or partnership is an informal or formal arrangement between two or more companies with a common business objective. In the case of the highly competitive service industry of banking which is continually expanding with new entrants, particularly from the insurance and building society sector like Standard Life Bank, the competition to maintain competitive advantage becomes more difficult. Many companies are forming strategic alliances as one way of **maintaining competitive advantage** and **reducing their risk**.

Motivations for Strategic Alliances

Strategic alliances can be motivated by a desire to achieve some of the following benefits:

(a) **Strategic advantage**. This may offer greater market control. In the case of the bank and mobile phone company by offering a wider spread of service for its customers.

(b) **Marketing Advantage.** An alliance with the mobile phone company would gain access to new markets and customers.

(c) **Gain access to a needed technology.** The opportunity to access the latest technology with no initial financial investment.

(d) **Growth and profit.** The main aim for many companies is to increase profit and gain market share. An alliance can provide this by reducing costs and increasing sales, for example, in the case of this alliance, the mobile phone operator could have access to the bank's large database and be able to use the premises for promotional activity. The bank on the other hand can offer existing and new customers access to the latest on-line banking facilities.

(e) **Customer service.** A partnership between the two companies could improve and extend their customer service as well as adding value to both products.

All of the above will enable the bank to maintain competitive advantage by combining those resources and expertise in a partnership which will create new and effective barriers against the competition.

Constructing the alliance

There are four main types of marketing alliances that can be adopted:

- Product and/or service
- Logistics
- Promotional
- Pricing collaborations

One or more can be used to suit the needs of both companies, but before any commitment takes place an agreement needs to be reached on several key issues. Some of these key issues are listed below:

- Both sides understand and agree to their partners long and short term plans
- The scope of the alliance does not create any major conflicts of interest for either side
- Both sides are clear about the extent and limits of the intended alliance
- The imagery and associations of our two brands do not clash
- The partners have assets which the other does not have and cannot access without help.

Conclusion

Over the years there has been major failures as well as successes with strategic partnerships. Rover had a successful alliance with Honda but a failure with BMW. Dixons and Cellnet had a successful alliance with venture Link. Aakers (1998) suggests that for an alliance to work, most of the following needs to take place:

(a) **Balance.** A major problem with strategic alliances occurs when the relative contribution of the partners becomes unbalanced over time and one partner no longer has any proprietary assets and competencies to contribute.

(b) **Compatibility.** When the motivation of one partner is to avoid investment and achieve attractive short-term returns while the other seeks to develop assets and competencies over the longer term, the alliance will break down.

(c) **Culture.** The joint venture must be allowed to evolve with its own culture and values as the existing cultures of the partners will probably not work even if they are compatible with each other.

(d) **Management.** The management and power structure from the two partners must be balanced with project champions as leaders, particularly during difficult times. Without people committed to making the venture happen, it will not happen. It is vital that methods are developed to resolve problems and to allow change over time. It is unrealistic to expect any strategy, organisation, or implementation to exist without evolving and changing. Partners and the organisation thus need to be flexible enough to allow change to occur.

Even if these four factors are considered and planned for, success is not guaranteed.

7

Report

To: Marketing Director
From: Consultant
Subject: Scenario Planning

Introduction

Uncertainty and change is evident everywhere in the business world. To help minimise the risks arising from this uncertainty, forecasting has become an essential tool for organisations. Forecasting techniques are divided into two types, quantitative and qualitative.

Quantitative projections are based on numerical data, usually historical. Qualitative projections are based on explicit assumptions and judgements made about them by groups or individuals. Qualitative forecasting is crucial in supporting the future strategic direction of the organisation, as often hard data is likely to be unavailable or questionable at this level.

Types of Forecasting

There are several well known forecasting techniques. These are the main ones to consider:

(a) **Trend extrapolation.** Uses historical trends over time and extrapolates the information onto a trend line to predict the future.

(b) **Delphi technique.** A group of experts in the field are assembled and a member of the group becomes the project leader. A questionnaire containing a series of problem scenarios on the subject is sent to all members. Each individual responds, usually via the computer to the project leader. The answers are refined and a new series of questions are sent out. The objective is to focus the questions more tightly after each round, so a consensus of opinion is reached, within a given time frame.

(c) **Jury method.** Like the Delphi method it relies of a panel of experts. The difference is they meet as a committee and the majority decision carries the day.

(d) **Individual forecasting.** A popular method, where an individual uses their experience and expertise to forecast future trends.

Scenario Planning

Scenario planning process is not concerned with single estimates of the future. It is the construction of several sets of circumstances which could arise. Each set of circumstances is called a scenario and stems from a series of assumptions about the future. The future is then represented by several alternative scenarios rather than one single view.

The essence of scenario planning is the expression of a wide range of situations which could apply in the future, and which describe the boundaries within which contingency planning can take place. This process is usually carried out by a whole or cross-section of a management group that are familiar with the external environment.

A four stage model shows how to develop simple scenarios:

- Identify the critical variables
- Develop possible strings of events
- Refine the scenarios
- Identify the issues arising

For example, suppose an exporting company is trying to forecast sales of its products in a South East Asian country in ten years time. One set of assumptions could be that at that time there will be a pro-Western government and a strong world economy. In addition, there may be specific assumptions about inflation rates, exchange rates or technological changes. These assumptions are translated into a scenario which shows the sales, prices, costs, manpower and competition relating to the products. A second scenario is formed from a second and different set of assumptions. The process continues and more scenarios are formed until all sets of assumptions which could reasonably be expected to apply have been exhausted.

The most robust of scenarios that have survived this process are evaluated to see what outcomes have been identified and their possible impact on the organisation. Scenario planning is not a detailed technique nor does it pretend to be accurate or predict the possibility of any scenario happening. Rather, it recognises the difficulty of making a definite forecast.

Instead, the emphasis is on covering the range of possibilities and forming flexible plans which can cope with all of them. Its advantage is that it leads to a realistic perspective on future uncertainty. It can also be combined with more techniques for translating assumptions into quantified scenarios. It is particularly useful in the most difficult type of forecasting, for example where the time horizon is long and there are many uncertainties.

Benefits for academic book publishing company

The advent of new technology can impact adversely on this industry, for example, consider Encyclopaedia Brittanica who decided in the mid 90's not to extend to CD Roms. This decision almost eliminated their total sales operation in the USA.

Scenario planning could help the book publishing company to avoid similar mistakes by:

- Alerting the organisation to the most important drivers for change
- Identifying that publishing may take other forms (CD Roms, Internet)
- Help the organisation understand the critical issues for the future of the organisation
- Create a framework from which events can sequentially evolve
- Highlight crucial strategic issues for the management team.

This process could offer the best assessment of the future for the company, and be the basis for key strategic marketing decisions, enabling the company to react faster to the changing dynamics of the market.

Topic index

Topic index

Aims, 88
Aldi, 79, 104
Amstrad, 79
Ansoff, 85
Apple computers, 80

Bath, 87
Body Works, 87
Bodyshop, 87
Boots, 79
Booz, Allen and Hamilton, 121
Boston Consulting Group Matrix, 85
British Airways, 83
British Telecom, 86
Budgets, 16, 133
Buyer behaviour, 6, 42, 47

Coats Viyella, 86
Competitive advantage, 103, 173
Competitive strategy, 11, 79
Competitor response profiles, 48
Corporate planning, 4, 29
Corporate strategy, 4, 30
Cost drivers, 174
Cost leadership, 174
Critical factors for success, 13, 107
Culture, 47
Customer orientation, 35

Decision making unit, 42
Decline, 70
Delphi technique, 75
Developing a strategy, 101
Differentiation, 174

EasyJet, 178
Encyclopaedia Britannica, 86
Evaluation criteria, 13, 111
External environmental analysis, 41

Feasibility studies and risk evaluation, 124
Feasibility studies and risk evaluation, 14

Haji-Ioannou, 179
Heinz, 181

IBM, 86
Implementation problems, 134
Individual forecasting, 75
Industrial segmentation, 12, 92
Internal company analysis, 41
Internal marketing, 16, 136

Jury method, 75

Kellogg's, 181
Kotler, 38
Kwik Save, 79

Laura Ashley, 84
Life cycles, 32
Lord King, 83

Marconi, 86
Market fragmentation, 32
Marketing audit, 6, 40
Marketing concept, 34
Marketing orientation, 4, 34, 35
Marketing plan, 11, 77
Marketing planning, 29
Marks and Spencer, 81, 86
Mcdonalds, 80
Mission, 87
Mission and objectives, 11

New product development, 11, 81
New product development process, 121

Objectives, 87, 88
Organisational buying, 42

Piercy, 76
Policy, 88
Proctor and Gamble, 181
Product orientation, 34
Psychological factors, 48

Reference groups, 47
Richard Branson, 83
Rover, 93

Sainsbury's, 84
Sales forecast, 56
Sales forecasting, 8, 56
Scenario planning, 75
Seat, 181
Shell, 104
Skoda, 181
Skoda cars, 79
Sony, 76
Stella Artois, 104
Strategic wear-out, 86
Swot analysis, 8, 54

Tesco, 79

Topic index

Textile industry, 86
Trend extrapolation, 75

Unilever, 181

Value chain, 179
Vauxhall, 79
Virgin, 83, 104, 181
Volkswagen, 181

CIM Order

To BPP Publishing Ltd, Aldine Place, London W12 8AA
Tel: 020 8740 2211. Fax: 020 8740 1184

Mr/Mrs/Ms (Full name) _____
Daytime delivery address _____
_____ Postcode _____
Daytime Tel _____ Date of exam (month/year) _____

POSTAGE & PACKING

Study Texts

	First	Each extra	
UK	£3.00	£2.00	£ ____
Europe*	£5.00	£4.00	£ ____
Rest of world	£20.00	£10.00	£ ____

Kits/Passcards/Success Tapes

	First	Each extra	
UK	£2.00	£1.00	£ ____
Europe*	£2.50	£1.00	£ ____
Rest of world	£15.00	£8.00	£ ____

Grand Total (Cheques to *BPP Publishing*) I enclose a cheque for (incl. Postage) £ _____

Or charge to Access/Visa/Switch

Card Number ☐☐☐☐ ☐☐☐☐ ☐☐☐☐ ☐☐☐☐

Expiry date ☐☐☐☐ Start Date ☐☐☐☐

Issue Number (Switch Only) ☐☐

Signature _____

		5/00 Texts	9/00 Kits	Tapes
CERTIFICATE				
1	Marketing Environment	£17.95 ☐	£8.95 ☐	£12.95 ☐
2	Customer Communications in Marketing	£17.95 ☐	£8.95 ☐	£12.95 ☐
3	Marketing in Practice	£17.95 ☐	£8.95 ☐	£12.95 ☐
4	Marketing Fundamentals	£17.95 ☐	£8.95 ☐	£12.95 ☐
ADVANCED CERTIFICATE				
5	The Marketing Customer Interface	£17.95 ☐	£8.95 ☐	£12.95 ☐
6	Management Information for Marketing Decisions	£17.95 ☐	£8.95 ☐	£12.95 ☐
7	Effective Management for Marketing	£17.95 ☐	£8.95 ☐	£12.95 ☐
8	Marketing Operations	£17.95 ☐	£8.95 ☐	£12.95 ☐
DIPLOMA				
9	Integrated Marketing Communications	£17.95 ☐	£8.95 ☐	£12.95 ☐
10	International Marketing Strategy	£17.95 ☐	£8.95 ☐	£12.95 ☐
11	Strategic Marketing Management: Planning and Control	£17.95 ☐	£8.95 ☐	£12.95 ☐
12	Strategic Marketing Management: Analysis and Decision (9/00)	£24.95 ☐		

SUBTOTAL £ _____

We aim to deliver to all UK addresses inside 5 working days. A signature will be required. Orders to all EU addresses should be delivered within 6 working days.

All other orders to overseas addresses should be delivered within 8 working days.

* Europe includes the Republic of Ireland and the Channel Islands.

CIM - Diploma: Strategic marketing management: Planning and control (9/00)

REVIEW FORM & FREE PRIZE DRAW

All original review forms from the entire BPP range, completed with genuine comments, will be entered into one of two draws on 31 January 2001 and 31 July 2001. The names on the first four forms picked out on each occasion will be sent a cheque for £50.

Name: _____ Address: _____

_____

_____

How have you used this Kit?
(Tick one box only)

☐ Home study (book only)
☐ On a course: college _____
☐ With 'correspondence' package
☐ Other _____

Why did you decide to purchase this Kit?
(Tick one box only)

☐ Have used complementary Study Text
☐ Have used BPP Kits in the past
☐ Recommendation by friend/colleague
☐ Recommendation by a lecturer at college
☐ Saw advertising
☐ Other _____

During the past six months do you recall seeing/receiving any of the following?
(Tick as many boxes as are relevant)

☐ Our advertisement in *Marketing Success*
☐ Our advertisement in *Marketing Business*
☐ Our brochure with a letter through the post
☐ Our brochure with *Marketing Business*

Which (if any) aspects of our advertising do you find useful?
(Tick as many boxes as are relevant)

☐ Prices and publication dates of new editions
☐ Information on Kit content
☐ Facility to order books off-the-page
☐ None of the above

Have you used the companion Study Text for this subject?   ☐ Yes   ☐ No

Your ratings, comments and suggestions would be appreciated on the following areas

	Very useful	Useful	Not useful
Introductory section (Study advice, key questions checklist, etc)	☐	☐	☐
'Do you know' checklists	☐	☐	☐
Tutorial questions	☐	☐	☐
Examination-standard questions	☐	☐	☐
Content of suggested answers	☐	☐	☐
Quiz	☐	☐	☐
Test paper	☐	☐	☐
Structure and presentation	☐	☐	☐

	Excellent	Good	Adequate	Poor
Overall opinion of this Kit	☐	☐	☐	☐

Do you intend to continue using BPP Study Texts/Kits?   ☐ Yes   ☐ No

Please note any further comments and suggestions/errors on the reverse of this page.

Please return to: Kate Machattie, BPP Publishing Ltd, FREEPOST, London, W12 8BR

REVIEW FORM & FREE PRIZE DRAW (continued)

Please note any further comments and suggestions/errors below

FREE PRIZE DRAW RULES

1. Closing date for 31 January 2001 draw is 31 December 2000. Closing date for 31 July 2001 draw is 30 June 2001.

2. Restricted to entries with UK and Eire addresses only. BPP employees, their families and business associates are excluded.

3. No purchase necessary. Entry forms are available upon request from BPP Publishing. No more than one entry per title, per person. Draw restricted to persons aged 16 and over.

4. Winners will be notified by post and receive their cheques not later than 6 weeks after the relevant draw date.

5. The decision of the promoter in all matters is final and binding. No correspondence will be entered into.